BEARING

Also by Henry Louis Gates, Jr.

The Signifying Monkey: A Theory of Afro-American Literary Criticism

Edited by Henry Louis Gates, Jr.

Our Nig: Sketches from the Life of a Free Black
by Harriet Wilson

Race, Writing, and Difference

The Classic Slave Narratives

BEARING WITNESS

Selections from African-American Autobiography in the Twentieth Century

Edited by
HENRY LOUIS GATES, JR.

PANTHEON BOOKS, NEW YORK

Acknowledgments to reprint previously published material appear on pages 381–83. Photo credits are on page 384.

Library of Congress Cataloging-in-Publication Data

Gates, Henry Louis.
    Bearing Witness: Selections from African-American Autobiography in the Twentieth Century / ed. Henry Louis Gates, Jr.
       p. cm.
      1. Afro-Americans—Biography. 2. Autobiographies—United States. 3. United States—Biography. I. Title.
    E185.96.G38 1991 920'.009296073—dc20   90-52538
    [B]
    ISBN 0-679-73520-8

Book Design by Linda Herman + Company
Manufactured in the United States of America

9876

For Arnold Rampersad

Contents

Contents

Contents

I wish to thank the following people
for all their help on this book:
William Andrews, Henry Finder,
Lisa Gates, Candy Heinemann,
Frances Jalet-Miller,
Nancy Martin, and James Olney.

BEARING WITNESS

Introduction:
On Bearing Witness

Histories cannot be more certain than when he who creates the things also narrates them.

—Vico

OF THE VARIOUS genres that comprise the African-American literary tradition, none has played a role as central as has black autobiography. For hundreds of black authors, the most important written statement that they could make seems to have been the publication of their life stories. Through autobiography, these writers could, at once, shape a public "self" in language, and protest the degradation of their ethnic group by the multiple forms of American racism. The ultimate form of protest, certainly, was to register in print the existence of a "black self" that had transcended the limitations and restrictions that racism had placed on the personal development of the black individual.

The African-American tradition is distinctive in that an author typically publishes as a *first* book her or his autobiography, establishing her or his presence and career as a writer through this autobiographical act—rather than, as for most authors, at or near the end of a productive career, or at least after an author's other works have, as it were, generated sufficient interest in the life that has generated the author's oeuvre. A familiar example of this phenomenon is Maya Angelou, who emerged as a major American author with her marvelously compelling and lyrical *I Know Why the Caged Bird Sings* (1968, excerpted here), but this is true as well for many of the most promi-

3

nent figures in the African-American tradition, from Frederick Douglass to Itabari Njeri.

And curiously enough, the structural similarities among these autobiographies suggest that black writers turn to autobiographical texts written by other black writers to pattern their own narratives. Claude Brown, the author of *Manchild in the Promised Land* (1965, excerpted here), told a New York audience in 1990 that, when faced with the task of creating his autobiography, he carefully analyzed Frederick Douglass's slave narrative and Richard Wright's *Black Boy* to learn how other blacks had solved difficult matters of language and form, and then emulated the structure of their narratives. The evidence gained from reading hundreds of black autobiographies indicates that most of their authors underwent a similar process.

Deprived of access to literacy, the tools of citizenship, denied the rights of selfhood by law, philosophy, and pseudo-science, and denied as well the possibility, even, of possessing a collective history as a people, black Americans—commencing with the slave narratives in 1760—published their *individual* histories in astonishing numbers, in a larger attempt to narrate the collective history of "the race." If the individual black self could not exist before the law, it could, and would, be forged in language, as a testimony at once to the supposed integrity of the black self and against the social and political evils that delimited individual and group equality for all African-Americans. The will to power for black Americans was the will to write; and the predominant mode that this writing would assume was the shaping of a black self in words. And while fiction would seem to be the major genre practiced by black writers today, the impulse to testify, to chart the peculiar contours of the individual protagonist on the road to becoming, clearly undergirds even the fictional tradition of black letters, as the predominance of the first-person form attests. Constructed upon an ironic foundation of autobiographical narratives written by ex-slaves, the African-American tradition, more clearly and directly than most, traces its lineage—in the act of declaring the existence of a surviving, enduring ethnic self—to this impulse of autobiography.

But the potency of black autobiography is hardly restricted to the realm of high culture. I remember when Sammy Davis, Jr.'s, first autobiography, *Yes I Can!,* was published in 1965 and quickly became a bestseller, such a bestseller in fact that I was able to purchase it at our local newsstand in Piedmont, West Virginia, soon after the Watts riots. Davis's tale of woe and triumph was inspirational for me, and led me to search for other black autobiographies.

Searching for a key to unlock the madness of American racism, and strategies for my own survival of it, I avidly read, first, *The Autobiography of Malcolm X,* then Claude Brown's *Manchild in the Promised Land,* as did everyone else in my family. It was through *Manchild* that I first encountered the careful record of a sensitive and articulate black adolescent's quest for selfhood and dignity in an urban world so very far away from my village in the hills of West Virginia. That the book nevertheless captured the terrors that every adolescent encounters on the crooked path to adulthood is perhaps most crudely evidenced by the fact that his book sold three million copies and was translated into fourteen languages in 1965.

The burden of the past plays itself out rather differently in the white and black literary traditions. For the scholar of Western literature, the weight of the authority of canonized texts and canonical critical inter-pretations can prove to be a confining barrier to creativity, innovation, and even improvisation, delimiting ways of seeing and restricting modes of analysis. The curse that the scholar of Western culture bears, then, is the presence of an enshrined collective cultural mem-ory, one that can confine and delimit just as surely as it preserves continuity and enables the extension of tradition.

Paradoxically, however, the curse that the scholar of African and African-American Studies bears is the *absence* of a printed, cata-logued, collective cultural memory. Despite the enormous interest in Black Studies since the late sixties, we still have relatively few of the sort of reference works—such as biographical dictionaries; annotated bibliographies; histories of disciplines; and especially encyclopedias, concordances, and dictionaries of black-language use—that allow the scholar to presume so very much about the subject at hand. These sorts of data, readily accessible to scholars in the traditional disciplines, can be enabling tools, allowing for the production of more sophisticated modes of analysis than are possible otherwise, when a scholar is forced virtually always to re-create from degree zero the historical and critical context in which she or he is working. The excitement generated by the production of scholarship in Black Studies stems from the certain knowledge that virtually all that one sees and writes can be novel and different, free of this burden of the canonized past, the prison-house of tradition. While historical and archival scholarship in Black Studies is revealing our traditions to be much fuller than we ever dreamed them to be, there nevertheless persists the suspicion that all we think, and see, and write is somehow new. Publishing criticism, for our generation of commentators, still feels like an inscription upon a small section of a large and black tabula rasa.

And yet *remembering* is one of the cardinal virtues emphasized by the culture itself—from subtle narrative devices such as repetition of line and rhythm (the sermon, black music, oral narration) to more public pageant modes of commemoration such as the observation of particular "black" holidays ("Juneteenth," Black History Month, Kwaanza) or their particular ways of observing, such as eating "Hoppin' John" on New Year's Day or reinterpreting the Fourth of July to make it analogous to Good Friday rather than to Easter. From Founder's Day ceremonies and family reunions, to the naming of black institutions after black historical figures—Wheatley, Carver, Dunbar, and Washington public schools have long been familiar, and now, of course, Martin Luther King schools and boulevards abound—or what we might think of as historical concepts or metaphors, such as the African Methodist Episcopal Church, African-Americans have been overtly concerned with what Toni Morrison has described in an apt phrase as "rememory," the systematic remembrance of things past.

Remembering has been encoded within the culture as a process precisely because blacks were denied access to their history systematically, both under slavery and after slavery. Under slavery, of course, they were denied access to the tools of formal memory—reading and writing. They were also denied access to their native languages and often even to the drum (deemed "subversive" by many masters, and correctly so, since it was the "home" of repetition and contained the code of a Pan-African language that all blacks could understand). Without a written language, as Hegel had it, there could be no ordered repetition or memory, and without memory, there could be no history. Without history, there could be no self. One abolitionist described in his memoirs an encounter with a slave that illustrates this point nicely: when the abolitionist asked after the slave's "self," he responded, "I ain't got no self." Without hesitation, the abolitionist responded to the black man, "Slave are you?" "That's what I is."

This connection among language, memory, and the self has been of signal importance to African-Americans, intent as they have had to be upon demonstrating both common humanity with whites and upon demonstrating that their "selves" were, somehow, as whole, integral, educable, and as noble as were those of any other American ethnic group. Scholars have long registered the relation in the African-American tradition between the declaration of selfhood and the public act of publication. Deprived of formal recognition of their subjectivity in Western arts and letters, in jurisprudence, and in all that signals full citizenship, African-Americans sought out the permanence of the book to write a rhetorical self into the nonexistence of language. "I write my self, therefore I am" could very well be taken as the motto of "the race" in this country. The perilous journey from object to subject is strewn with black autobiographies. "Unscathed by Slavery" could very well be the subtitle of the hundreds of slave narratives published by ex-slaves between 1760 and Booker T. Washington's *Up From Slavery* in 1901.

I was once led to speculate whether the very vitality of autobiography produced a concomitant nonvitality of the individualized black biography; whether the requisite energy necessary to proclaim that "I am" could not be dissipated in making that claim for another. In the African-American tradition, it appears, the channel of existence had to be transgressed by one's self, without the agency of a midwife. One's public initiation was a private act. One crossed that abyss by an act of individual will, positing humanity, selfhood, and citizenship with the stroke of a pen. Only in the biographical dictionary could these requisites of isolated initiation be transcended, biography as an iconographic act of hero-production was collective, a testament to the existence of "the negro," rather than isolated Negroes; parts, in the arbitrariness of alphabetical order, amounting to an African-American whole. Nurses and churchmen; club women and fraternal orders; free citizens of Cincinnati and freemasons—each had their collective biographical testimony, intended to create the collective features of "the race." But the black individual's concern was to create herself or himself, in words. As Barbara Mellix has put it so well, "I came to comprehend more fully the generative power of language. I discovered . . . that through writing one can continually bring new selves into being, each with new responsibilities and difficulties, but also with new possibilities. Remarkable power, indeed. I write and continually give birth to myself."

Bearing Witness is a collection of autobiographical statements written by black women and men between 1904 and 1990, ranging from Fannie Barrier Williams's *A Northern Negro's Autobiography* (1904) to Itabari Njeri's *Every Good-Bye Ain't Gone* (1990).

The field of African-American autobiography is especially rich. Accordingly, this anthology would have been considerably longer—indeed at least twice as long—had I been able to include all of the selections that I believe merit the designation "canonical" texts in the tradition. For obvious reasons, however, this could not be. I would have liked to have included selections from the slave narratives, as well as the writings of such people as: James Weldon Johnson, William Pickens, Billie Holiday, Theodore Rosengarten, Dorothy West, and Barbara Mellix among several others. No doubt each reader will have suggestions for additions and complaints about omissions, but I have tried to edit a collection of autobiographical writing in the twentieth century more representative of gender differences than has heretofore been the case. Included among the contributors are scholars, politicians, creative writers, and journalists. Despite differences of occupation, class, gender, and chronology, these fragments provide intimate and fascinating portraits of outstanding individual black Americans.

But they also, taken together, amount to a collective portrait of the African-American people, revealing how they kept the faith against what often seemed like the insuperable odds of racism and sexism in a society where being black (and a woman) were enormous barriers to realizing the dream of individual accomplishment.

These testaments reveal that answers to questions of African-American identity in American society are not static, that they are dynamic constructions reflecting, and responding to, the dramatic changes in black-white and male-female American relations between antebellum America and the post–civil rights era. Despite shared concerns about the relation of the individual black talent to racist and sexist social structures evinced in all of this writing—and despite the formal relations that obtain among these texts—the pattern of response by black writers is full of infinite improvisation, like variations on two great themes. The silences that a contemporary reader may remark in the narrative of the ex-slave—silences on, for example, his or her own sexuality and misogyny—become, for a later generation, fundamental moments of revelation. We have come a long way from Samuel Delany's very personal account of his discovery of his own homosexuality or Itabari Njeri's frank account of her cousin's turn to the streets at age thirteen. And while the concern with literacy—from learning the ABCs to the immersion in the world's great literatures—and its relation to freedom is one of the leitmotifs of this volume, we can safely say that what it means to be a black person in America has proven richly various. As James Baldwin put it so well, "While the tale of how we suffer, and how we are delighted, and how we may triumph is never new, it always must be heard. There isn't any other to tell, it's the only light we've got in all this darkness . . . and this tale, according to that face, that body, those strong hands on those strings, has another aspect in every country, and a new depth in every genera-tion." These stories endure as chronicles not merely of personal achievement, but of the impulse *to bear witness.*

Fannie Barrier Williams, lecturer and feminist, was born a free
black in New York in 1855. Her writings include "The Intellectual Progress of the Colored Women of the United States Since
the Emancipation Proclamation" and "Social Bonds in the Black
Belt of Chicago." She died in New York in 1944.

FANNIE BARRIER WILLIAMS

A Northern Negro's Autobiography

(1904)

IN THE INDEPENDENT of March 17th last I read, with a great deal of interest, three contributions to the so-called race problem, to be found in the experiences of a Southern colored woman, a Southern white woman and a Northern white woman.

I am a Northern colored woman, a mulatto in complexion, and was born since the war in a village town of Western New York. My parents and grandparents were free people. My mother was born in New York State and my father in Pennsylvania. They both attended the common schools and were fairly educated. They had a taste for good books and the refinements of life, were public spirited and regarded as good citizens. My father moved to this Western New York village when he was quite a boy and was a resident of the town for over fifty years; he was married to my mother in this town and three

[The three articles that we printed in THE INDEPENDENT last March called forth more replies than any articles we have recently published. We were obliged to reject all of them, however, except the following, which discusses a phase of the negro problem not touched upon by the three anonymous women, and often generally overlooked by the American people. This article therefore supplements the others, and the four taken together picture the negro problem from the feminine standpoint in the most genuine and realistic manner shown in any articles we have seen in print.—Editor, *The Independent*] children were born to them; he created for himself a good business and was able to take good care of his family. My parents were strictly religious people and were members of one of the largest white churches in the village. My father, during his membership in this church, held successively almost every important office open to a layman, having been clerk, trustee, treasurer and deacon, which office he held at the time of his death, in 1890. He was for years teacher of an adult Bible class composed of some of the best men and women of the village, and my mother is still a teacher of a large Bible class of women in the same Sunday school. Ours was the only colored family in the church, in fact, the only one in the town for many years, and certainly there could not have been a relationship more cordial, respectful and intimate than that of our family and the white people of this community. We three children were sent to school as soon as we were old enough, and remained there until we were graduated. During our school days our associates, schoolmates and companions were all white boys and girls. These relationships were natural, spontaneous and free from all restraint. We went freely to each other's houses, to parties, socials, and joined on equal terms in all school entertainments with perfect comradeship. We suffered from no discriminations on account of color or "previous condition," and lived in blissful ignorance of the fact that we were practicing the unpardonable sin of "social equality." Indeed, until I became a young woman and went South to teach I had never been reminded that I belonged to an "inferior race."

After I was graduated from school my first ambition was to teach. I could easily have obtained a position there at my own home, but I wanted to go out into the world and do something large or out of the ordinary. I had known of quite a number of fine young white women who had gone South to teach the freedmen, and, following my race instinct, I resolved to do the same. I soon obtained a situation in one of the ex–slave States. It was here and for the first time that I began life as a colored person, in all that that term implies. No one but a colored woman, reared and educated as I was, can ever know what it means to be brought face to face with conditions that fairly overwhelm you with the ugly reminder that a certain penalty must be suffered by those who, not being able to select their own parentage, must be born of a dark complexion. What a shattering of cherished ideals! Everything that I learned and experienced in my innocent social relationships in New York State had to be unlearned and readjusted to these lowered standards and changed conditions. The Bible that I had been taught, the preaching I had heard, the philosophy and ethics and the rules of conduct that I had been so sure of, were all to be discounted. All truth seemed here only half truths. I found that, instead of there being a unity of life common to all intelligent, respectable and ambitious people, down South life was divided into white and black lines, and that in every direction my ambitions and aspirations were to have no beginnings and no chance for development. But, in spite of all this, I tried to adapt myself to these hateful conditions. I had some talent for painting, and in order to obtain further instruction I importuned a white art teacher to admit me into one of her classes, to which she finally consented, but on the second day of my appearance in the class I chanced to look up suddenly and was amazed to find that I was completely surrounded by screens, and when I resented the apparent insult, it was made the condition of my remaining in the class. I had missed the training that would have made this continued humiliation possible; so at a great sacrifice I went to a New England city, but even here, in the very cradle of liberty, white Southerners were there before me, and to save their feelings I was told by the principal of the school, a man who was descended from a long line of abolition ancestors, that it would imperil the interests of the school if I remained, as all of his Southern pupils would leave, and again I had to submit to the tyranny of a dark complexion. But it is scarcely possible to enumerate the many ways in which an ambitious colored young woman is prevented from being all that she might be in the higher directions of life in this country. Plainly I would have been far happier as a woman if my life up to the age of eighteen years had not been so free, spontaneous and unhampered by race prejudice. I have still many white friends and the old home and school associations are still sweet and delightful and always renewed with pleasure, yet I have never quite recovered from the shock and pain of my first bitter realization that to be a colored woman is to be discredited, mistrusted and often meanly hated. My faith in the verities of religion, in justice, in love and many sacredly taught sentiments has greatly decreased since I have learned how little even these stand for when you are a colored woman.

After teaching a few years in the South, I went back to my home in New York State to be married. After the buffetings, discouragements and discourtesies that I had been compelled to endure, it was almost as in a dream that I saw again my schoolmates gather around me, making my home beautiful with flowers, managing every detail of preparation for my wedding, showering me with gifts, and joining in the ceremony with tears and blessings. My own family and my husband were the only persons to lend color to the occasion. Minister, attendants, friends, flowers and hearts were of purest white. If this be social equality, it certainly was not of my own seeking and I must say that no one seemed harmed by it. It seemed all a simple part of the natural life we lived where people are loved and respected for their worth, in spite of their darker complexions.

After my marriage my husband and I moved to one of the larger cities of the North, where we have continued to live. In this larger field of life and action I found myself, like many another woman, becoming interested in many things that come within the range of woman's active sympathy and influence.

My interest in various reform work, irrespective of color, led me frequently to join hand in hand with white women on a common basis of fellowship and helpfulness extended to all who needed our sympathy and interest. I experienced very few evidences of race prejudice and perhaps had more than my share of kindness and recognition. However, this kindness to me as an individual did not satisfy me or blind me to the many inequalities suffered by young colored women seeking employment and other advantages of metropolitan life. I soon discovered that it was much easier for progressive white women to be considerate and even companionable to one colored woman whom they chanced to know and like than to be just and generous to colored young women as a race who needed their sympathy and influence in securing employment and recognition according to their tastes and ability. To this end I began to use my influence and associations to further the cause of these helpless young colored women, in an effort to save them to themselves and society, by finding, for those who must work, suitable employment. How surprisingly difficult was my task may be seen in the following instances selected from many of like nature:

I was encouraged to call upon a certain bank president, well known for his broad, humane principles and high-mindedness. I told him what I wanted, and how I thought he could give me some practical assistance, and enlarged upon the difficulties that stand in the way of ambitious and capable young colored women. He was inclined to think, and frankly told me, that he thought I was a little overstating the case, and added, with rather a triumphant air, so sure he was that I could not make good my statements as to ability, fitness, etc., "We need a competent stenographer right here in the bank now; if you will send to me the kind of a young colored woman you describe, that is thoroughly equipped, I think I can convince you that you are wrong." I ventured to tell him that the young woman I had in mind did not show much color. He at once interrupted me by saying, "Oh, that will not cut any figure; you send the young woman here." I did so and allowed a long time to elapse before going to see him again. When I did call, at the young woman's request, the gentleman said, with deep humiliation, "I am ashamed to confess, Mrs. ———, that you were right and I was wrong. I felt it my duty to say to the directors that this young woman had a slight trace of negro blood. That settled it. They promptly said, 'We don't want her, that's all.'" He gave the names of some of the directors and I recognized one of them as a man of long prayers and a heavy contributor to the Foreign Mission Fund; another's name was a household word on account of his financial interest in Home Missions and Church extension work. I went back to the young woman and could but weep with her because I knew that she was almost in despair over the necessity of speedily finding something to do. The only consolation I could offer was that the president declared she was the most skillful and thoroughly competent young woman who had ever applied for the position.

I tried another large establishment and had a pleasant talk with the manager, who unwittingly committed himself to an overwhelming desire "to help the colored people." He said that his parents were staunch abolitionists and connected with the underground railway, and that he distinctly remembered that as a child he was not allowed to eat sugar that had been cultivated by the labor of the poor slave or to wear cotton manufactured by slave labor, and his face glowed as he told me how he loved his "black mammie," and so on *ad nauseam*. I began to feel quite elated at the correctness of my judgment in seeking him out of so many. I then said: "I see that you employ a large number of young women as clerks and stenographers. I have in mind some very competent young colored women who are almost on the verge of despair for lack of suitable employment. Would you be willing to try one of them should you have a vacancy?" The grayness of age swept over his countenance as he solemnly said: "Oh, I wish you had not asked me that question. My clerks would leave and such an innovation would cause a general upheaval in my business." "But," I said, "your clerks surely do not run your business!" "No," he said, "you could not understand." Knowing that he was very religious, my almost forgotten Bible training came to mind. I quoted Scripture as to "God being no respecter of persons," and reminded him that these young women were in moral danger through enforced idleness, and quoted the anathema of offending one of "these little ones" whom Christ loved. But he did not seem to fear at all condemnation from that high tribunal. His only reply was, "Oh, that is different," and I turned away, sadly thinking "Is it different?"

This still remains a sad chapter in my experience, even tho I have been successful in finding a few good positions for young colored women, not one of whom has ever lost her position through any fault of hers. On the contrary, they have become the prize workers wherever they have been employed. One of them became her employer's private secretary, and he told me with much enthusiasm that her place could scarcely be filled, she had become so efficient and showed such an intelligent grasp upon the requirements of the position. My plea has always been simply to give these girls a chance and let them stand or fall by any test that is not merely a color test.

I want to speak of one other instance. It sometimes happens that after I have succeeded in getting these girls placed and their competency has been proved they are subjected to the most unexpected humiliations. A young woman of very refined and dignified appearance and with only a slight trace of African blood had held her position for some time in an office where she had been bookkeeper, stenographer and clerk, respectively, and was very highly thought of both by her employer and her fellow clerks. She was sitting at her desk one day when a man entered and asked for her employer. She told him to be seated, that Mr. ———— would be back in a moment. The man walked around the office, then came back to her and said: "I came from a section of the country where we make your people know their places. Don't you think you are out of yours?" She merely looked up and said, "I think I know my place." He strolled about for a moment, then came back to her and said: "I am a Southern man, I am, and I would like to know what kind of a man this is that employs a 'nigger' to sit at a desk and write." She replied: "You will find Mr. ———— a perfect gentleman." The proprietor came in, in a moment, and ushered the man into his private office. The Southern gentleman came out of the office very precipitately. It evidently only took him a few seconds to verify the clerk's words that "her employer was a perfect gentleman."

It may be plainly seen that public efforts of this kind and a talent for public speaking and writing would naturally bring to me a recognition and association independent of any self-seeking on my own account. It, therefore, seemed altogether natural that some of my white friends should ask me to make application for membership in a prominent woman's club on the ground of mutual helpfulness and mutual interest in many things. I allowed my name to be presented to the club without the slightest dream that it would cause any opposition or even discussion. This progressive club has a membership of over eight hundred women, and its personality fairly represents the wealth, intelligence and culture of the women of the city. When the members of this great club came to know the color of its new applicant there was a startled cry that seemed to have no bounds. Up to this time no one knew that there was any anti-negro sentiment in the club. Its purposes were so humane and philanthropic and its grade of individual membership so high and inclusive of almost every nationality that my endorsers thought that my application would only be subject to the club's test of eligibility, which was declared to be "Character, intelligence and the reciprocal advantage to the club and the individual, without regard to race, color, religion or politics." For nearly fourteen months my application was fought by a determined minority. Other clubs throughout the country took up the matter, and the awful example was held up in such a way as to frighten many would-be friends. The whole anti-slavery question was fought over again in the same spirit and with the same arguments, but the common sense of the members finally prevailed over their prejudices. When the final vote was taken I was elected to membership by a decisive majority.

Before my admission into the club some of the members came to me and frankly told me that they would leave the club, much as they valued their membership, if I persisted in coming in. Their only reason was that they did not think the time had yet come for that sort of equality. Since my application was not of my own seeking I refused to recognize their unreasonable prejudices as something that ought to be fostered and perpetuated; beside, I felt that I owed something to the friends who had shown me such unswerving loyalty through all those long and trying months, when every phase of my public and private life was scrutinized and commented upon in a vain effort to find something in proof of my ineligibility. That I should possess any finer feeling that must suffer under this merciless persecution and unwelcome notoriety seemed not to be thought of by those who professed to believe that my presence in a club of eight hundred women would be at a cost of their fair self-respect. I cannot say that I have experienced the same kind of humiliations as recited in the pathetic story of a Southern colored woman in THE INDEPENDENT of March 17th, but I can but believe that the prejudice that blights and hinders is quite as decided in the North as it is in the South, but does not manifest itself so openly and brutally.

Fortunately, since my marriage I have had but little experience south of Mason and Dixon's line. Some time ago I was induced by several clubs in different States and cities of the South to make a kind of lecture tour through that section. I knew, of course, of the miserable separations, "Jim Crow" cars, and other offensive restrictions and resolved to make the best of them. But the "Jim Crow" cars were almost intolerable to me. I was fortunate enough to escape them in every instance. There is such a cosmopolitan population in some of the Southwestern States, made up of Spanish, Mexican and French nationalities, that the conductors are very often deceived; beside, they know that an insult can scarcely go further than to ask the wrong person if he or she be colored. I made it a rule always to take my seat in the first-class car, to which I felt I was entitled by virtue of my first-class ticket. However, adapting one's self to these false conditions does not contribute to one's peace of mind, self-respect or honesty. I remember that at a certain place I was too late to procure my ticket at the station, and the conductor told me that I would have to go out at the next station and buy my ticket, and then, despite my English book, which I was very ostentatiously reading, he stepped back and quickly asked me, "Madame, are you colored?" I as quickly replied, "Je suis Français." "Français?" he repeated. I said, "Oui." He then called to the brakeman and said, "Take this lady's money and go out at the next station and buy her ticket for her," which he kindly did, and I as kindly replied, as he handed me the ticket, "Merci." Fortunately their knowledge of French ended before mine did or there might have been some embarrassments as to my further unfamiliarity with my mother tongue. However, I quieted my conscience by recalling that there was quite a strain of French blood in my ancestry, and too that their barbarous laws did not allow a lady to be both comfortable and honest. It is needless to say that I traveled undisturbed in the cars to which my ticket entitled me after this success, but I carried an abiding heartache for the refined and helpless colored women who must live continuously under these repressive and unjust laws. The hateful interpretation of these laws is to make no distinction between the educated and refined and the ignorant and depraved negro.

Again, the South seems to be full of paradoxes. In one city of the far South I was asked to address a club of very aristocratic white women, which I did with considerable satisfaction to myself because it gave me an opportunity to call the attention of these white women to the many cultured and educated colored women living right there in their midst, whom they did not know, and to suggest that they find some common ground of fellowship and helpfulness that must result in the general uplift of all women. These women gave me a respectful and appreciative hearing, and the majority of them graciously remained and received an introduction to me after the address. A curious feature of the meeting was that, altho it had been announced in all the papers as a public meeting, not a colored person was present except myself, which shows how almost insurmountable a color line can be.

In another city I had a very different experience, which betrayed my unconscious fear of the treachery of Southern prejudice, tho following so closely upon the pleasant experience above related. I noticed, while on my way to the church where I was advertised to speak to a colored audience, that we were being followed by a half a dozen of what seemed to me the typical Southern "cracker," red shirt and all. I was not thinking of moonshiners, but of Ku-Klux clans, midnight lynching parties, etc. My fears were further increased when they suddenly stopped and separated, so that my friends and myself were obliged to pass between the lines of three so made. My friends tried to reassure me, but I fancied with trembling tones, but my menacing escort then closed up ranks and again followed on. Finally they beckoned to the only gentleman with us and asked him what I was going to talk about. He told them the subject and hastened to console me. When we got to the church and just before I rose to speak these six men all filed in and sat down near the platform, accompanied by another individual even more fierce in appearance than they were, whom I afterward learned was the deputy sheriff of the town. My feelings are better imagined than described, but I found myself struggling to hold the attention only of this menacing portion of my audience. They remained to the close of the lecture and as they went out expressed appreciation of my "good sense," as they termed it.

This recital has no place in this article save to show the many contrasts a brief visit to the Southland is capable of revealing. It is only just to add that I have traveled in the first-class—that is, white— cars all through the South, through Texas, Georgia and as far as Birmingham, Ala., but I have never received an insult or discourtesy from a Southern white man. While, fortunately, this has been my experience, still I believe that in some other localities in the South such an experience would seem almost incredible.

I want to refer briefly to the remarks of one of the writers in THE INDEPENDENT with reference to the character strength of colored women. I think it but just to say that we must look to American slavery as the source of every imperfection that mars the character of the colored American. It ought not to be necessary to remind a Southern woman that less than 50 years ago the ill-starred mothers of this ransomed race were not allowed to be modest, not allowed to follow the instincts of moral rectitude, and there was no living man to whom they could cry for protection against the men who not only owned them, body and soul, but also the souls of their husbands, their brothers, and, alas, their sons. Slavery made her the only woman in America for whom virtue was not an ornament and a necessity. But in spite of this dark and painful past, I believe that the sweeping assertions of this writer are grossly untrue and unjust at least to thousands of colored women in the North who were free from the debasing influence of slavery, as well as thousands of women in the South, who instinctively fought to preserve their own honor and that of their unfortunate offspring. I believe that the colored women are just as strong and just as weak as any other women with like education, training and environment.

It is a significant and shameful fact that I am constantly in receipt of letters from the still unprotected colored women of the South, begging me to find employment for their daughters according to their ability, as domestics or otherwise, to save them from going into the homes of the South as servants, as there is nothing to save them from dishonor and degradation. Many prominent white women and ministers will verify this statement. The heartbroken cry of some of these helpless mothers bears no suggestion of the "flaunting pride of dishonor" so easily obtained, by simply allowing their daughters to enter the homes of the white women of the South. Their own mothers cannot protect them and white women will not, or do not. The moral feature of this problem has complications that it would seem better not to dwell on. From my own study of the question, the colored woman deserves greater credit for what she has done and is doing than blame for what she cannot so soon overcome.

As to the negro problem, the only things one can be really sure of is that it has a beginning, and we know that it is progressing some way, but no one knows the end. Prejudice is here and everywhere, but it may not manifest itself so brutally as in the South. The chief interest in the North seems to be centered in business, and it is in business where race prejudice shows itself the strongest. The chief interest in the South is social supremacy, therefore prejudice manifests itself most strongly against even an imaginary approach to social contact. Here in the Northern States I find that a colored woman of character and intelligence will be recognized and respected, but the white woman who will recognize and associate with her in the same club or church would probably not tolerate her as a fellow clerk in office. . . .

The conclusion of the whole matter seems to be that whether I live in the North or the South, I cannot be counted for my full value, be that much or little. I dare not cease to hope and aspire and believe in human love and justice, but progress is painful and my faith is often strained to the breaking point.

CHICAGO, ILL.

Marita Bonner was born in Boston in 1899. She contributed
several stories, including "The Purple Flower," to the magazines
Crisis and *Opportunity*. Her collected works are published as
Frye Street and Environs: The Collected Works of Marita Bonner.
She died in 1971.

2

MARITA BONNER

From Frye Street and Environs: The Collected Works of Marita Bonner

On Being Young—a Woman—and Colored

(1925)

YOU START OUT after you have gone from kindergarten to sheepskin covered with sundry Latin phrases.

At least you know what you want life to give you. A career as fixed and as calmly brilliant as the North Star. The one real thing that money buys. Time. Time to do things. A house that can be as delectably out of order and as easily put in order as the doll-house of "playing-house" days. And of course, a husband you can look up to without looking down on yourself.

Somehow you feel like a kitten in a sunny catnip field that sees sleek, plump brown field mice and yellow baby chicks sitting coyly, side by side, under each leaf. A desire to dash three or four ways seizes you.

That's Youth.

But you know that things learned need testing—acid testing—to see if they are really after all, an interwoven part of you. All your life you have heard of the debt you owe "Your People" because you have managed to have the things they have not largely had.

So you find a spot where there are hordes of them—of course below the Line—to be your catnip field while you close your eyes to mice and chickens alike.

If you have never lived among your own, you feel prodigal. Some warm untouched current flows through them—through you—and drags you out into the deep waters of a new sea of human foibles and mannerisms; of a peculiar psychology and prejudices. And one day you find yourself entangled—enmeshed—pinioned in the seaweed of a Black Ghetto.

Not a Ghetto, placid like the Strasse that flows, outwardly unperturbed and calm in a stream of religious belief, but a peculiar group. Cut off, flung together, shoved aside in a bundle because of color and with no more in common.

Unless color is, after all, the real bond.

Milling around like live fish in a basket. Those at the bottom crushed into a sort of stupid apathy by the weight of those on top. Those on top leaping, leaping; leaping to scale the sides; to get out.

There are two "colored" movies, innumerable parties—and cards. Cards played so intensely that it fascinates and repulses at once.

Movies.

Movies worthy and worthless—but not even a low-caste spoken stage.

Parties, plentiful. Music and dancing and much that is wit and color and gaiety. But they are like the richest chocolate; stuffed costly chocolates that make the taste go stale if you have too many of them. That make plain whole bread taste like ashes.

There are all the earmarks of a group within a group. Cut off all around from ingress from or egress to other groups. A sameness of type. The smug self-satisfaction of an inner measurement; a measurement by standards known within a limited group and not those of an unlimited, seeing, world. . . . Like the blind, blind mice. Mice whose eyes have been blinded.

Strange longing seizes hold of you. You wish yourself back where you can lay your dollar down and sit in a dollar seat to hear voices, strings, reeds that have lifted the World out, up, beyond things that have bodies and walls. Where you can marvel at new marbles and bronzes and flat colors that will make men forget that things exist in a flesh more often than in spirit. Where you can sink your body in a cushioned seat and sink your soul at the same time into a section of life set before you on the boards for a few hours.

You hear that up at New York this is to be seen; that, to be heard.

You decide the next train will take you there.

You decide the next second that that train will not take you, nor the next—nor the next for some time to come.

For you know that—being a woman—you cannot twice a month or twice a year, for that matter, break away to see or hear anything in a city that is supposed to see and hear too much.

That's being a woman. A woman of any color.

You decide that something is wrong with a world that stifles and chokes; that cuts off and stunts; hedging in, pressing down on eyes, ears and throat. Somehow all wrong.

You wonder how it happens there that—say five hundred miles from the Bay State—Anglo Saxon intelligence is so warped and stunted.

How judgment and discernment are bred out of the race. And what has become of discrimination? Discrimination of the right sort. Discrimination that the best minds have told you weighs shadows and nuances and spiritual differences before it catalogues. The kind they have taught you all of your life was best: that looks clearly past generalization and past appearance to dissect, to dig down to the real heart of matters. That casts aside rapid summary conclusions, drawn from primary inference, as Daniel did the spiced meats.

Why can't they then perceive that there is a difference in the glance from a pair of eyes that look, mildly docile, at "white ladies" and those that, impersonally and perceptively—aware of distinctions—see only women who happen to be white?

Why do they see a colored woman only as a gross collection of desires, all uncontrolled, reaching out for their Apollos and the Quasimodos with avid indiscrimination?

Why unless you talk in staccato squawks—brittle as seashells—unless you "champ" gum—unless you cover two yards square when you laugh—unless your taste runs to violent colors—impossible perfumes and more impossible clothes—are you a feminine Caliban craving to pass for Ariel?

An empty imitation of an empty invitation. A mime; a sham; a copy-cat. A hollow re-echo. A froth, a foam. A fleck of the ashes of superficiality?

Everything you touch or taste now is like the flesh of an unripe persimmon.

. . . Do you need to be told what that is being . . . ?

Old ideas, old fundamentals seem worm-eaten, out-grown, worthless, bitter; fit for the scrap-heap of Wisdom.

What you had thought tangible and practical has turned out to be a collection of "blue-flower" theories.

If they have not discovered how to use their accumulation of facts, they are useless to you in Their world.

Every part of you becomes bitter.

But—"In Heaven's name, do not grow bitter. Be bigger than they are"—exhort white friends who have never had to draw breath in a Jim-Crow train. Who have never had petty putrid insult dragged over them—drawing blood—like pebbled sand on your body where the skin is tenderest. On your body where the skin is thinnest and tenderest.

You long to explode and hurt everything white; friendly; unfriendly. But you know that you cannot live with a chip on your shoulder even if you can manage a smile around your eyes—without getting steely and brittle and losing the softness that makes you a woman.

For chips make you bend your body to balance them. And once you bend, you lose your poise, your balance, and the chip gets into you. The real you. You get hard.

. . . And many things in you can ossify . . .

And you know, being a woman, you have to go about it gently and quietly, to find out and to discover just what is wrong. Just what can be done.

You see clearly that they have acquired things.

Money; money. Money to build with, money to destroy. Money to swim in. Money to drown in. Money.

An ascendancy of wisdom. An incalculable hoard of wisdom in all fields, in all things collected from all quarters of humanity.

A stupendous mass of things.

Things.

So, too, the Greeks . . . Things.

And the Romans. . . .

And you wonder and wonder why they have not discovered how to handle deftly and skillfully, Wisdom, stored up for them—like the honey for the Gods on Olympus—since time unknown.

You wonder and you wonder until you wander out into Infinity, where—if it is to be found anywhere—Truth really exists.

The Greeks had possessions, culture. They were lost because they did not understand.

The Romans owned more than anyone else. Trampled under the heel of Vandals and Civilization, because they would not understand.

Greeks. Did not understand.

Romans. Would not understand.

"They." Will not understand.

So you find they have shut Wisdom up and have forgotten to find the key that will let her out. They have trapped, trammeled, lashed her to themselves with thews and thongs and theories. They have ransacked sea and earth and air to bring every treasure to her. But she sulks and will not work for a world with a whitish hue because it has snubbed her twin sister, Understanding.

You see clearly—off there is Infinity—Understanding. Standing alone, waiting for someone to really want her.

But she is so far out there is no way to snatch at her and really drag her in.

So—being a woman—you can wait.

You must sit quietly without a chip. Not sodden—and weighted as if your feet were cast in the iron of your soul. Not wasting strength in enervating gestures as if two hundred years of bonds and whips had really tricked you into nervous uncertainty.

But quiet; quiet. Like Buddha—who brown like I am—sat entirely at ease, entirely sure of himself; motionless and knowing, a thousand years before the white man knew there was so very much difference between feet and hands.

Motionless on the outside. But on the inside?

Silent.

Still . . . "Perhaps Buddha is a woman."

So you too. Still; quiet; with a smile, ever so slight, at the eyes so that Life will flow into and not by you. And you can gather, as it passes, the essences, the overtones, the tints, the shadows; draw understanding to yourself.

And then you can, when Time is ripe, swoop to your feet—at your full height—at a single gesture.

Ready to go where?

Why . . . Wherever God motions.

Zora Neale Hurston, folklorist, anthropologist, and writer, was born in the all-black town of Eatonville, Florida, in 1891. Hurston wrote both fiction—stories, novels, and plays—and nonfiction books on folklore and black culture. Her works include *Jonah's Gourd Vine, Mules and Men, Their Eyes Were Watching God, Tell My Horse, Moses, Man of the Mountain, Dust Tracks on a Road,* and *Seraph on the Suwanee.* She died in Fort Pierce, Florida, in 1960.

3

ZORA NEALE HURSTON

How It Feels to Be Colored Me

(1928)

I AM COLORED but I offer nothing in the way of extenuating circumstances except the fact that I am the only Negro in the United States whose grandfather on the mother's side was *not* an Indian chief.

I remember the very day that I became colored. Up to my thirteenth year I lived in the little Negro town of Eatonville, Florida. It is exclusively a colored town. The only white people I knew passed through the town going to or coming from Orlando. The native whites rode dusty horses, the Northern tourists chugged down the sandy village road in automobiles. The town knew the Southerners and never stopped cane chewing[1] when they passed. But the Northerners were something else again. They were peered at cautiously from behind curtains by the timid. The more venturesome would come out on the porch to watch them go past and got just as much pleasure out of the tourists as the tourists got out of the village.

The front porch might seem a daring place for the rest of the town, but it was a gallery seat for me. My favorite place was atop the gate-post. Proscenium box for a born first-nighter. Not only did I enjoy the show, but I didn't mind the actors knowing that I liked

---

[1]Chewing sugar cane.

it. I usually spoke to them in passing. I'd wave at them and when they returned my salute, I would say something like this: "Howdy-do-well-I-thank-you-where-you-goin'?" Usually automobile or the horse paused at this, and after a queer exchange of compliments, I would probably "go a piece of the way" with them, as we say in farthest Florida. If one of my family happened to come to the front in time to see me, of course negotiations would be rudely broken off. But even so, it is clear that I was the first "welcome-to-our-state" Floridian, and I hope the Miami Chamber of Commerce will please take notice.

During this period, white people differed from colored to me only in that they rode through town and never lived there. They liked to hear me "speak pieces" and sing and wanted to see me dance the parse-me-la, and gave me generously of their small silver for doing these things, which seemed strange to me for I wanted to do them so much that I needed bribing to stop. Only they didn't know it. The colored people gave no dimes. They deplored any joyful tendencies in me, but I was their Zora nevertheless. I belonged to them, to the nearby hotels, to the county—everybody's Zora.

But changes came in the family when I was thirteen, and I was sent to school in Jacksonville. I left Eatonville, the town of the olean-ders,[2] as Zora. When I disembarked from the river-boat at Jacksonville, she was no more. It seemed that I had suffered a sea change. I was not Zora of Orange County any more, I was now a little colored girl. I found it out in certain ways. In my heart as well as in the mirror, I became a fast brown—warranted not to rub nor run.

But I am not tragically colored. There is no great sorrow dammed up in my soul, nor lurking behind my eyes. I do not mind at all. I do not belong to the sobbing school of Negrohood who hold that nature somehow has given them a lowdown dirty deal and whose feelings are all hurt about it. Even in the helter-skelter skirmish that is my life, I have seen that the world is to the strong regardless of a little

[2]Fragrant tropical flowers.

pigmentation more or less. No, I do not weep at the world—I am too busy sharpening my oyster knife.[3]

Someone is always at my elbow reminding me that I am the granddaughter of slaves. It fails to register depression with me. Slavery is sixty years in the past. The operation was successful and the patient is doing well, thank you. The terrible struggle[4] that made me an American out of a potential slave said "On the line!" The Reconstruction said "Get set!"; and the generation before said "Go!" I am off to a flying start and I must not halt in the stretch to look behind and weep. Slavery is the price I paid for civilization, and the choice was not with me. It is a bully adventure and worth all that I have paid through my ancestors for it. No one on earth ever had a greater chance for glory. The world to be won and nothing to be lost. It is thrilling to think—to know that for any act of mine, I shall get twice as much praise or twice as much blame. It is quite exciting to hold the center of the national stage, with the spectators not knowing whether to laugh or to weep.

The position of my white neighbor is much more difficult. No brown specter pulls up a chair beside me when I sit down to eat. No dark ghost thrusts its leg against mine in bed. The game of keeping what one has is never so exciting as the game of getting.

I do not always feel colored. Even now I often achieve the unconscious Zora of Eatonville before the Hegira.[5] I feel most colored when I am thrown against a sharp white background.

For instance at Barnard.[6] "Beside the waters of the Hudson" I feel my race. Among the thousand white persons, I am a dark rock surged upon, and overswept, but through it all, I remain myself. When covered by the waters, I am; and the ebb but reveals me again.

[3]Cf. the popular expression "The world is my oyster."
[4]I.e., the Civil War. The Reconstruction was the period immediately following the war; one of its better effects was that Northern educators came south to teach newly freed slaves.
[5]I.e., a journey undertaken away from a dangerous situation into a more highly desirable one (literally, the flight of Mohammed from Mecca in A.D. 622).
[6]American women's college in New York City, near the Hudson River (cf. the psalmist's "by the waters of Babylon").

★★★

Sometimes it is the other way around. A white person is set down in our midst, but the contrast is just as sharp for me. For instance, when I sit in the drafty basement that is The New World Cabaret with a white person, my color comes. We enter chatting about any little nothing that we have in common and are seated by the jazz waiters. In the abrupt way that jazz orchestras have, this one plunges into a number. It loses no time in circumlocutions, but gets right down to business. It constructs the thorax and splits the heart with its tempo and narcotic harmonies. This orchestra grows rambunctious, rears on its hind legs and attacks the tonal veil with primitive fury, rending it, clawing it until it breaks through to the jungle beyond. I follow those heathen—follow them exultingly. I dance wildly inside myself; I yell within, I whoop; I shake my assegai[7] above my head, I hurl it true to the mark *yeeeeooww!* I am in the jungle and living in the jungle way. My face is painted red and yellow and my body is painted blue. My pulse is throbbing like a war drum. I want to slaughter something— give paid, give death to what, I do not know. But the piece ends. The men of the orchestra wipe their lips and rest their fingers. I creep back slowly to the veneer we call civilization with the last tone and find the white friend sitting motionless in his seat, smoking calmly.

"Good music they have here," he remarks, drumming the table with his fingertips.

Music. The great blobs of purple and red emotion have not touched him. He has only heard what I felt. He is far away and I see him but dimly across the ocean and the continent that have fallen between us. He is so pale with his whiteness then and I am *so* colored.

At certain times I have no race, I am *me*. When I set my hat at a certain angle and saunter down Seventh Avenue, Harlem City, feeling as snooty as the lions in front of the Forty-second Street Library, for instance. So far as my feelings are concerned, Peggy Hopkins Joyce[8] on the Boule Mich with her gorgeous raiment, stately carriage, knees

[7]South African hunting spear.
[8]Peggy Hopkins Joyce: American beauty and fashion-setter of the twenties; the Boule Mich is the Boulevard Saint-Michel, a fashionable Parisian street.

knocking together in a most aristocratic manner, has nothing on me. The cosmic Zora emerges. I belong to no race nor time. I am the eternal feminine with its string of beads.

I have no separate feeling about being an American citizen and colored. I am merely a fragment of the Great Soul that surges within the boundaries. My country, right or wrong.

Sometimes, I feel discriminated against, but it does not make me angry. It merely astonishes me. How *can* any deny themselves the pleasure of my company? It's beyond me.

But in the main, I feel like a brown bag of miscellany propped against a wall. Against a wall in company with other bags, white, red and yellow. Pour out the contents, and there is discovered a jumble of small things priceless and worthless. A first-water diamond, an empty spool, bits of broken glass, lengths of string, a key to a door long since crumbled away, a rusty knife-blade, old shoes saved for a road that never was and never will be, a nail bent under the weight of things too heavy for any nail, a dried flower or two still a little fragrant. In your hand is the brown bag. On the ground before you is the jumble it held—so much like the jumble in the bags, could they be emptied, that all might be dumped in a single heap and the bags refilled without altering the content of any greatly. A bit of colored glass more or less would not matter. Perhaps that is how the Great Stuffer of Bags filled them in the first place—who knows?

Richard Wright, writer and social critic, was born in 1908. Wright is most famous for his influential novel *Native Son.* His other books include *Black Boy, Uncle Tom's Children, The Outsider, Savage Holiday,* and *White Man, Listen!* Wright left the United States in 1947; he died in Paris in 1960.

4

RICHARD WRIGHT

From Uncle Tom's Children

The Ethics of Living Jim Crow:
An Autobiographical Sketch

(1937)

MY FIRST LESSON in how to live as a Negro came when I was quite small. We were living in Arkansas. Our house stood behind the railroad tracks. Its skimpy yard was paved with black cinders. Nothing green ever grew in that yard. The only touch of green we could see was far away, beyond the tracks, over where the white folks lived. But cinders were good enough for me and I never missed the green growing things. And anyhow cinders were fine weapons. You could always have a nice hot war with huge black cinders. All you had to do was crouch behind the brick pillars of a house with your hands full of gritty ammunition. And the first woolly black head you saw pop out from behind another row of pillars was your target. You tried your very best to knock it off. It was great fun.

I never fully realized the appalling disadvantages of a cinder environment till one day the gang to which I belonged found itself engaged in a war with the white boys who lived beyond the tracks. As usual we laid down our cinder barrage, thinking that this would wipe the white boys out. But they replied with a steady bombardment of broken bottles. We doubled our cinder barrage, but they hid behind trees, hedges, and the sloping embankments of their lawns. Having no such fortifications, we retreated to the brick pillars of our homes.

During the retreat a broken milk bottle caught me behind the ear, opening a deep gash which bled profusely. The sight of blood pouring over my face completely demoralized our ranks. My fellow-combatants left me standing paralyzed in the center of the yard, and scurried for their homes. A kind neighbor saw me and rushed me to a doctor, who took three stitches in my neck.

I sat brooding on my front steps, nursing my wound and waiting for my mother to come from work. I felt that a grave injustice had been done me. It was all right to throw cinders. The greatest harm a cinder could do was leave a bruise. But broken bottles were danger-ous; they left you cut, bleeding, and helpless.

When night fell, my mother came from the white folks' kitchen. I raced down the street to meet her. I could just feel in my bones that she would understand. I knew she would tell me exactly what to do next time. I grabbed her hand and babbled out the whole story. She examined my wound, then slapped me.

"How come yuh didn't hide?" she asked me. "How come yuh awways fightin'?"

I was outraged, and bawled. Between sobs I told her that I didn't have any trees or hedges to hide behind. There wasn't a thing I could have used as a trench. And you couldn't throw very far when you were hiding behind the brick pillars of a house. She grabbed a barrel stave, dragged me home, stripped me naked, and beat me till I had a fever of one hundred and two. She would smack my rump with the stave, and while the skin was still smarting, impart to me gems of Jim Crow wisdom. I was never to throw cinders any more. I was never to fight any more wars. I was never, never, under any conditions, to fight *white* folks again. And they were absolutely right in clouting me with the broken milk bottle. Didn't I know she was working hard every day in the hot kitchens of the white folks to make money to take care of me? When was I ever going to learn to be a good boy? She couldn't be bothered with my fights. She finished by telling me that I ought to be thankful to God as long as I lived that they didn't kill me.

All that night I was delirious and could not sleep. Each time I closed my eyes I saw monstrous white faces suspended from the ceiling, leering at me.

From that time on, the charm of my cinder yard was gone. The green trees, the trimmed hedges, the cropped lawns grew very meaningful, became a symbol. Even today when I think of white folks, the hard, sharp outlines of white houses surrounded by trees, lawns, and hedges are present somewhere in the background of my mind. Through the years they grew into an overreaching symbol of fear.

It was a long time before I came in close contact with white folks again. We moved from Arkansas to Mississippi. Here we had the good fortune not to live behind the railroad tracks, or close to white neighborhoods. We lived in the very heart of the local Black Belt. There were black churches and black preachers; there were black schools and black teachers; black groceries and black clerks. In fact, everything was so solidly black that for a long time I did not even think of white folks, save in remote and vague terms. But this could not last forever. As one grows older one eats more. One's clothing costs more. When I finished grammar school I had to go to work. My mother could no longer feed and clothe me on her cooking job.

There is but one place where a black boy who knows no trade can get a job, and that's where the houses and faces are white, where the trees, lawns, and hedges are green. My first job was with an optical company in Jackson, Mississippi. The morning I applied I stood straight and neat before the boss, answering all his questions with sharp yessirs and nosirs. I was very careful to pronounce my *sirs* distinctly, in order that he might know that I was polite, that I knew where I was, and that I knew he was a *white* man. I wanted that job badly.

He looked me over as though he were examining a prize poodle. He questioned me closely about my schooling, being particularly insistent about how much mathematics I had had. He seemed very pleased when I told him I had had two years of algebra.

"Boy, how would you like to learn something around here?" he asked me.

"I'd like it fine, sir," I said, happy. I had visions of "working my way up." Even Negroes have those visions.

"All right," he said. "Come on."

I followed him to the small factory.

"Pease," he said to a white man of about thirty-five, "this is Richard. He's going to work for us."

Pease looked at me and nodded.

I was then taken to a white boy of about seventeen.

"Morrie, this is Richard, who's going to work for us."

"Whut yuy sayin' there, boy!" Morrie boomed at me.

"Fine!" I answered.

The boss instructed these two to help me, teach me, give me jobs to do, and let me learn what I could in my spare time.

My wages were five dollars a week.

I worked hard, trying to please. For the first month I got along O.K. Both Pease and Morrie seemed to like me. But one thing was missing. And I kept thinking about it. I was not learning anything and nobody was volunteering to help me. Thinking they had forgotten that I was to learn something about the mechanics of grinding lenses, I asked Morrie one day to tell me about the work. He grew red.

"Whut yuh tryin' t' do, nigger, get smart?" he asked.

"Naw; I ain't tryin' t' git smart," I said.

"Well, don't, if yuh know whut's good for yuh!"

I was puzzled. Maybe he just doesn't want to help me, I thought. I went to Pease.

"Say, are yuh crazy, you black bastard?" Pease asked me, his gray eyes growing hard.

I spoke out, reminding him that the boss had said I was to be given a chance to learn something.

"Nigger, you think you're *white,* don't you?"

"Naw, sir!"

"Well, you're acting mighty like it!"

"But, Mr. Pease, the boss said . . ."

Pease shook his fist in my face.

"This is a *white* man's work around here, and you better watch yourself!"

From then on they changed toward me. They said good-morning no more. When I was a bit slow performing some duty, I was called a lazy black son-of-a-bitch.

Once I thought of reporting all this to the boss. But the mere idea of what would happen to me if Pease and Morrie should learn that I had "snitched" stopped me. And after all the boss was a white man, too. What was the use?

The climax came at noon one summer day. Pease called me to his work-bench. To get to him I had to go between two narrow benches and stand with my back against a wall.

"Yes, sir," I said.

"Richard, I want to ask you something," Pease began pleasantly, not looking up from his work.

"Yes, sir," I said again.

Morrie came over, blocking the narrow passage between the benches. He folded his arms, staring at me solemnly.

I looked from one to the other, sensing that something was coming.

"Yes, sir," I said for the third time.

Pease looked up and spoke very slowly.

"Richard, *Mr.* Morrie here tells me you called me *Pease.*"

I stiffened. A void seemed to open up in me. I knew this was the show-down.

He meant that I had failed to call him Mr. Pease. I looked at Morrie. He was gripping a steel bar in his hands. I opened my mouth to speak, to protest, to assure Pease that I had never called him simply *Pease,* and that I had never had any intentions of doing so, when Morrie grabbed me by the collar, ramming my head against the wall.

"Now, be careful, nigger!" snarled Morrie, baring his teeth. *"I* heard yuh call 'im *Pease!* 'N' if you say yuh didn't, yuh're callin' me a *lie,* see?" He waved the steel bar threateningly.

If I had said: No, sir, Mr. Pease, I never called you *Pease,* I would have been automatically calling Morrie a liar. And if I had said: Yes, sir, Mr. Pease, I called you *Pease,* I would have been pleading guilty to having uttered the worst insult that a Negro can utter to a southern white man. I stood hesitating, trying to frame a neutral reply.

"Richard, I asked you a question!" said Pease. Anger was creeping into his voice.

"I don't remember calling you *Pease,* Mr. Pease," I said cautiously. "And if I did, I sure didn't mean . . ."

"You black son-of-a-bitch! You called me *Pease,* then!" he spat, slapping me till I bent sideways over a bench. Morrie was on top of me, demanding:

"Didn't yuh call 'im *Pease?* If yuh say yuh didn't I'll rip yo' gut string loose with this bar, yuh black granny dodger! Yuh can't call a white man a lie 'n' git erway with it, you black son-of-a-bitch!"

I wilted. I begged them not to bother me. I knew what they wanted. They wanted me to leave.

"I'll leave," I promised. "I'll leave right *now.*"

They gave me a minute to get out of the factory. I was warned not to show up again, or tell the boss.

I went.

When I told the folks at home what had happened, they called me a fool. They told me that I must never again attempt to exceed my boundaries. When you are working for white folks, they said, you got to "stay in your place" if you want to keep working.

My Jim Crow education continued on my next job, which was portering in a clothing store. One morning, while polishing brass out front, the boss and his twenty-year-old son got out of their car and half dragged and half kicked a Negro woman into the store. A policeman standing at the corner looked on, twirling his night-stick. I watched out of the corner of my eye, never slackening the strokes of my chamois upon the brass. After a few minutes, I heard shrill screams coming from the rear of the store. Later the woman stumbled out, bleeding, crying, and holding her stomach. When she reached the end of the block, the policeman grabbed her and accused her of being drunk. Silently, I watched him throw her into a patrol wagon.

When I went to the rear of the store, the boss and his son were washing their hands in the sink. They were chuckling. The floor was bloody and strewn with wisps of hair and clothing. No doubt I must have appeared pretty shocked, for the boss slapped me reassuringly on the back.

"Boy, that's what we do to niggers when they don't want to pay their bills," he said, laughing.

His son looked at me and grinned.

"Here, hava cigarette," he said.

Not knowing what to do, I took it. He lit his and held the match for me. This was a gesture of kindness, indicating that even if they had beaten the poor old woman, they would not beat me if I knew enough to keep my mouth shut.

"Yes, sir," I said, and asked no questions.

After they had gone, I sat on the edge of a packing box and stared at the bloody floor till the cigarette went out.

That day at noon, while eating in a hamburger joint, I told my fellow Negro porters what had happened. No one seemed surprised. One fellow, after swallowing a huge bite, turned to me and asked:

"Huh! Is tha' all they did t' her?"

"Yeah. Wasn't tha' enough?' I asked.

"Shucks! Man, she's a lucky bitch!" he said, burying his lips deep into a juicy hamburger. "Hell, it's a wonder they didn't lay her when they got through."

I was learning fast, but not quite fast enough. One day, while I was delivering packages in the suburbs, my bicycle tire was punctured. I walked along the hot, dusty road, sweating and leading my bicycle by the handle-bars.

A car slowed at my side.

"What's the matter, boy?" a white man called.

I told him my bicycle was broken and I was walking back to town.

"That's too bad," he said. "Hop on the running board."

He stopped the car. I clutched hard at my bicycle with one hand and clung to the side of the car with the other.

"All set?"

"Yes, sir," I answered. The car started.

It was full of young white men. They were drinking. I watched the flask pass from mouth to mouth.

"Wanna drink, boy?" one asked.

I laughed as the wind whipped my face. Instinctively obeying the freshly planted precepts of my mother, I said:

"Oh, no!"

The words were hardly out of my mouth before I felt something hard and cold smash me between the eyes. It was an empty whisky bottle. I saw stars, and fell backwards from the speeding car into the dust of the road, my feet becoming entangled in the steel spokes of my bicycle. The white men piled out and stood over me.

"Nigger, ain' yuh learned no better sense'n tha' yet?" asked the man who hit me. "Ain' yuh learned t' say *sir* t' a white man yet?"

Dazed, I pulled to my feet. My elbows and legs were bleeding. Fists doubled, the white man advanced, kicking my bicycle out of the way.

"Aw, leave the bastard alone. He's got enough," said one.

They stood looking at me. I rubbed my shins, trying to stop the flow of blood. No doubt they felt a sort of contemptuous pity, for one asked:

"Yuh wanna ride t' town now, nigger? Yuh reckon yuh know enough t' ride now?"

"I wanna walk," I said, simply.

Maybe it sounded funny. They laughed.

"Well, walk, yuh black son-of-a-bitch!"

When they left they comforted me with:

"Nigger, yuh sho better be damn glad it wuz us yuh talked t' tha' way. Yuh're a lucky bastard, 'cause if yuh'd said tha' t' somebody else, yuh might've been a dead nigger now."

Negroes who have lived South know the dread of being caught alone upon the streets in white neighborhoods after the sun has set. In such a simple situation as this the plight of the Negro in America is graphically symbolized. While white strangers may be in these neighborhoods trying to get home, they can pass unmolested. But the color of a Negro's skin makes him easily recognizable, makes him suspect, converts him into a defenseless target.

Late one Saturday night I made some deliveries in a white neighborhood. I was pedaling my bicycle back to the store as fast as I could, when a police car, swerving toward me, jammed me into the curbing.

"Get down and put up your hands!" the policemen ordered.

I did. They climbed out of the car, guns drawn, faces set, and advanced slowly.

"Keep still!" they ordered.

I reached my hands higher. They searched my pockets and packages. They seemed dissatisfied when they could find nothing incriminating. Finally, one of them said:

"Boy, tell your boss not to send you out in white neighborhoods after sundown."

As usual, I said:

"Yes, sir."

My next job was a hall-boy in a hotel. Here my Jim Crow education broadened and deepened. When the bell-boys were busy, I was often called to assist them. As many of the rooms in the hotel were occupied by prostitutes, I was constantly called to carry them liquor and cigarettes. These women were nude most of the time. They did not bother about clothing, even for bell-boys. When you went into their rooms, you were supposed to take their nakedness for granted, as though it startled you no more than a blue vase or a red rug. Your presence awoke in them no sense of shame, for you were not regarded as human. If they were alone, you could steal side-long glimpses at them. But if they were receiving men, not a flicker of your eyelids could show. I remember one incident vividly. A new woman, a huge, snowy-skinned blonde, took a room on my floor. I was sent to wait upon her. She was in bed with a thick-set man; both were nude and uncovered. She said she wanted some liquor and slid out of bed and waddled across the floor to get her money from a dresser drawer. I watched her.

"Nigger, what in hell are you looking at?" the white man asked me, raising himself upon his elbows.

"Nothing," I answered, looking miles deep into the blank wall of the room.

"Keep your eyes where they belong, if you want to be healthy!" he said.

"Yes, sir."

★★★

One of the bell-boys I knew in this hotel was keeping steady company with one of the Negro maids. Out of a clear sky the police descended upon his home and arrested him, accusing him of bastardy. The poor boy swore he had had no intimate relations with the girl. Nevertheless, they forced him to marry her. When the child arrived, it was found to be much lighter in complexion than either of the two supposedly legal parents. The white men around the hotel made a great joke of it. They spread the rumor that some white cow must have scared the poor girl while she was carrying the baby. If you were in their presence when this explanation was offered, you were supposed to laugh.

One of the bell-boys was caught in bed with a white prostitute. He was castrated and run out of town. Immediately after this all the bell-boys and hall-boys were called together and warned. We were given to understand that the boy who had been castrated was a "mighty, mighty lucky bastard." We were impressed with the fact that next time the management of the hotel would not be responsible for the lives of "trouble-makin' niggers." We were silent.

One night just as I was about to go home, I met one of the Negro maids. She lived in my direction, and we fell in to walk part of the way home together. As we passed the white night-watchman, he slapped the maid on her buttock. I turned around, amazed. The watchman looked at me with a long, hard, fixed-under stare. Suddenly he pulled his gun and asked:

"Nigger, don't yuh like it?"

I hesitated.

"I asked yuh don't yuh like it?" he asked again, stepping forward.

"Yes, sir," I mumbled.

"Talk like it, then!"

"Oh, yes, sir!" I said with as much heartiness as I could muster.

Outside, I walked ahead of the girl, ashamed to face her. She caught up with me and said:

"Don't be a fool! Yuh couldn't help it!"

This watchman boasted of having killed two Negroes in self-defense.

Yet, in spite of all this, the life of the hotel ran with an amazing smoothness. It would have been impossible for a stranger to detect anything. The maids, the hall-boys, and the bell-boys were all smiles. They had to be.

I had learned my Jim Crow lessons so thoroughly that I kept the hotel job till I left Jackson for Memphis. It so happened that while in Memphis I applied for a job at a branch of the optical company. I was hired. And for some reason, as long as I worked there, they never brought my past against me.

Here my Jim Crow education assumed quite a different form. It was no longer brutally cruel, but subtly cruel. Here I learned to lie, steal, to dissemble. I learned to play that dual role which every Negro must play if he wants to eat and live.

For example, it was almost impossible to get a book to read. It was assumed that after a Negro had imbibed what scanty schooling the state furnished he had no further need for books. I was always borrowing books from men on the job. One day I mustered enough courage to ask one of the men to let me get books from the library in his name. Surprisingly, he consented. I cannot help but think that he consented because he was a Roman Catholic and felt a vague sympathy for Negroes, being himself an object of hatred. Armed with a library card, I obtained books in the following manner: I would write a note to the librarian, saying: "Please let this nigger boy have the following books." I would then sign it with the white man's name.

When I went to the library, I would stand at the desk, hat in hand, looking as unbookish as possible. When I received the books desired I would take them home. If the books listed in the note happened to be out, I would sneak into the lobby and forge a new one. I never took any chances guessing with the white librarian about what the fictitious white man would want to read. No doubt if any of the white patrons had suspected that some of the volumes they enjoyed had been in the home of a Negro, they would not have tolerated it for an instant.

The factory force of the optical company in Memphis was much larger than that in Jackson, and more urbanized. At least they liked to talk, and would engage the Negro help in conversation whenever possible. By this means I found that many subjects were taboo from the white man's point of view. Among the topics they did not like to discuss with Negroes were the following: American white women; the Ku Klux Klan; France, and how Negro soldiers fared while there; French women; Jack Johnson; the entire northern part of the United States; the Civil War; Abraham Lincoln; U. S. Grant; General Sherman; Catholics; the Pope; Jews; the Republican Party; slavery; social equality; Communism; Socialism; the 13th and 14th Amendments to the Constitution; or any topic calling for positive knowledge or manly self-assertion on the part of the Negro. The most accepted topics were sex and religion.

There were many times when I had to exercise a great deal of ingenuity to keep out of trouble. It is a southern custom that all men must take off their hats when they enter an elevator. And especially did this apply to us blacks with rigid force. One day I stepped into an elevator with my arms full of packages. I was forced to ride with my hat on. Two white men stared at me coldly. Then one of them very kindly lifted my hat and placed it upon my armful of packages. Now the most accepted response for a Negro to make under such circumstances is to look at the white man out of the corner of his eye and grin. To have said: "Thank you!" would have made the white man *think* that you *thought* you were receiving from him a personal service. For such an act I have seen Negroes take a blow in the mouth. Finding the first alternative distasteful, and the second dangerous, I hit upon an acceptable course of action which fell safely between these two poles. I immediately—no sooner than my hat was lifted—pretended that my packages were about to spill, and appeared deeply distressed with keeping them in my arms. In this fashion I evaded having to acknowledge his service, and, in spite of adverse circumstances, salvaged a slender shred of personal pride.

How do Negroes feel about the way they have to live? How do they discuss it when alone among themselves? I think this question can be answered in a single sentence. A friend of mine who ran an elevator once told me:

"Lawd, man! Ef it wuzn't fer them polices 'n' them ol' lynch-mobs, there wouldn't be nothin' but uproar down here!"

Mary Church Terrell, teacher, author, and civil rights leader, was born in 1863 in Tennessee. Terrell was active in the struggle for women's rights and formed the Colored Women's League of Washington, D.C., and the National Association of Colored Women in 1896. Her works include *Colored Women and World Peace, Harriet Beecher Stowe: An Appreciation,* and her autobiography, *A Colored Woman in a White World.* She died in 1954.

5

MARY CHURCH TERRELL

From A Colored Woman in a White World

My Parents

(1940)

TO TELL THE TRUTH, I came very near not being on this mundane sphere at all. In a fit of despondency my dear mother tried to end her life a few months before I was born. By a miracle she was saved, and I finally arrived on scheduled time none the worse for the prenatal experience which might have proved decidedly disagreeable, if not fatal, to my future.

I distinguished myself as a baby by having no hair on my head for a long time. I was perfectly bald till I was more than a year old. I have a picture of myself taken in those days when my little head looked for all the world like a billiard ball. I have often wondered why my mother, who usually had such excellent taste about everything, wanted to hand down to posterity such a bald-headed baby as I was. While I would hate to think that my mother was ashamed of her baby, I am sure she did not take the same pride in exhibiting me to her friends that she would have felt if my head had been covered by a reasonable amount of hair.

But babies who are born under far more favorable conditions than those which confronted me when I was ushered into the world do not have all the blessings of life showered upon them. Bald-headed though I was, the fates were kind to me in one particular at least. I was born at a time when I did not have to go through life as a slave. My parents were not so fortunate, for they were both slaves. I am thankful that I was saved from a similar fate.

I learned about my father's antecedents in a very matter of fact, natural sort of way. It was his custom to take me in his buggy to see Captain C. B. Church Sunday mornings when I was four or five years old. Captain Church always welcomed me cordially to his beautiful home, would pat me on the head affectionately, and usually filled my little arms with fruit and flowers when I left. "You've got a nice little girl here, Bob," he used to say to my father. "You must raise her right."

As for myself, I simply adored him. "Captain Church is certainly good to us, Papa," I said one day, just after Father had left his house. "And don't you know, Papa, you look just like Captain Church. I reckon you look like him because he likes you," I added, trying to explain in my childish way the striking resemblance between the two men. Then my father explained the relationship existing between Captain Church and himself, and told me how kind Captain Church had always been to him. "He raised me from a baby," said he. "He taught me to defend myself, and urged me never to be a coward. 'If anybody strikes you, hit him back,' said Captain Church, 'and I'll stand by you. Whatever you do, don't let anybody impose upon you.' " And my father was very obedient in this particular without a doubt.

Hanging on the wall of our home in Memphis, Tennessee, where I was born, near the close of the Civil War, there used to be a picture of Captain Church dressed as a Knight Templar, and near by one of my father wearing the same uniform. They looked exactly like the picture of the same man taken at different periods of his life. I have heard my father say that Captain Church's sympathy was on the side of the Union, even though he was a slaveholder, and that he suffered financially because he took this stand.

My father was so fair that no one would have supposed that he had a drop of African blood in his veins. As a matter of fact, he had very little. A few years ago I received a letter from a white man of whom I had never heard before, saying:

"Your grandmother Emmeline was my mother's nurse and life companion. My own mother died some two years ago at the age of 78 and but a short time previous to her death gave a sketch of some of her early life. I did not take down any of the scenes described, but one of them I remember very vividly, because there was such a beautiful touch of the polished fiction in real life connected with it. It was something of the early life of your great-grandmother as well as of your own grandmother, Emmeline.

"Your great-grandmother was not an African or of African descent, but a Malay princess brought over from the Island of San Domingo in captivity by a slave ship, bound for the United States from the shores of Africa. After the ship had secured its cargo of slaves, it touched at one of the ports of an island in San Domingo, at a time when the island was in a state of revolution. The revolution had in this particular instance overthrown the royal family, and had them in captivity.

"When the captain of the slaver went ashore, he found this state of affairs, and the Rebels had given the royal family, then in prison, the choice of either being sold into slavery or beheaded. Among those then in prison was a beautiful Malay girl, about 14 years old, a member of the royal family. Her complexion was a deep red and her hair was very straight and black. She had around her neck a beautiful coral chain attached to a gold cross, which her captors allowed her to retain. The captain of the slaver made a trade for her. She was not placed among the African slaves, but given a place in the cabin.

"Upon arrival at Norfolk, Va., one of the favorite ports of both entry and sale for the slavers in those days, she was sold to a rich tobacco merchant at what was then considered a fancy price. My grandfather had three plantations in Virginia at that time, and it was his custom to go down to Norfolk upon the arrival of these slavers and purchase more or less of these wild Africans. By distributing them among the other slaves on the plantations, they would in course of time become civilized. It was only after a very spirited bidding did he let the young princess go to her purchaser.

"She was taken into the family of this merchant as seamstress to his daughters, a position in those days of promise and distinction to any slave. In the course of a few years, after her daughter Emmeline was born and but a little girl, this tobacco merchant failed in business, and his slaves all had to be sold, including your grandmother and her mother.

"My grandfather went to Norfolk, and after assuring your great-grandparent that her little girl would be raised among his own daughters, he bought the very little girl, Emmeline, and gave her to my mother, who was then his baby girl. My mother's name was Rosalie and she and the little girl, Emmeline, were brought up more as two sisters than as mistress and maid.

"A planter from near Natchez, Miss., bought Emmeline's mother and she was given the position of seamstress to the household in his family. In fact, she was never treated as a slave and never had to do menial work. Besides speaking her own native language she had learned French while on the Island of San Domingo. All through her life she retained her talisman, the coral chain and cross, which her captors in San Domingo had allowed her to retain.

"My mother was married at the age of sixteen, after moving from Virginia to Holly Springs, Miss., and thence to Arkansas. Twenty years of her life were spent in New Orleans, where your grandmother, Emmeline, learned the French language and always passed as a creole. I have often heard my mother say she was the most beautiful type of creole she ever saw. The affection which existed between Mother and Emmeline was more on the order of sisters than mistress and maid. When Emmeline died Mother said she could never see as much sunshine in after years. Emmeline was a communicant of the Episcopal Church at the time of her death.

"You know we Southerners take much pleasure in watching the advancement and prosperity of even the younger generation of those whose parents were connected with our household and children's growth. I hope this little memo of history will be interesting to you. If it does, may I ask you to send me a photo of your own family, if possible, if not, of you and your husband. Now I wish you and yours many blessings of the future.

"I am most respectfully yours,"

When he wrote me this letter the man who says his mother owned my grandmother lived in Mammoth Springs, Ark., and so far as I know, his family resides there now.

Many a time I have lived over that parting scene when Emmeline, my grandmother, who was then only a small child, was sold from her mother never to see her again. Often have I suffered the anguish which I know that poor slave mother felt, when her little girl was torn from her arms forever.

When slavery is discussed and somebody rhapsodizes upon the

goodness and kindness of masters and mistresses toward their slaves in extenuation of the cruel system, it is hard for me to conceal my disgust. There is no doubt that some slaveholders were kind to their slaves. Captain Church was one of them, and this daughter of a slave father is glad thus publicly to express her gratitude to him. But the anguish of one slave mother from whom her baby was snatched away outweighs all the kindness and goodness which were occasionally shown a fortunate, favored slave.

My father was employed in various capacities on Captain Church's boats. From being a dishwasher he was finally elevated to the dignity of steward, which was as high a place as a slave could then occupy. In this capacity he naturally became accustomed to buying in large quantities. And the habit thus acquired followed him through life. In supplying his own home he never bought a little of anything. My earliest recollection is of seeing barrels of flour, firkins of butter, and large tins or wooden buckets of lard. He would buy turkeys and chickens by the crate. Bunches of bananas used to hang where we could easily get them in our house, and there was always a goodly supply of oranges and nuts.

My father was an excellent cook and enjoyed nothing more than coming into the kitchen to prepare dishes he liked. When I came home from school during summer vacations, one of the first things he used to do was to broil me a pompano, a fish which has a delightful flavor and is caught in the waters near New Orleans.

Although my father never went to school a day in his life, since there were no schools for slaves, he was unusually intelligent and thoughtful and reasoned exceedingly well. He learned to read by constantly perusing the newspapers and always kept abreast of the times. He taught himself to write his name legibly—even beautifully—but he never wrote a letter in his life to my knowledge. I do not know whether he would not or could not do this, but he always had an employee or a member of his family write his letters for him.

In conversing with my father, few would have suspected they were talking to an uneducated man except for an occasional mistake in grammar or the mispronunciation of a word, to which even educated people in the South are often addicted. I was never ashamed to have my father converse with anybody, no matter how highly educated or renowned that individual might be. I was always sure he would have something worth while to say and that he would express his thought very well.

When I was a mere slip of a girl I sometimes pitied other girls of my acquaintance because their parents made so many mistakes when they talked. But as I grew older I was not at all disturbed by the lapses in English made by those who were not responsible for their lack of education.

My father was rather reserved in his manner, was rarely familiar with anybody, and had a certain innate culture which men deprived of educational opportunities, as he was, rarely possess. He had business ability of high order and gave proof of that fact over and over again. It is a great temptation to say much about my father, for he was a remarkable man in many respects. I am not trying to paint him as a saint, for he was far from being one. He had the vices and defects common to men born at that time under similar circumstances, reared as a slave, and environed as he was for so many years, from necessity rather than choice, after he was freed.

My father had the most violent temper of any human being with whom I have come in contact. In a fit of anger he seemed completely to lose control of himself, and he might have done anything desperate in a rage. He was one of the most courageous men I have ever known. If it ever has been true of a human being that he knew no fear, it can be said of Robert Reed Church during the major portion of his life. As he grew older and feebler, he lost some of the fire and dash of youth, as was natural, but even then he had plenty. I could cite a number of cases in which my father faced danger fearlessly, but I shall refer only to two.

Shortly after the Civil War what is commonly called "the Irish Riot" occurred in Memphis. During that disturbance my father was shot in the back of his head at his place of business and left there for dead. He had been warned by friends that he was one of the colored men to be shot. They and my mother begged him not to leave his home that day. But he went to work as usual in spite of the peril he knew he faced. He would undoubtedly have been shot to death if the rioters had not believed they had finished him when he fell to the ground. Till the day of his death there was at the back of his head a hole left by the bullet which wounded him, into which one could easily insert the tip of the little finger. He suffered terribly from excruciating headaches which attacked him at intervals and lasted several days. Sometimes the pain was so great he threatened to take his life. Doctors told him these headaches were caused by the wound he received during the Irish Riot when he was a young man.

I want to relate just one other incident showing the fearlessness of my father. He had bought an unusually beautiful sleigh on one of his trips to the North, not because he needed it in the South, but because he admired it. His friends considered it a huge joke that he had brought such a sleigh to Memphis, but he insisted that he would have occasion to use it some day. And he did.

There came a heavy fall of snow in Memphis one winter, and everybody who owned a sleigh brought it out. My father drove up and down Main Street in his beautiful sleigh several times. It was drawn by a horse that was decidedly a high stepper. People were enjoying the unusual fall of snow immensely and were throwing snowballs at each other in the street with great glee. As Father drove up and down Main Street a shower of snowballs struck him. At first he took it good-naturedly and laughed with the crowd, although they hurt him and frightened his horse. He soon discovered that the innocent-looking snowballs were stones and rocks covered with snow and thrown at him to injure him. After he had been pelted with these missiles several times, a large rock was hurled at him and struck him in the face. Then he pulled out a revolver and shot into the crowd of men who had injured him. It was a desperate thing for a colored man to do anywhere, particularly in the South, and it is a great wonder he was not torn limb from limb, even though he was shooting in self-defense.

In temperament and dispostion my mother was as different from my father as one human being could well be from another. She irradiated good will and cheer upon all with whom she came into contact. She was a ray of sunshine all the time, and nobody, no matter how depressed he might be, could withstand the infection of her hearty, musical laugh. She had troubles of her own, to be sure, financial, domestic, and otherwise. But she could have said literally and truthfully with St. Paul, "None of these things move me."

Before her death she lived with me fifteen years in Washington, after she left New York City, which had been her home for a long time. I cannot recall that I ever saw her depressed but once, although she had lost all her worldly possessions and was in poor health. If I was gloomy or worried about anything and went to Mother's room to talk matters over with her, when I left her presence I always felt like a child who had hurt its finger and had its mother "kiss it well." She had a way of really convincing me (and I am not so easily "convinced") that the matter was not so bad as I thought it was, that the prospects didn't begin to be as gloomy as I had painted them, and that everything would turn out all right in the end.

As I look back upon my habit of confiding my troubles to my mother, I reproach myself severely for placing upon her mind and heart any burdens which she, herself, was not obliged to bear. It seems to me it was a weak and inconsiderate thing for a daughter to do. The only reason I can forgive myself for imposing my woes upon my mother was that she never seemed to let anything worry her at all.

She possessed artistic talent of a high order, and I believe she would have acquired considerable reputation as an artist if she had had a chance to study in her youth. When I had completed my sophomore year in college, I spent the summer vacation in Oberlin, Ohio, where I had been attending school. My mother came to see me and began to take lessons in painting. She was thoroughly absorbed in her work and did nothing from morning till night but paint. So enthusiastic and industrious was she in the pursuit of art, I was really concerned about her and feared she might be losing her mind. She painted pictures of birds, butterflies, and flowers, ad infinitum on little trays and articles of various kinds, till her room fairly overflowed with them. I have today a beautiful screen on which she painted wisteria, which has been highly commended by artists.

My mother also possessed remarkable business ability, and established a hair store in Memphis which was a brilliant success. I am sure she was the first colored woman in Memphis and among the first in the entire South to establish and maintain a store of such excellence as hers undoubtedly was. The élite of Memphis came to "Lou Church's" store to buy their hair goods. And 'way back in the 70's women had to buy a quantity of false hair to keep up with the prevailing style. There were waterfalls and curls galore hanging coquettishly under their chignons at the side of their heads. So fearfully and wonderfully made was the coiffure of the 1870's that my lady who could afford it always secured the services of a regular hairdresser and rarely attempted to do her hair herself for any important social function.

Lou Church was considered an artist, and her reputation as hair-dresser spread far and wide. She used to relate with pride that when the Duke Alexis came to Memphis, some of the ladies who were to attend the big ball given in his honor came to her store as early as seven o'clock in the morning to have her dress their hair, because when they put in their order she had so many engagements ahead of them that she had to start early and work hard all day till nearly midnight, so as to fill them all.

Mother's hair store was in the most exclusive business section of Memphis, right off Court Square. If she were alive today I doubt very much whether she or any other colored woman could rent a store in such a prominent business section.

To her husband Mother was a helpmeet indeed, for it was she who bought the first home and the first carriage we had. She was the most generous human being I have ever known. There are several people living who can testify to that fact. I am sure she would cheer-fully have given away the last cent she possessed, if she had thought it was necessary. And the individual who wanted to get it would not have had to argue or persuade much to convince her it was necessary. But, alas, she had less conception of the value of money or the necessity of saving it than anybody I have ever known. She lavished money on my brother and myself in buying us clothes and giving us everything the heart of children could desire. Not only did she spend money freely on her own children, when she happened to have it, but she delighted in making presents to her friends.

My mother and father separated when I was quite young. This pained and embarrassed me very much. In those days divorces were not so common as they are now, and no matter what caused the separation of a couple, the woman was usually blamed. The court gave my brother, who was four years my junior, and myself into the custody of my mother. My little brother had been living with my father, and Father wanted to keep him, but the court refused to grant his request.

I remember very distinctly the day the "hack" drove up to Mother's house on Court Street, a block below her hair store, and deposited my little brother, bag and baggage, on the sidewalk in front of our home. My joy knew no bounds.

Mother finally sold her store in Memphis and moved to New York City, where she established another on Sixth Avenue which she managed with brilliant success.

Although Mother had been a slave, she never referred to that fact. When I questioned her about it, she would usually say that her master had not only taught her to read and write, but had also given her lessons in French. She enjoyed relating that her wedding trousseau had been bought in New York by "Miss Laura," her master's daughter, who had gone there on a visit, and that she had been given a nice wedding at which a delicious repast had been served.

I cannot leave my forebears without saying a word about my dear grandmother on my mother's side. In complexion she was very dark brown, almost black, with a straight, shapely nose and a small mouth. In her manner she was quiet, refined, and reserved; she always spoke in a low tone of voice, and tried hard to teach her granddaughter to do the same thing. My grandmother was called "Aunt Liza" by everybody, black and white, old and young, and was generally beloved. When people in the neighborhood were ill, they always sent for "Aunt Liza." And she never failed them.

She could tell the most thrilling stories imaginable, and I listened to her by the hour. I wish I had inherited her gift. The story I liked best was the one which she told about a "hoop snake" which had spied some children walking through a wood, had decided to give them a good scare for being so far from home alone, and had put its tail in its mouth and rolled after them "jes' as hard as he could." One of the roving children happened to look back, saw the "hoop snake" pursuing them, and warned the others of their danger.

My eyes were as big as saucers and my hair stood on end at Grandmother's realistic imitation of the agonized tones of the eldest child as he called out, "Run, chillun, run, the hoop snake's after you! Run for your lives!"

Occasionally Grandmother told me tales of brutality perpetrated upon slaves who belonged to cruel masters. But they affected her and me so deeply she was rarely able to finish what she began. I tried to keep the tears back and the sobs suppressed, so that Grandmother would carry the story to the bitter end, but I seldom succeeded. Then she would stop abruptly and refuse to go on, promising to finish it another time. It nearly killed me to think that my dear grandmother, whom I loved so devotedly, had once been a slave. I do not know why the thought that my parents had once been slaves did not affect me in the same way. "Never mind, honey," she used to say to comfort me, "Gramma ain't a slave no more."

She had an unpleasant experience herself which it pained me to hear her relate. She was reared in the house and was the housekeeper for "ole miss," so she rarely came into contact with the overseer. But one day she went into the field on an errand and the overseer challenged her about something. She resented what he said and he threatened to whip her.

"I dared him to tech me," she said. "Then he started toward me raising his whip. I took out and run jes' as fast as ever I could and he right after me. When I got to the kitchen door I picked up a chair and said, ef you come a step nearer, I'll knock your brains out with this here chair. An' he never come a step nearer, neither."

James Wilson, my father's brother, was as fair as a lily, with eyes as blue as the sky, and was as perfect a specimen of the Caucasian as could be found anywhere in the world. Uncle Jim was forced to fight in the Confederate Army very much against his will. Although he was usually cool and calm, nothing riled him so quickly as a reference to what he considered that painful and disgraceful episode in his life.

Not many people have fewer relatives than myself. Until my father married a second time, for many years our entire family consisted of my mother, father, brother and myself.

Langston Hughes, a major poet and playwright during the Harlem Renaissance, was born in Joplin, Missouri, in 1902. His prodigious writings include the volumes of poetry *The Weary Blues, Montage of a Dream,* and *The Panther and the Lash*; his autobiographies *The Big Sea* and *I Wonder As I Wander*; the novels *Not Without Laughter* and *Tambourines to Glory*; and several plays, works of nonfiction, short stories, translations, and poems. He was awarded the NAACP Spingarn Medal and the Hammond Gold Award for *Not Without Laughter*; he was elected to the National Institute of Arts and Letters. Hughes died in 1967.

6

LANGSTON HUGHES

From The Big Sea

(1940)

... FINALLY IT CAME. At seven bells we went on toward Africa, the engines chugging soft and serene.

The next day was Sunday and the missionaries wanted everybody to come to prayers in the saloon, but nobody went except the Captain and the Chief Mate. The bo'sun said he'd go if the missionaries had any communion wine, but the missionaries didn't have any, so he didn't go.

When we got to Teneriffe, in the Canary Islands, it was mid-afternoon and very bright. The Canaries looked like fairy islands, all sharp peaks of red rock and bright sandy beaches and little green fields dropped like patchwork between the beaches and the rocks, with the sea making a blue-white fringe around.

The Captain let us draw money—so Las Palmas seemed a gay city indeed. Ashore, three or four of us, including Ernesto and a Norwegian boy named Sven, had supper at a place with very bright lights, where they served huge platters of delicious mixed fish with big bottles of cool, white wine. Then we all went to a white villa by the sea, called *El Palacio de Amor* and stayed all night. In the morning very early, when the sun was just coming up, we drove back to the wharf in an open carriage. We kept thinking about the girls, who were

Spanish, and very young and pretty. And Sven said he would like to take one of them with him.

But all those days I was waiting anxiously to see Africa. And finally, when I saw the dust-green hills in the sunlight, something took hold of me inside. My Africa, Motherland of the Negro peoples! And me a Negro! Africa! The real thing, to be touched and seen, not merely read about in a book.

That first morning when we sighted the coast, I kept leaving my work to lean over the rail and look at Africa, dim and far away, off on the horizon in a haze of light, then gradually nearer and nearer, until you could see the color of the foliage on the trees.

We put in at the port of Dakar. There were lots of Frenchmen, and tall black Senegalese soldiers in red fezes, and Mohammedans in robes, so that at first you couldn't tell if the Mohammedans were men or women.

The next day we moved on. And farther down the coast it was more like the Africa I had dreamed about—wild and lovely, the people dark and beautiful, the palm trees tall, the sun bright, and the rivers deep. The great Africa of my dreams!

But there was one thing that hurt me a lot when I talked with the people. The Africans looked at me and would not believe I was a Negro.

Negro

You see, unfortunately, I am not black. There are lots of different kinds of blood in our family. But here in the United States, the word "Negro" is used to mean anyone who has *any* Negro blood at all in his veins. In Africa, the word is more pure. It means *all* Negro, therefore *black*.

I am brown. My father was a darker brown. My mother an olive-yellow. On my father's side, the white blood in his family came from a Jewish slave trader in Kentucky, Silas Cushenberry, of Clark County, who was his mother's father; and Sam Clay, a distiller of Scotch descent, living in Henry County, who was his father's father. So on my father's side both male great-grandparents were white, and

Sam Clay was said to be a relative of the great statesman, Henry Clay, his contemporary.

On my mother's side, I had a paternal great-grandfather named Quarles—Captain Ralph Quarles—who was white and who lived in Louisa County, Virginia, before the Civil War, and who had several colored children by a colored housekeeper, who was his slave. The Quarles traced their ancestry back to Francis Quarles, famous Jacobean poet, who wrote *A Feast for Wormes*.

On my maternal grandmother's side, there was French and Indian blood. My grandmother looked like an Indian—with very long black hair. She said she could lay claim to Indian land, but that she never wanted the government (or anybody else) to give her anything. She said there had been a French trader who came down the St. Lawrence, then on foot to the Carolinas, and mated with her grandmother, who was a Cherokee—so all her people were free. During slavery, she had free papers in North Carolina, and traveled about free, at will. Her name was Mary Sampson Patterson, and in Oberlin, Ohio, where she went to college, she married a free man named Sheridan Leary.

She was with child in Oberlin when Sheridan Leary went away, and nobody knew where he had gone, except that he told her he was going on a trip. A few weeks later his shawl came back to her full of bullet holes. He had been killed following John Brown in that historic raid at Harpers Ferry. They did not hang him. He had been killed that first night in the raid—shot attacking, believing in John Brown. My grandmother said Sheridan Leary always did believe people should be free.

She married another man who believed the same thing. His name was Charles Langston, my grandfather. And in the '70's the Langstons came out to Kansas where my mother was born on a farm near Lawrence.

My grandfather never made much money. But he went into politics, looking for a bigger freedom than the Emancipation Proclamation had provided. He let his farm and his grocery store in Lawrence run along, and didn't much care about making money. When he died, none of the family had any money. But he left some fine speeches behind him.

His brother, John Mercer Langston, left a book of speeches, too, and an autobiography, *From a Virginia Plantation to the National Capital.* But he was much better than Charles at making money, so he left a big house as well, and I guess some stocks and bonds. When I was small, we had cousins in Washington, who lived a lot better than we did in Kansas. But my grandmother never wrote them for anything. John Mercer Langston had been a Congressman from Virginia, and later United States Minister to Haiti, and Dean of the first Law School at Howard University. He had held many high positions—very high positions for a Negro in his day, or any day in this rather difficult country. And his descendants are still in society.

We were never very much "in society" in Kansas, because we were always broke, and the families of the Negro doctors and lawyers lived much better than we did. One of the first things I remember is my grandmother worrying about the mortgage on our house. It was always very hard for her to raise the money to pay the interest. And when my grandmother died, the house went right straight to the mortgage man, quickly.

I was born in Joplin, Missouri, in 1902, but I grew up mostly in Lawrence, Kansas. My grandmother raised me until I was twelve years old. Sometimes I was with my mother, but not often. My father and mother were separated. And my mother, who worked, always traveled about a great deal, looking for a better job. When I first started to school, I was with my mother a while in Topeka. (And later, for a summer in Colorado, and another in Kansas City.) She was a stenographer for a colored lawyer in Topeka, named Mr. Guy. She rented a room near his office, downtown. So I went to a "white" school in the downtown district.

At first, they did not want to admit me to the school, because there were no other colored families living in that neighborhood. They wanted to send me to the colored school, blocks away down across the railroad tracks. But my mother, who was always ready to do battle for the rights of a free people, went directly to the school board, and finally got me into the Harrison Street School—where all the teachers were nice to me, except one who sometimes used to make remarks about my being colored. And after such remarks, occasionally the kids would grab stones and tin cans out of the alley and chase me home.

But there was one little white boy who would always take up for me. Sometimes others of my classmates would, as well. So I learned early not to hate *all* white people. And ever since, it has seemed to me that *most* people are generally good, in every race and in every country where I have been.

The room my mother lived in in Topeka was not in a house. It was in a building, upstairs over a plumbing shop. The other rooms on that floor facing a long hall were occupied by a white architect and a colored painter. The architect was a very old man, and very kind. The colored painter was young, and used to paint marvelous lions and tigers and jungle scenes. I don't know where he saw such things in Topeka, but he used to paint them. Years later, I saw him paint them on the walls of cheap barrooms in Chicago and New York. I don't know where he is now.

My mother had a small monkey-stove in our room for both heating and cooking. You could put only one pot on the stove at a time. She used to send me through the downtown alleys every day after the stores closed to pick up discarded boxes to burn in our stove. Sometimes we would make a great racket, cutting kindling with a hatchet in our room at night. If it was a tough box we could not break up, we would put a whole piece of board in the stove, and it would stick out through the top, and my mother would call it "long-branch kindling." When she would go away and leave me alone, she would warn me about putting "long-branch kindling" in the stove, because it might burn until it broke off, and fall, and catch the rug on fire.

My mother used to take me to see all the plays that came to Topeka like *Buster Brown, Under Two Flags,* and *Uncle Tom's Cabin.* We were very fond of plays and books. Once we heard *Faust.*

When I was about five or six years old, my father and mother decided to go back together. They had separated shortly after I was born, because my father wanted to go away to another country, where a colored man could get ahead and make money quicker, and my mother did not want to go. My father went to Cuba, and then to Mexico, where there wasn't any color line, or any Jim Crow. He finally sent for us, so we went there, too.

But no sooner had my mother, my grandmother, and I got to Mexico City than there was a big earthquake, and people ran out from their houses into the Alameda, and the big National Opera House they were building sank down into the ground, and tarantulas came out of the walls—and my mother said she wanted to go back home at once to Kansas, where people spoke English or something she could understand and there were no earthquakes. So we went. And that was the last I saw of my father until I was seventeen.

When I was in the second grade, my grandmother took me to Lawrence to raise me. And I was unhappy for a long time, and very lonesome, living with my grandmother. Then it was that books began to happen to me, and I began to believe in nothing but books and the wonderful world in books—where if people suffered, they suffered in beautiful language, not in monosyllables, as we did in Kansas. And where almost always the mortgage got paid off, the good knights won, and the Alger boy triumphed.

Our mortgage never got paid off—for my grandmother was not like the other colored women of Lawrence. She didn't take in washing or go out to cook, for she had never worked for anyone. But she tried to make a living by renting rooms to college students from Kansas University; or by renting out half her house to a family; or sometimes she would move out entirely and go to live with a friend, while she rented the whole little house for ten or twelve dollars a month, to make a payment on the mortgage. But we were never quite sure the white mortgage man was not going to take the house. And sometimes, on that account, we would have very little to eat, saving to pay the interest.

I remember one summer a friend of my mother's in Kansas City sent her son to pass a few weeks with me at my grandmother's home in Lawrence. But the little boy only stayed a few days, then wrote his mother that he wanted to leave, because we had nothing but salt pork and wild dandelions to eat. The boy was right. But being only eight or nine years old, I cried when he showed me the letter he was writing his mother. And I never wanted my mother to invite any more little boys to stay with me at my grandmother's house.

You see, my grandmother was very proud, and she would never beg or borrow anything from anybody. She sat, looking very much like an Indian, copper-colored with long black hair, just a little gray in places at seventy, sat in her rocker and read the Bible, or held me on her lap and told me long, beautiful stories about people who wanted to make the Negroes free, and how her father had had apprenticed to him many slaves in Fayetteville, North Carolina, before the War, so that they could work out their freedom under him as stone masons. And once they had worked out their purchase, he would see that they reached the North, where there was no slavery.

Through my grandmother's stories always life moved, moved heroically toward an end. Nobody ever cried in my grandmother's stories. They worked, or schemed, or fought. But no crying. When my grandmother died, I didn't cry, either. Something about my grandmother's stories (without her ever having said so) taught me the uselessness of crying about anything.

She was a proud woman—gentle, but Indian and proud. I remember once she took me to Osawatomie, where she was honored by President Roosevelt—Teddy—and sat on the platform with him while he made a speech; for she was then the last surviving widow of John Brown's raid.

I was twelve when she died. I went to live with a friend of my grandmother's named Auntie Reed. Auntie Reed and her husband had a little house a block from the Kaw River, near the railroad station. They had chickens and cows. Uncle Reed dug ditches and laid sewer pipes for the city, and Auntie Reed sold milk and eggs to her neighbors. For me, there have never been any better people in the world. I loved them very much. Auntie Reed let me set the hens, and Uncle Reed let me drive the cows to pasture. Auntie Reed was a Christian and made me go to church and Sunday school every Sunday. But Uncle Reed was a sinner and never went to church as long as he lived, nor cared anything about it. In fact, he washed his overalls every Sunday morning (a grievous sin) in a big iron pot in the back yard, and then just sat and smoked his pipe under the grape arbor in summer, in winter on a bench behind the kitchen range. But both of them were very good and kind—the one who went to church and the one who didn't. And no doubt from them I learned to like both Christians and sinners equally well.

Salvation

I was saved from sin when I was going on thirteen. But not really saved. It happened like this. There was a big revival at my Auntie Reed's church. Every night for weeks there had been much preaching, singing, praying, and shouting, and some very hardened sinners had been brought to Christ, and the membership of the church had grown by leaps and bounds. Then just before the revival ended, they held a special meeting for children, "to bring the young lambs to the fold." My aunt spoke of it for days ahead. That night I was escorted to the front row and placed on the mourners' bench with all the other young sinners, who had not yet been brought to Jesus.

My aunt told me that when you were saved you saw a light, and something happened to you inside! And Jesus came into your life! And God was with you from then on! She said you could see and hear and feel Jesus in your soul. I believed her. I had heard a great many old people say the same thing and it seemed to me they ought to know. So I sat there calmly in the hot, crowded church, waiting for Jesus to come to me.

The preacher preached a wonderful rhythmical sermon, all moans and shouts and lonely cries and dire pictures of hell, and then he sang a song about the ninety and nine safe in the fold, but one little lamb was left out in the cold. Then he said: "Won't you come? Won't you come to Jesus? Young lambs, won't you come?" And he held out his arms to all us young sinners there on the mourners' bench. And the little girls cried. And some of them jumped up and went to Jesus right away. But most of us just sat there.

A great many old people came and knelt around us and prayed, old women with jet-black faces and braided hair, old men with work-gnarled hands. And the church sang a song about the lower lights are burning, some poor sinners to be saved. And the whole building rocked with prayer and song.

Still I kept waiting to *see* Jesus.

Finally all the young people had gone to the altar and were saved, but one boy and me. He was a rounder's son named Westley. Westley and I were surrounded by sisters, and deacons praying. It was very hot in the church, and getting late now. Finally Westley said to me in a whisper: "God damn! I'm tired o' sitting here. Let's get up and be saved." So he got up and was saved.

Then I was left all alone on the mourners' bench. My aunt came and knelt at my knees and cried, while prayers and songs swirled all around me in the little church. The whole congregation prayed for me alone, in a mighty wail of moans and voices. And I kept waiting serenely for Jesus, waiting, waiting—but he didn't come. I wanted to see him, but nothing happened to me. Nothing! I wanted something to happen to me, but nothing happened.

I heard the songs and the minister saying: "Why don't you come? My dear child, why don't you come to Jesus? Jesus is waiting for you. He wants you. Why don't you come? Sister Reed, what is this child's name?"

"Langston," my aunt sobbed.

"Langston, why don't you come? Why don't you come and be saved? Oh, Lamb of God! Why don't you come?"

Now it was really getting late. I began to be ashamed of myself, holding everything up so long. I began to wonder what God thought about Westley, who certainly hadn't seen Jesus either, but who was now sitting proudly on the platform, swinging his knickerbockered legs and grinning down at me, surrounded by deacons and old women on their knees praying. God had not struck Westley dead for taking his name in vain or for lying in the temple. So I decided that maybe to save further trouble, I'd better lie, too, and say that Jesus had come, and get up and be saved.

So I got up.

Suddenly the whole room broke into a sea of shouting, as they saw me rise. Waves of rejoicing swept the place. Women leaped in the air. My aunt threw her arms around me. The minister took me by the hand and led me to the platform.

When things quieted down, in a hushed silence, punctuated by a few ecstatic "Amens," all the new young lambs were blessed in the name of God. Then joyous singing filled the room.

That night, for the last time in my life but one—for I was a big boy twelve years old—I cried. I cried, in bed alone, and couldn't stop. I buried my head under the quilts, but my aunt heard me. She woke up and told my uncle I was crying because the Holy Ghost had come into my life, and because I had seen Jesus. But I was really crying because I couldn't bear to tell her that I had lied, that I had deceived everybody in the church, that I hadn't seen Jesus, and that now I didn't believe there was a Jesus any more, since he didn't come to help me.

The Mother of the Gracchi

My Auntie Reed cooked wonderful salt pork and greens with corn dumplings. There were fresh peas and young onions right out of the garden, and milk with cream on it. There were ho-cakes, and sorghum molasses, and apple dumplings with butter sauce. And she and Uncle Reed owned their own home without a mortgage on it, clear.

In the spring I used to collect maple seeds and sell them to the seed store. I delivered papers for a while and sold the *Saturday Evening Post*. For a few weeks I also sold the *Appeal to Reason* for an old gentleman with a white beard, who said his paper was trying to make a better world. But the editor of the local daily told me to stop selling the *Appeal to Reason*, because it was a radical sheet and would get colored folks in trouble. Besides, he said I couldn't carry his papers and that one, too. So I gave up the *Appeal to Reason*.

On Saturdays I went to football games at the University of Kansas and heard the students yelling:

Walk-Chalk!
Jay Hawk! K. U.!

And I felt bad if Nebraska or Missouri beat Kansas, as they usually did.

When I was in the seventh grade, I got my first regular job, cleaning up the lobby and toilets of an old hotel near the school I attended. I kept the mirrors and spittoons shined and the halls scrubbed. I was paid fifty cents a week, with which I went to see Mary Pickford and Charlie Chaplin and Theda Bara on the screen. Also Pearl White in *The Clutching Claw,* until the theater (belonging to a lady named Mrs. Pattee) put up a sign: NO COLORED ADMITTED. Then I went to see road shows like *The Firefly* and *The Pink Lady* and Sothern and Marlowe when they came to town, sitting up in the gallery of the Opera House all by myself, thrilled at the world across the footlights.

But there was a glamour in the real world, too. For a while there had been a poet in Lawrence who had left his mark on the town. I remember my mother, when I was a small child, pointing him out to me on the street. His name was Harry Kemp, but I don't remember clearly how he looked.

The great Negro actor, Nash Walker, of "Bon Bon Buddy, the Chocolate Drop" fame, had lived in Lawrence, too. And my Uncle Nat (before he died) had taught him music, long before I was born. I saw Nash Walker only once, because he was off in the East with the great Williams and Walker shows, since he was a partner of Bert Williams, but I often heard the local people speak of him. And I vaguely remember that he brought to Lawrence the first phonograph I had ever seen, when he came back ill to his mother at the end. He gave a concert at my aunt's church on the phonograph, playing records for the benefit of the church mortgage fund one night. I remember my mother said she had had dinner with Nash Walker and his mother, while he was ill, and that they ate from plates with gold edging. Then Nash (George Walker, as he was known in the theater) died and there was a big funeral for him and I got my hand slapped for pointing at the flowers, because it was not polite for a child to point.

When I went to live with Auntie Reed, whose house was near the depot, I used to walk down to the Santa Fe station and stare at the railroad tracks, because the railroad tracks ran to Chicago, and Chicago was the biggest town in the world to me, much talked of by the people in Kansas. I was glad when my mother sent for me to come to Lincoln, Illinois, where she was then living, not far from Chicago. I was going on fourteen. And the papers said the Great War had begun in Europe.

My mother had married again. She had married a chef cook named Homer Clark. But like so many cooks, as he got older he couldn't stand the heat of the kitchen, so he went to work at other things. Odd jobs, the steel mills, the coal mines. By now I had a little brother. I liked my step-father a great deal, and my baby brother, also; for I had been very lonesome growing up all by myself, the only child, with no father and no mother around.

But ever so often, my step-father would leave my mother and go away looking for a better job. The day I graduated from grammar school in Lincoln, Illinois, he had left my mother, and was not there to see me graduate.

I was the Class Poet. It happened like this. They had elected all the class officers, but there was no one in our class who looked like a poet, or had ever written a poem. There were two Negro children in the class, myself and a girl. In America most white people think, of course, that *all* Negroes can sing and dance, and have a sense of rhythm. So my classmates, knowing that a poem had to have rhythm, elected me unanimously—thinking, no doubt, that I had some, being a Negro.

The day I was elected, I went home and wondered what I should write. Since we had eight teachers in our school, I thought there should be one verse for each teacher, with an especially good one for my favorite teacher, Miss Ethel Welsh. And since the teachers were to have eight verses, I felt class should have eight, too. So my first poem was about the longest poem I ever wrote—sixteen verses, which were later cut down. In the first half of the poem, I said that our school had the finest teachers there ever were. And in the latter half, I said our class was the greatest class ever graduated. So at graduation, when I read the poem, naturally everybody applauded loudly.

That was the way I began to write poetry.

It had never occurred to me to be a poet before, or indeed a writer of any kind. But my mother had often read papers at the Inter-State Literary Society, founded by my grandfather in Kansas. And occasionally she wrote original poems, too, that she gave at the Inter-State. But more often, she recited long recitations like "Lasca" and "The Mother of the Gracchi," in costume. As Lasca she dressed as a cowgirl. And as Cornelia, the mother of the Gracchi, she wore a sheet like a Roman matron.

On one such occasion, she had me and another little boy dressed in half-sheets as her sons—jewels, about to be torn away from her by a cruel Spartan fate. My mother was the star of the program and the church in Lawrence was crowded. The audience hung on her words; but I did not like the poem at all, so in the very middle of it I began to roll my eyes from side to side, round and round in my head, as though in great distress. The audience tittered. My mother intensified her efforts, I, my mock agony. Wilder and wilder I mugged, as the poem mounted, batted and rolled my eyes, until the entire assemblage burst into uncontrollable laughter.

My mother, poor soul, couldn't imagine what was wrong. More fervently than ever, she poured forth her lines, grasped us to her breast, and begged heaven for mercy. But the audience by then couldn't stop giggling, and with the applause at the end, she was greeted by a mighty roar of laughter. When the program was over and my mother found out what had happened, I got the worst whipping I ever had in my life. Then and there I learned to respect other people's art.

Nevertheless, the following spring, at a Children's Day program at my aunt's church, I, deliberately and with malice aforethought, forgot a poem I knew very well, having been forced against my will to learn it. I mounted the platform, said a few lines, and then stood there—much to the embarrassment of my mother, who had come all the way from Kansas City to hear me recite. My aunt tried to prompt me, but I pretended I couldn't hear a word. Finally I came down to my seat in dead silence—and I never had to recite a poem in church again.

The only poems I liked as a child were Paul Lawrence Dunbar's. And *Hiawatha*. But I liked any kind of stories. I read all of my mother's novels from the library: *The Rosary, The Mistress of Shenstone, Freckles,* Edna Ferber, all of Harold Bell Wright, and all of Zane Grey. I thought *Riders of the Purple Sage* a wonderful book and still think so, as I remember it.

In Topeka, as a small child, my mother took me with her to the little vine-covered library on the grounds of the Capitol. There I first fell in love with librarians, and I have been in love with them ever since—those very nice women who help you find wonderful books! The silence inside the library, the big chairs, and long tables, and the fact that the library was always there and didn't seem to have a mortgage on it, or any sort of insecurity about it—all of that made me love it. And right then, even before I was six, books began to happen to me, so that after a while, there came a time when I believed in books more than in people—which, of course, was wrong. That was why, when I went to Africa, I threw all the books into the sea.

J. Saunders Redding, born in Delaware in 1906, wrote exten-
sively on the African-American experience and literature. His
works include *No Day of Triumph, They Came in Chains, On
Being Negro in America,* and *The Lonesome Road.* He was
awarded both Rockefeller and Guggenheim fellowships, and he
taught and lectured widely. He died in 1988.

7

J. SAUNDERS REDDING

From No Day of Triumph

(1942)

MY MOTHER WAS tall, with a smooth, rutilant skin and a handsome figure. Her hair began to whiten in her late twenties and whitened very rapidly. I especially liked to be on the street with her, for I enjoyed the compliment of staring which was paid to her. I think she was not aware of these stares. There was pride in her, a kind of glowing consciousness that showed in her carriage in exactly the same way that good blood shows in a horse. But she had no vanity. Her pride gave to everything she did a certain ritualistic élan.

It is surprising to me now how little I learned about my mother in the sixteen years she lived after my birth. It was not that I lacked opportunity, but insight. She was never withdrawn or restrained, purposefully shading out her personality from us. And her speech and actions seemed to have the simple directness and the sharp impact of thrown stones. But she was a woman of many humors, as if, knowing her time to be short, she would live many lives in one. Gaiety and soberness, anger and benignity, joy and woe possessed her with equal force. In all her moods there was an intensity as in a spinning top.

I vividly recall the day when in rage and tears she stormed because another Negro family moved into our neighborhood. When her rage had passed and she had dropped into that stilly tautness that sometimes kept her strained for days, she said to my father:

"That's all it takes, Fellow. Today our house is worth one-third of what it was last night. When those people . . ." She shrugged her wide shoulders and stared at my father.

"Oh, Girl! Girl!" my father said gently. "You mustn't be so hard on them. They may be respectable people."

"Hard! Hard! And respectable people!" She laughed brittlely. "What has respectability got to do with it?"

Then she tried to find the words for what she thought, for we children were present and she did not wish to appear unreasonable before us. The subject of race was for her a narrow bridge over a chasmal sea, and the walking of it was not a part of her daily living. Only when she felt she must save herself from the abyss did she venture to walk. At other times she ignored it, not only in word, but I think in thought as well. She knew the speeches of John Brown and Wendell Phillips, the poetry of Whittier and Whitman, but not as my father knew them; not as battering stones hurled against the strong walls of a prison. She was not imprisoned. Stones, perhaps, but dropped into a dark sea whose tides licked only at the farthest shores of her life. She took this for reasonableness.

I remember she laughed a brittle laugh and said, "The first thing they moved in was one of those pianola things. Oh, we shall have music," she said bitterly, "morning, noon, and midnight. And they're not buying. They're renting. Why can't they stay where they belong!"

"Belong?" my father said.

"Yes. Over the bridge."

"They are our people, Girl," my father said.

My mother looked at him, tears of vexation dewing her eyes. She blinked back the tears and looked fixedly at my father's dark face shining dully under the chandelier, his bald head jutting back from his forehead like a brown rock. As if the words were a bad taste to be rid of, she said:

"Yours maybe. But not mine."

"Oh, Girl. Girl!"

But Mother had already swept from the dining room.

It is strange how little my deep affection for my mother (and hers for all of us) taught me about her while she lived. I have learned much more about her since her death. It is as if the significance of remembered speech and action unfolded to me gradually a long time after. My mother was the most complex personality I have ever known.

But no will of my mother's could abate the heave of the social tide just then beginning to swell. Our new neighbors were the first that we saw of that leaderless mass of blacks that poured up from the South during and after the war years. It was a trickle first, and then a dark flood that soon inundated the east side and burbled restively at our street. Within five months of the time my mother had raged, the whites were gone. But rents and prices in our street were too high for the laborers in morocco and jute mills, shipyards and foundries, the ditch-diggers, coal-heavers, and the parasites. They crowded sometimes as many as eight to a room in the houses below us, and I knew of at least one house of six small rooms in which fifty-one people lived.

Our street and the diagonal street above it were a more exclusive preserve. A few middle-class Jews, a clannish community of Germans clustered about their Turn Hall, and some Catholic Irish lived there. But they were nudged out. The Germans first, for they became the victims of mass hatred during the war, and the last German home was stoned just before the day of the Armistice. Landlords and realtors inflated prices to profit by Negro buyers who clamored for houses as if for heaven. Into our street moved the prosperous class of mulattoes, a physician and a dentist, a minister, an insurance agent, a customs clerk, a well-paid domestic, and several school teachers. Nearly all of these were buying at prices three times normal.

The atmosphere of our street became purely defensive. No neighborhood in the city was so conscious of its position and none, trapped in a raw materialistic struggle between the well-being of the west side and the grinding poverty of the east, fought harder to maintain itself. This struggle was the satanic bond, the blood-pact that held our street together.

But there was also the spiritual side to this struggle. It remained for me for a long time undefined but real. It was not clear and cold in the brain as religion was and taxes and food to eat and paint to buy. It was in the throat like a warm clot of phlegm or blood that no expectorant could dislodge. It was in the bowels and bone. It was memory and history, the pound of the heart, the pump of the lungs. It was Weeping Joe making bursting flares of words on the Court House wall and murmuring like a priest in funeral mass on our back steps of summer evenings. It was east side, west side, the white and the black, the word nigger, the cry of exultation, of shame, of fear when black Lemuel Price shot and killed a white policeman. It was Paul Dunbar, whose great brooding eyes spirit-flowed from his drawn face in a photograph over our mantel. It was sleeping and waking. It was Wilson and Hughes in 1917, Harding and Cox in 1921. It was a science teacher saying sarcastically, "Yes. I know. They won't hire you because you're colored," and, "Moreover, the dog licked Lazarus' wounds," and getting very drunk occasionally and reeling about, his yellow face gone purple, blubbering, "A good chemist, God damn it. A Goddamn good chemist! And here I am teaching a school full of niggers. Oh, damn my unwhite skin! And God damn it!" It was the music of pianolas played from dusk to dawn. And it was books read and recited and hated and loved: fairy tales, *Up From Slavery, Leaves of Grass, Scaramouche, Othello, The Yoke, Uncle Tom's Cabin, The Heroic Story of the Negro in the Spanish-American War, The Leopard's Spots, Door of the Night, Sentimental Tommy, The Negro, Man or Beast?,* and the rolling apostrophes of the *World's Best Orations.*

And on this plane allegiances were confused, divided. There was absolute cleavage between those spiritual values represented by Grandma Conway, who thought and lived according to ideas and ideals inherited from a long line of free ancestors and intimates (her father had been white, her mother part Irish, Indian, Negro. Her first husband was a mulatto carriage maker with a tradition of freedom three generations old) and those ill-defined, uncertain values represented by Grandma Redding and which, somehow, seemed to be close to whatever values our neighbors on the east held. What these were I never knew, nor, I suspect, did Grandma Redding. Certainly she would have cast equal scorn on the east side's black Lizzie Gunnar, who ran a whore house and who two days before every Christmas gathered up all the Negro children she could find and led them to the Court House for the city's party to the poor, because, "Nigghas is jus' about de poores' folks dere is," and white and foreign-born Weeping Joe, who spoke of linking the spirits of men together in the solvent bond of Christ. Her closeness to them was more a sympathetic prepossession than an alliance. They were her people, whether their values were the same as hers or not. Blood was stronger than ideal, and the thing that was between them sprang from emotion rather than mind. It was unreasoning, and as ineluctable as the flight of time. Grandma Redding was the outright inheritor of a historical situation.

But not so Grandma Conway. She had assumed—not to say usurped—both the privileges and the penalties of a tradition that was hers only disingenuously, and therefore all the more fiercely held. The privileges gave her power; the penalties strength. She was certain of her values and she held them to be inviolate. She believed in a personal God and that He was in His heaven and all was right with the world. She believed in a rigid code of morality, but in a double standard, because she believed that there was something in the male animal that made him naturally incontinent, and that some women, always of a class she scornfully pitied, had no other purpose in life than to save good women from men's incontinence. In her notion, such women were not loose any more than rutting bitches were loose. A loose woman was a woman of her own class who had wilfully assumed the privileges and shunned the penalities of her birth. Such women she hated with face-purpling hatred. She believed in banks and schools and prisons. She believed that the world was so ordered that in the end his just deserts came to every man. This latter belief was very comprehensive, for she thought in terms of reciprocal responsibility of man and his class—that man did not live for himself alone and that he could not escape the general defections (she called it "sin") of the group into which he was born.

These beliefs must have been conspicuous to Grandma Conway's most casual acquaintance, but to me—and I have no doubt, to the rest of us long familiar with them—they were past both realizing and remarking, like the skin of one's body.

But realization of her most occult belief must have come quite early. Perhaps it came to me in 1917, when, on one of her visits, she first found the lower boundary of our neighborhood roiling with strange black folk and brazen with conspicuous life. It may have come to me imperceptibly, along with the consciousness of the stigma attaching to blackness of skin. But this stigma was a blemish, not a taint. A black skin was uncomely, but not inferior. My father was less beautiful than my mother, but he was not inferior to her. There were soot-black boys whom I knew in school who could outrun, outplay, and outthink me, but they were less personable than I. And certainly we did not think in any conscious way that Grandma Redding was a lesser person than Grandma Conway. The very core of awareness was this distinction.

But gradually, subtly, depressingly and without shock there entered into my consciousness the knowledge that Grandma Conway believed that a black skin was more than a blemish. In her notion it was a taint of flesh and bone and blood, varying in degree with the color of the skin, overcome sometimes by certain material distinctions and the grace of God, but otherwise fixed in the blood.

To Grandma Conway, as to my mother, our new neighbors on the east were a threat.

In our house a compromise was struck. No one ever talked about it. In the careless flow of our talk, it was the one subject avoided with meticulous concern. My parents were stern disciplinarians, and this subject was so fraught with punishable possibilities and yet so conscious a part of our living that by the time the three older ones of us were in grammar and high school our care for the avoidance of it took on at times an almost hysterical intensity. Many a time, as we heard schoolmates do and as we often did ourselves outside, one or the other of us wished to hurl the epithet "black" or "nigger," or a combination, and dared only sputter, "You, you . . . monkey!" For being called a monkey was not considered half so grave an insult as being called the other; and it was at least as grave a sin to avoid as using the Lord's name in vain. My parents, of course, never used either black or nigger, and avoided mentioning color in describing a person. One was either dark or light, never black or yellow—and between these two was that indeterminate group of browns of which our family was largely composed. We grew up in the very center of a complex.

I think my older brother and sister escaped most of the adolescent emotional conflict and vague melancholy (it came later to them, and especially to my brother, and in decidedly greater force) which were the winds of my course through teenhood. For me it was a matter of choices, secret choices really. For them there was no choice. And yet I had less freedom than they. They went off to a New England college in 1919. Up to then their associates had been first the white and then the mulatto children on our street. Even the children whom they met in high school were largely of the mulatto group, for the dark tide of migration had not then swept the schools. Going to school was distinctly an upper-class pursuit, and the public school was almost as exclusive as the summer playground which Miss Grinnage conducted along stubbornly select lines for "children of the best blood" (it was her favorite phrase), almost as exclusive as the Ethical Culture lectures we attended once each month, or the basement chapel of St. Andrew's Episcopal church, where Father Tatnall held segregated services for us twice a month. For my older brother and sister, the road through childhood was straight, without sideroads or crossings.

But by the time I reached high school in the fall of 1919, life was undergoing a tumultuous change. It was as if a placid river had suddenly broken its banks and in blind and senseless rage was destroying old landmarks, leveling the face of the country farther and farther beyond the shore line.

The migrants not only discovered our neighborhood, they discovered the church where we went to Sunday school and where my father was superintendent. They discovered the vast, beautiful reaches of the Brandywine where we used to walk on fair Sundays. They discovered the school. I remember the sickening thrill with which I heard a long-headed black boy arraign the mulatto teachers for always giving the choice parts in plays, the choice chores, the cleanest books to mulatto children. He called the teachers "color-struck," a phrase that was new to me, and "sons-of-bitches," a phrase that was not. He was put out of school. Many black children were put out of school, or not encouraged to continue. Two incidents stand out in my mind.

In my first oratorical competition, I knew—as everyone else knew—that the contestant to beat was a gangling dark fellow named Tom Cephus. He had a fervor that I did not have and for which I was taught to substitute craft. His voice, already changed, boomed with a vibrant quality that was impressive to hear. Moreover, he was controlled, self-possessed, and I was not. For days before the competition I was unable to rest, and when I did finally face the audience, I uttered a sentence or two and from sheer fright and nervous exhaustion burst into uncontrollable tears. Somehow, bawling like a baby, I got through. I was certain that I had lost.

Cephus in his turn was superb. The greater part of the audience was with him. Beyond the first rows of benches, which were friendly to me, stretched row after increasingly dark row of black faces and beaming eyes. It was more than an oratorical contest to them. It was a class and caste struggle as intense as any they would ever know, for it was immediate and possible of compromise and assuagement, if not of victory. Mouths open, strained forward, they vibrated against that booming voice, transfixed in ecstasy. The applause was deafening and vindicative. In the back of the crowded hall someone led three cheers for Cephus (a wholly unheard-of thing) and while the teacher-judges were conferring, cheer after cheer swelled from the audience like the approaching, humming, booming bursting of ocean waves.

A pulsing hush fell on them when the judges returned. They watched the announcer as leashed and hungry dogs watch the approach of food. But the judge was shrewd. She wanted that excitement to simmer down. Flicking a smile at the first rows, she calmly announced the singing of a lullaby and waited, a set smile on her face, until three verses had been sung. Then icily, in sprung-steel Bostonian accents, she announced to an audience whose soft-skinned faces gradually froze in spastic bewilderment, "Third place, Edith Miller. Second place, Thomas Cephus. First place . . ." My name was lost in a void of silence. "Assembly dismissed!"

Stunned beyond expression and feeling, the back rows filed out. The front rows cheered. Cephus's lips worked and he looked at me. I could not look at him. I wanted to fall on my knees.

I was truant from school for a week. When my parents discovered it, I took my punishment without a word. A little later that year, Cephus dropped out of school.

But I was stubborn in my resistance to these lessons. My stubbornness was not a rational thing arrived at through intellection. It was not as simple and as hard as that. I was not a conscious rebel. I liked people, and, for all the straitening effects of environment, I was only lightly color-struck. A dark skin was perhaps not as comely as a brown or yellow, but it was sometimes attractive. In matters of class mortality and custom and thought I was perhaps too young to make distinctions. I liked people. When I was sixteen and a senior in high school, I liked a doe-soft black girl named Viny. After school hours, Viny was a servant girl to kindly, dumpy, near-white Miss Kruse, the school principal, who lived across the street from us. I saw a good bit of Viny, for I ran Miss Kruse's confidential errands and did innumerable small things for her. There was nothing clandestine about my relations with her servant girl. We talked and joked in the kitchen. We sometimes walked together from school. We were frequently alone in the house.

But one day Miss Kruse called me to the front porch, where in fine, warm weather she ensconced herself in a rocker especially braced to support her flabby weight. She sat with her back turned squarely to the street. She was very fair, and because she ate heavily of rich, heavy foods, at forty-five she was heavy-jowled, with a broad, pleasant, doughy face. A sack of flesh swelled beneath her chin and seemed to hold her mouth open in a tiny O. She was reading.

"Sit down," she said.

I sat in the chair next to hers, but facing the street, so that we could look directly at each other. Both sides of the street were still lined with trees at that time, and it was June. Hedges were green. Miss Kruse read for a while longer, then she crumpled the paper against herself and folded her fingers over it.

"You like Viny, don't you?" she asked, looking at me with a heavy frown.

"Yes, ma'am," I said.

"Well, you be careful. She'll get you in trouble," she said.

"Trouble?"

"How would you like to marry her?"

I did not answer, for I did not know what to say.

"How?"

"I don't know'm."

This provoked her. She threw the newspaper on the floor. The network of fine pink veins on the lobes of her nose turned purple.

"Well, let her alone! Or she'll trap you to marry her. And what would you look like married to a girl like that?" she said bitingly. "No friends, no future. You might as well be dead! How would you like to spend the rest of your life delivering ice or cleaning outdoor privies? Don't you know girls like her haven't any shame, haven't any decency? She'll get you in trouble."

I stared stupidly at her. I do not know what my reaction was. I remember being confused and hotly embarrassed, and after that a kind of soggy lethargy settled in my stomach, like indigestible food. I distinctly remember that I felt no resentment and no shock, and that my confusion was due less to this first frank indictment of blackness than to the blunt reference to sex. Boys talked about sex in giggly whispers among themselves, but between male and female talk of sex was taboo. In the midst of my embarrassment, I heard Miss Kruse's voice again, calm and gentle now, persuasive, admonitory.

"You're going to college. You're going to get a fine education. You're going to be somebody. You'll be ashamed you ever knew Viny. There'll be fine girls for you to know, to marry."

She sighed, making a round sound of it through her O-shaped mouth, and rubbing her hands hard together as if they were cold.

"Viny. Well, Viny won't ever be anything but what she is already."

And what is she? And what and where are the others? One, who wore the flashy clothes and made loud laughter in the halls, is now a man of God, a solemn, earnest pulpiteer. Cephus, the boy who won and lost, is dead. And Pogie Walker's dead. It is remarkable how many of those I came to know in 1919 are dead. Birdie, Sweetie Pie, and Oliver. Viny? After she quit and moved away, she used to write me once a year on cheap, lined paper. "I'm doing alrite." (She never learned to spell.) "I'm living alrite. I gess I'm geting along alrite. How do these few lines fine you?" And Brunson, the smartest of that migrant lot, who outran, outfought, outthought all of us. He was expelled for writing a letter and passing it among the students. Most of the things he said were true—the exclusion of the very black from the first yearbook, the way one teacher had of referring to the black-skinned kids as "You, Cloudy, there," and never remembering their names. Well, Brunson is a week-end drunk. At other times he's very bitter. Not long ago I saw him. I spoke to him. "You don't remember me," I said. "Yeah. I remember you all right. So what?" He lives down on the east side, way down, where in the spring the river comes. . . .

Margaret Walker, an educator and poet, was born in Alabama in 1915. She has contributed poems to numerous anthologies, and is the author of *Prophets for a New Day* and *Jubilee,* among other books. For her poetry, she has received the Yale Award for Younger Poets and several writing fellowships, including a Ford fellowship.

8

MARGARET WALKER

From How I Wrote Jubilee and Other Essays on Life and Literature

Growing Out of Shadow

(1943)

WHEN I WAS FIVE, I was busy discovering my world, and it was a place of happiness and delight. Then, one day, a white child shouted in my ears "nigger" as if he were saying "cur," and I was startled. I had never heard the word before, and I went home and asked what it meant, and my parents looked apprehensively at each other as if to say, "It's come." Clumsily, without adding hurt to the smart I was already suffering, they sought to explain, but they were unable to destroy my pain. I could not understand my overwhelming sense of shame, as if I had been guilty of some unknown crime. I did not know why I was suffering, what brought this vague uneasiness, this clutching for understanding.

When I went to school, I read the history books that glorify the white race and describe the Negro either as a clown and a fool or a beast capable of very hard work in excessive heat. I discovered the background of chattel slavery behind this madness of race prejudice. Once we were slaves and now we are not, and the South remains angry. But when I went home to the good books and the wonderful music and the gentle, intelligent parents, I could see no reason for prejudice on the basis of a previous condition of servitude.

I went to church and I wondered why God let this thing continue.

Why were there segregated churches and segregated hospitals and cemeteries and schools? Why must I ride behind a Jim Crow sign? Why did a full-grown colored man sit meekly behind a Jim Crow sign and do nothing about it? What could he do? Then I decided perhaps God was on the side of the white people because after all God was white. The world was white, and I was Black.

Then I began to daydream: It will not always be this way. Someday, just as chattel slavery ended, this injustice will also end; this internal suffering will cease; this ache inside for understanding will exist no longer. Someday, I said, when I am fully grown, I will understand, and I will be able to do something about it. I will write books that will prove the history texts were distorted. I will write books about colored people who have colored faces, books that will not make me ashamed when I read them.

But always I was seeking for the real answer, not the daydream. Always I wanted to know. I lay awake at night pondering in my heart, "Why? Why? Why?"

I heard Roland Hayes and Marian Anderson sing, and James Weldon Johnson and Langston Hughes read poetry. In the audiences were well-dressed, well-behaved colored people. They were intelligent, yet they were not allowed to sit beside white people at concerts and recitals. Why? Every night Negro cooks and maids and chauffeurs and nursemaids returned home from the white people's houses where their employers were not afraid to sit beside them.

I learned of race pride and consciousness and the contribution of the Negro to American culture. Still I was bewildered. America was a place of strange contradictions. The white grocery man at the corner who was so friendly when I was in his store thought it a crime for a white and a colored boxer to fight in the ring together. But he did not think it a crime for a Negro to be drafted to fight for America.

I decided vaguely that the white man must think these things because of fear; because he felt insecure. Perhaps he was a little afraid of what would happen in a free America. How did I first discover the color of my skin? I had only to look in my mirror every morning to know. I must say it appeared to me a good healthy color. But there is a difference in knowing you are Black and in understanding what it means to be Black in America. Before I was ten I knew what it was to step off the sidewalk to let a white man pass; otherwise he might knock me off. I had had a sound thrashing by white boys while Negro men looked on helplessly. I was accustomed to riding in the Jim Crow streetcars with the Negro section marked off by iron bars that could not be moved. For a year and a half I went to school in a one-room wooden shack. One year when my father's schoolwork took him out of town constantly, my mother lived in fear of our lives because there was no man in the house to protect us against the possibility of some attack. Once, we climbed the fire escape to see a movie, because there was no Negro entrance, and after that we saw no movies. Another time my mother stood for hours upstairs in a darkened theatre to hear a recital by Rachmaninoff, because there were no seats for colored. My father was chased home one night at the point of a gun by a drunken policeman who resented seeing a fountain pen in a "nigger's" pocket. My grandmother told the story of a woman tarred and feathered in the neighborhood. A mob came and took her from her home because it was rumored that a white man was visiting her. Although they took her deep into the woods, her screams were heard by relatives and neighbors. My grandmother heard them, too. Next day the woman's family went to the woods and brought her home. She was still alive, so they removed the tar and feathers with turpentine. She was horribly burned and scarred.

And always the answer and the question in a child's mind to each of these was "Why? Why do they do these things?"

Negroes congregating on a city block to argue and talk about the race question imitated what they heard from the pulpits or what the white folks told them: "The trouble with the Negro problem in America is just we needs to git together . . . We don't co-operate . . . We always kicking one another . . . This is a white man's country and Black man ain't got no place in it . . . We just cursed by God, sons of Ham, hewers of wood and drawers of water . . . Our leaders are crooked and they betray us . . . We need to get a little money and make ourselves independent of the white man . . . If it wasn't for the white man we'd be way back in the jungles of Africa somewhere . . . We oughta thank the white man for bringing us to this country and making us civilized . . . Trouble is we scared to fight, scared to stick up for our rights . . . We'll fight for the white man but we won't fight for ourselves . . . All the progress we've made we owe to the white man . . . I hates a white man worsener I hates poison, left to me I'd kill up every paleface in the world . . . Don't let 'em fool you when they grinning in your face, they want something . . . Only God can help us . . . It takes time, that's all, to solve the Negro problem . . . All we got to do is humble ourselves and do right and we'll win out . . . Colored man hurts hisself most of the time . . . All we got to do is do like the children of Israel and the slaves done way back yonder, pray . . . Colored people oughta get out of the notion that they are Negroes . . . That word *Negroes* is what hurts us. . . ."

But all of it was no real answer to the anxious questioning of a child burdened constantly with the wonder of what race prejudice is.

When I went away to college in my teens, I left the South with mingled emotions. I had been told that Negroes in the North were better off than Negroes down South; they had more sense and more opportunities; they could go any place, enjoy recreational facilities such as parks and movies, eat in restaurants without discrimination; there were no Jim Crow transportation restrictions, and if Negroes were subjected to any indignity, they could sue the person or company involved; there was no such thing as lynching. Best of all, Negroes could vote.

I was, nevertheless, shy and afraid over the prospect of going to a white school; I might prove backward as a result of my southern training. I had also perforce become somewhat antiwhite myself and I feared coming into close contact with white people. Yet I anticipated a new kind of freedom once I crossed the Mason-Dixon Line.

Imagine my great hurt to discover that few of the wonderful promises came true. I was refused service in restaurants in Evanston and Chicago time and time again. In the South I had suffered no similar embarrassment because there I had known what to expect. I discovered that most of the Negroes in the northern colleges and universities were from the South, for the majority of Negroes in the Middle West had no money with which to take advantage of higher education.

What was most amazing was my discovery of my own prejudices and my first realization of the economic problem.

Because of the nature of segregated life in America many Negroes have misconceptions of white life. I was no exception. As servants, Negroes know certain elements of white life and characterize the whole in this way. My first step toward understanding what it means to be Black in America was understanding the economics of the United States.

In the South I had always thought that, naturally, white people had more money than colored people. Poor white trash signified for me the lazy scum of the marginal fringe of society with no excuse for poverty. Now I discovered there were poor white working people exploited by rich white people. I learned that all Jews were not rich. I discovered that all Negroes were not even in the same economic class. While there were no Negro multi-millionaires, there were many wealthy Negroes who made money by exploiting poor Negroes, who had some of the same attitudes toward them that rich whites had toward poor whites and that prejudiced whites have toward all Negroes. Imagine my amazement to hear a white girl tell me she was forced to leave Northwestern because she had no money. But I, a poor Negro girl, had stayed even when I had no money. They never threatened me with expulsion. Yet I did not find a white school in the Middle West free of prejudice. All around me was prejudice. To understand the issues out of which it grew became my life's preoccupation.

A year out of college found me working with poor whites—Jew and Gentile—and poor Negroes, too. In Chicago, for the first time I began to see that Negroes, as almost entirely a working-class people, belong with organized labor. My background was so thoroughly petty-bourgeois, with parents who belonged to a professional small-salaried class, that I had not understood that people who worked with their brains were also workers. I knew we were poor and decent, and that was all I knew. In the South, many, if not most, petty-bourgeois Negroes are antiunion, antistrike, and antiwhite. This, of course, is not strange when one considers the history of Negroes in unions in the South, their forced role as scabs, the brutal treatment they received as such, prior to the Congress of Industrial Organizations (CIO), the general nature of Negro life in the South, threatened always by sinister undertones of white violence.

Thus there began for me in Chicago a period in which I learned about class in the United States. As soon as I began working in close contact with whites, I discovered startling things peculiar to both racial groups, all adding up to one main conclusion: that whites suffer psychologically from the problem of race prejudice as much as Negroes. I began to see race prejudice as a definite tool to keep people divided and economically helpless: Negroes hating whites and whites hating Blacks, with conditions of both groups pitiful, both economically and psychologically. I saw, too, that it was not beyond the ability of both groups to reach understanding and to live peaceably side by side, that the organization of Negroes and whites by labor was certainly one step forward toward that end.

The second step toward understanding what it means to be Black in America came in understanding the political problem. By 1932 and 1936, Negroes had, out of the dire necessity of destitution, become politically conscious even in the Deep South, where they had no real voice in politics. In the North, the East, and particularly the Middle West, the Negro vote assumed significant proportions and in many instances proved effective in the balance of power.

In 1936 I cast my first vote in Chicago in a Presidential election. It was a great time to come of age. There had been four years of the New Deal, and many of the ills and evils of our society, as they immediately touched Negroes and all poor people, had been somewhat alleviated. We had benefited from the Works Progress Administration (WPA), the National Youth Administration (NYA), the Federal Housing and Federal Farm Administration, Social Security, the WPA adult education program; we had benefited in many instances where there had previously been evil practices of discrimination. I began to dig into the historical background of politics in America, to read the record where Negroes were concerned. I began to see parallels. When the thirteen colonies revolted, they revolted on the premise that taxation without representation is tyranny. Yet that is precisely what the Negro suffered in the South still. Moreover, poor white people as well had no voice in their government. If the truth were nationally known and understood, the small number of votes cast in electing southern representatives and senators to Congress, as compared with the population, would not merely appear ridiculous but alarming. Not that these citizens of America were too indifferent to vote; they were disfranchised under the pretense of a poll tax not paid or a grandfather clause. The old saying that a voteless people is a helpless people became a basic fact in my understanding of the Negro problem.

A third step came from a growing world perspective. As a child, reading the history books in the South, I was humiliated by some unhappy picture or reference to a Negro. Such items made me burn all over. It was as if we were cut off from humanity, without sensitivity. I could make no connection between my life as a Negro child in the South and the life of Chinese children or Indian children or children in South Africa. I grew up and became self-supporting, yet I had not connected myself with working women all over the world, with poor peasant women who are white as well as Black. Now I began to reach out. I saw it was eternally to the credit of Negroes in America that we were represented in Spain on the side of the Loyalists with soldiers, nurses, volunteer workers, our humble gift of an ambulance, our moral support. We can be proud that Ethiopia found a willing ear for help from us. While white America is far too prone to appreciate the struggle of people in distant lands and forget the problems on its own doorstep, its disadvantaged groups are often too obsessed with their own problems to see further than the bridge of their nose. I realized it was essential for Negroes to be identified with every heroic struggle of an oppressed people, with the brave Chinese, the Indians, the South Africans, the Negroes in the West Indies who fight for liberty. Now that we are engaged in a global war, it is even more essential that all peoples of the earth gain a world perspective and become conscious of our common humanity and man's struggle to be free.

Yet I am sure that economic, political, and social understanding is not all. There is need for a new type of spiritual understanding, and

I use the word not in its narrow religious meaning. I am concerned with something far more meaningful in the lives of individual men and women, of greater practical value and far better potentialities for personal and social growth. Once the human spirit is washed clean of prejudices, once the basic needs of people are considered, and not the pocketbooks of the few nor the power of a handful; once institutionalized religion is liberated into religious meaning, of necessity there must begin to bloom upon the earth something spiritually more durable than any of the mystic conceptions of religion that humankind has thus far brought forth. Then no person will look at another with fear, patronage, condescension, hatred, or disparagement, under pain of one's own spiritual death.

W.E.B. DuBois, scholar and civil rights leader, was born in 1868 in Massachusetts. After receiving his Ph.D. from Harvard in 1896, DuBois cofounded the National Negro Committee, which later became the NAACP; for several years he taught economics and history at Atlanta University. DuBois served as the editor of *The Crisis* and published *The Souls of Black Folks, What the Negro Wants, John Brown,* and *The Black Flame,* among other works. DuBois received the International Peace Prize in 1952; he later moved to Ghana, where he died in 1963.

9

W.E.B. DUBOIS

From What the Negro Wants

My Evolving Program for Negro Freedom

(1944)

My Midnight Classmate

ONCE UPON A TIME, I found myself at midnight on one of the swaggering streetcars that used to roll out from Boston on its way to Cambridge. It must have been in the Spring of 1890, and quite accidentally I was sitting by a classmate who would graduate with me in June. As I dimly remember, he was a nice-looking young man, almost dapper; well-dressed, charming in manner. Probably he was rich or at least well-to-do, and doubtless belonged to an exclusive fraternity, although that I do not know. Indeed I have even forgotten his name. But one thing I shall never forget and that was his rather regretful admission (that slipped out as we gossiped) that he had no idea as to what his life-work would be, because, as he added, "There's nothing which I am particularly interested in!"

I was more than astonished—I was almost outraged to meet any human being of the mature age of twenty-two who did not have his life all planned before him, at least in general outline; and who was not supremely, if not desperately, interested in what he planned to do.

Since then, my wonder has left my classmate, and been turned in and backward upon myself: how long had I been sure of my life-work and how had I come so confidently to survey and plan it? I now realize that most college seniors are by no means certain of what they want to do or can do with life; but stand rather upon a hesitating threshold, awaiting will, chance or opportunity. Because I had not mingled intimately or understandingly with my Harvard classmates, I did not at the time realize this, but thought my rather unusual attitude was general. How had this attitude come to seem normal to me?

My Early Youth

The small western New England town where I was born, and several generations of my fathers before me, was a middle-class community of Americans of English and Dutch descent, with an Irish laboring class and a few remnants of Negro working folk of past centuries. Farmers and small merchants predominated, with a fringe of decadent Americans; with mill-hands, railroad laborers and domestics. A few manufacturers formed a small aristocracy of wealth. In the public schools of this town, I was trained from the age of six to sixteen, and in its schools, churches and general social life I gained my patterns of living. I had almost no experience of segregation or color discrimination. My schoolmates were invariably white; I joined quite naturally all games, excursions, church festivals; recreations like coasting, skating and ball-games. I was in and out of the homes of nearly all my mates, and ate and played with them. I was a boy unconscious of color discrimination in any obvious and specific way.

I knew nevertheless that I was exceptional in appearance and that this riveted attention upon me. Less clearly, I early realized that most of the colored persons I saw, including my own folk, were poorer than the well-to-do whites; lived in humbler houses, and did not own stores; this was not universally true: my cousins, the Crispels, in West Stockbridge, had one of the most beautiful homes in the village. Other cousins, in Lenox, were well-to-do. On the other hand, none of the colored folk I knew were so poor, drunken and sloven as some of the lower Americans and Irish. I did not then associate poverty or ignorance with color, but rather with lack of opportunity; or more often with lack of thrift, which was in strict accord with the philosophy of New England and of the Nineteenth Century.

On the other hand, much of my philosophy of the color line must have come from my family group and their friends' experience. My father dying early, my immediate family consisted of my mother and her brother and my older half-brother most of the time. Near to us in space and intimacy were two married aunts with older children, and a number of cousins, in various degrees removed, living scattered through the county and state. Most of these had been small farmers, artisans, laborers and servants. With few exceptions all could read and write, but few had training beyond this. These talked of their work and experiences, of hindrances which colored people encountered, of better chances in other towns and cities. In this way I must have gotten indirectly a pretty clear outline of color bars which I myself did not experience. Moreover, it was easy enough for me to rationalize my own case, because I found it easy to excel most of my schoolmates in studies if not in games. The secret of life and the loosing of the color bar, then, lay in excellence, in accomplishment; if others of my family, of my colored kin, had stayed in school, instead of quitting early for small jobs, they could have risen to equal whites. On this my mother quietly insisted. There was no real discrimination on account of color—it was all a matter of ability and hard work.

This philosophy was saved from conceit and vainglory by rigorous self-testing, which doubtless cloaked some half-conscious misgivings on my part. If visitors to school saw and remarked my brown face, I waited in quiet confidence. When my turn came, I recited glibly and usually correctly because I studied hard. Some of my mates did not care, some were stupid; but at any rate I gave the best a hard run, and then sat back complacently. Of course I was too honest with myself not to see things which desert and even hard work did not explain or solve: I recognized ingrained difference in gift; Art Gresham could draw caricatures for the *High School Howler,* published occasionally in manuscript, better than I; but I could express meanings in words better than he; Mike McCarthy was a perfect marble player, but dumb in Latin. I came to see and admit all this, but I hugged my own gifts and put them to test.

When preparation for college came up, the problem of poverty began to appear. Without conscious decision on my part, and probably because of continuous quiet suggestion from my High School principal, Frank Hosmer, I found myself planning to go to college; how or where, seemed an unimportant detail. A wife of one of the cotton mill owners, whose only son was a pal of mine, offered to see that I got lexicons and texts to take up the study of Greek in High School, without which college doors in that day would not open. I accepted the offer as something normal and right; only after many years did I realize how critical this gift was for my career. I am not yet sure how she came to do it; perhaps my wise principal suggested it. Comparatively few of my white classmates planned or cared to plan for college—perhaps two or three in a class of twelve.

I collected catalogues of colleges and over the claims of Williams and Amherst, nearest my home, I blithely picked Harvard, because it was oldest and largest, and most widely known. My mother died a few months after my graduation, just as though, tired of the long worry and pull, she was leaving me alone at the post, with a certain characteristic faith that I would not give up.

I was, then, an orphan, without a cent of property, and with no relative who could for a moment think of undertaking the burden of my further education. But the family could and did help out and the town in its quiet and unemotional way was satisfied with my record and silently began to plan. First, I must go to work at least for a season and get ready for college in clothes and maturity, as I was only sixteen. Then there was the question of where I could go and how the expenses could be met.

The working out of these problems by friends and relatives brought me face to face, for the first time, with matters of income and wealth. A place was secured for me as time-keeper, during the building of a mansion by a local millionaire, in whose family an ancestor of mine had once worked. My job brought me for the first time in close contact with organized work and wage. I followed the building and its planning: I watched the mechanics at their work; I knew what they earned, I gave them their weekly wage and carried the news of their dismissal. I saw the modern world at work, mostly with the hands, and with few machines.

Meantime in other quarters a way was being made for me to go to college. The father of one of my schoolmates, the Reverend C. C. Painter, was once in the Indian Bureau. There and elsewhere he saw the problem of the reconstructed South, and conceived the idea that there was the place for me to be educated, and there lay my future field of work. My family and colored friends rather resented the idea. Their Northern Free Negro prejudice naturally revolted at the idea of sending me to the former land of slavery, either for education or for living. I am rather proud of myself that I did not agree with them. That I should always live and work in the South, I did not then stop to decide; that I would give up the idea of graduating from Harvard, did not occur to me. But I wanted to go to Fisk, not simply because it was at least a beginning of my dream of college, but also, I suspect, because I was beginning to feel lonesome in New England; because, unconsciously, I realized, that as I grew older, the close social intermingling with my white fellows would grow more restricted. There were meetings, parties, clubs, to which I was not invited. Especially in the case of strangers, visitors, newcomers to the town was my presence and friendship a matter of explanation or even embarrassment to my schoolmates. Similar discriminations and separations met the Irish youth, and the cleft between rich and poor widened.

On the other hand, the inner social group of my own relatives and colored friends always had furnished me as a boy most interesting and satisfying company; and now as I grew, it was augmented by visitors from other places. I remember a lovely little plump and brown girl who appeared out of nowhere, and smiled at me demurely; I went to the East to visit my father's father in New Bedford, and on that trip saw well-to-do, well-mannered colored people; and once, at Rocky Point, Rhode Island, I viewed with astonishment 10,000 Negroes of every hue and bearing. I was transported with amazement and dreams; I apparently noted nothing of poverty or degradation, but only extraordinary beauty of skin-color and utter equality of men, with absence so far as I could see of even the shadow of the line of race. Gladly and armed with a scholarship, I set out for Fisk.

At Fisk University

Thus in the Fall of 1885 and at the age of seventeen, I was tossed boldly into the "Negro Problem." From a section and circumstances where the status of me and my folk could be rationalized as the result of poverty and limited training, and settled essentially by schooling and hard effort, I suddenly came to a region where the world was split into white and black halves, and where the darker half was held back by race prejudice and legal bonds, as well as by deep ignorance and dire poverty.

But facing this was not a little lost group, but a world in size and a civilization in potentiality. Into this world I leapt with provincial enthusiasm. A new loyalty and allegiance replaced my Americanism: henceforward I was a Negro.

To support and balance this, was the teaching and culture background of Fisk of the latter Nineteenth Century. All of its teachers but one where white, from New England or from the New Englandized Middle West. My own culture background thus suffered no change nor hiatus. Its application only was new. This *point d'appui* was not simply Tennessee, which was never a typical slave state, but Georgia, Alabama, Mississippi, Louisiana and Texas, whence our students came; and who as mature men and women, for the most part from five to ten years older than I, could paint from their own experience a wide and vivid picture of the post-war South and of its black millions. There were men and women who had faced mobs and seen lynchings; who knew every phase of insult and repression; and too there were sons, daughters and clients of every class of white Southerner. A relative of a future president of the nation had his dark son driven to school each day.

The college curriculum of my day was limited but excellent. Adam Spence was a great Greek scholar by any comparison. Thomas Chase with his ridiculously small laboratory nevertheless taught us not only chemistry and physics but something of science and of life.

In after years I used Bennett's German in Germany, and with the philosophy and ethics of Cravath, I later sat under William James and George Palmer at Harvard. The excellent and earnest teaching, the small college classes; the absence of distractions, either in athletics or society, enabled me to re-arrange and re-build my program for freedom and progress among Negroes. I replaced my hitherto egocentric world by a world centering and whirling about my race in America. To this group I transferred my plan of study and accomplishment. Through the leadership of men like me and my fellows, we were going to have these enslaved Israelites out of the still enduring bondage in short order. It was a battle which might conceivably call for force, but I could think it confidently through mainly as a battle of wits; of knowledge and deed, which by sheer reason and desert, must eventually overwhelm the forces of hate, ignorance and reaction.

Always in my dreaming, a certain redeeming modicum of common sense has usually come to my rescue and brought fantasy down to the light of common day: I was not content to take the South entirely by hearsay; and while I had no funds to travel widely, I did, somewhat to the consternation of both teachers and fellow-students, determine to go out into the country and teach summer school. I was only eighteen and knew nothing of the South at first hand, save what little I had seen in Nashville. There to be sure I had stared curiously at the bullet holes in the door of the City Hall where an editor had been murdered in daylight and cold blood. It was the first evidence of such physical violence I had ever seen. I had once made the tragic mistake of raising my hat to a white woman, whom I had accidentally jostled on the public street. But I had not seen anything of the small Southern town and the countryside, which are the real South. If I could not explore Darkest Mississippi, at least I could see West Tennessee, which was not more than fifty miles from the college.

Needless to say the experience was invaluable. I traveled not only in space but in time. I touched the very shadow of slavery. I lived and taught school in log cabins built before the Civil War. My school was the second held in the district since emancipation. I touched intimately the lives of the commonest of mankind—people who ranged from bare-footed dwellers on dirt floors, with patched rags for clothes, to rough, hard-working farmers, with plain, clean plenty. I saw and talked with white people, noted now their unease, now their truculence and again their friendliness. I nearly fell from my horse when the first school commissioner whom I interviewed invited me to stay to dinner. Afterward I realized that he meant me to eat at the second, but quite as well-served, table.

The net result of the Fisk interlude was to broaden the scope of my program of life, not essentially to change it; to center it in a group of educated Negroes, who from their knowledge and experience would lead the mass. I never for a moment dreamed that such leadership could ever be for the sake of the educated group itself, but always for the mass. Nor did I pause to enquire in just what ways and with what technique we would work—first, broad, exhaustive knowledge of the world; all other wisdom, all method and application would be added unto us.

In essence I combined a social program for a depressed group with the natural demand of youth for "Light, more Light." Fisk was a good college; I liked it; but it was small, it was limited in equipment, in laboratories, in books; it was not a university. I wanted the largest and best in organized learning. Nothing could be too big and thorough for training the leadership of the American Negro. There must remain no suspicion of part-knowledge, cheap equipment, for this mighty task. The necessity of earning a living scarcely occurred to me. I had no need for or desire for money.

I turned with increased determination to the idea of going to Harvard. There I was going to study the science of sciences—philosophy. Vainly did Chase point out, as James did later, that the world was not in the habit of paying philosophers. In vain did the president offer me a scholarship at Hartford Theological Seminary. I believed too little in Christian dogma to become a minister. I was not without Faith: I never stole material nor spiritual things; I not only never lied, but blurted out my conception of the truth on the most untoward occasions; I drank no alcohol and knew nothing of women, physically or psychically, to the incredulous amusement of most of my more experienced fellows: I above all believed in work—systematic and tireless.

I went to Harvard. Small difference it made if Harvard would only admit me to standing as a college junior; I earned $100 by summer work: I received Price Greenleaf Aid to the amount of $250, which seemed a very large sum. Of the miracle of my getting anything, of the sheer luck of being able to keep on studying with neither friends nor money, I gave no thought.

The Enlargement at Harvard and Berlin

Fortunately I did not fall into the mistake of regarding Harvard as the beginning rather than the continuing of my college training. I did not find better teachers at Harvard, but teachers better known, with wider facilities and in broader atmosphere for approaching truth. Up to this time, I had been absorbing a general view of human knowledge: in ancient and modern literatures; in mathematics, physics and chemistry and history. It was all in vague and general terms—interpretations of what men who knew the facts at first hand, thought they might mean. With the addition of a course in chemistry in a Harvard laboratory under Hill, some geology under Shaler and history under Hart, I was in possession of the average educated man's concept of this world and its meaning. But now I wanted to go further: to know what man could know and how to collect and interpret facts face to face. And what "facts" were.

Here I revelled in the keen analysis of William James, Josiah Royce and young George Santayana. But it was James with his pragmatism and Albert Bushnell Hart with his research method, that turned me back from the lovely but sterile land of philosophic speculation, to the social sciences as the field for gathering and interpreting that body of fact which would apply to my program for the Negro.

I began with a bibliography of Nat Turner and ended with a history of the suppression of the African Slave Trade to America; neither needed to be done again at least in my day. Thus in my quest for basic knowledge with which to help guide the American Negro, I came to the study of sociology, by way of philosophy and history rather than by physics and biology, which was the current approach; moreover at that day, Harvard recognized no "science" of sociology and for my doctorate, after hesitating between history and economics, I chose history. On the other hand, psychology, hovering then at the threshold of experiment under Münsterberg, soon took a new orientation which I could understand from the beginning.

My human contacts at Harvard were narrow, and if I had not gone immediately to Europe, I was about to encase myself in a completely colored world, self-sufficient and provincial, and ignoring just as far as possible the white world which conditioned it. This was self-protective coloration, with perhaps an inferiority complex, but more of increasing belief in the ability and future of black folk. I sought at Harvard no acquaintanceship with white students and only such contacts with white teachers as lay directly in the line of my work. I joined certain clubs like the Philosophical Club; I was a member of the Foxcroft dining club because it was cheap. James and one or two other teachers had me at their homes at meal and reception.

Nevertheless my friends and companions were taken from the colored students of Harvard and neighboring institutions, and the colored folk of Boston and other cities. With them I led a happy and inspiring life. There were among them many educated and well-to-do folk; many young people studying or planning to study; many charming young women. We met and ate, danced and argued and planned a new world. I was exceptional among them, in my ideas on voluntary race segregation; they for the most part saw salvation only in integration at the earliest moment and on almost any terms in white culture; I was firm in my criticism of white folk and in my more or less complete dream of a Negro self-sufficient culture even in America.

In Germany, on the other hand, where after a stiff fight for recognition of my academic work, I went on fellowship in 1892, the situation was quite different. I found myself on the outside of the American world, looking in. With me were white folk—students, acquaintances, teachers—who viewed the scene with me. They did not pause to regard me as a curiosity, or something sub-human; I was just a man of the somewhat privileged student rank, with whom they were glad to meet and talk over the world; particularly, the part of the world whence I came. I found to my gratification that they with me

did not regard America as the last word in civilization. Indeed I
derived a certain satisfaction in learning that the University of Berlin
did not recognize a degree even from Harvard University, no more
than from Fisk. Even I was a little startled to realize how much that
I had regarded as white American, was white European and not
American at all: America's music is German, the Germans said; the
Americans have no art, said the Italians; and their literature, remarked
the English, is English; all agreed that Americans could make money
but did not care how they made it. And the like. Sometimes their
criticism got under even my anti-American skin, but it was refreshing
on the whole to hear voiced my own attitude toward so much that
America had meant to me.

In my study, I came in contact with several of the great leaders
of the developing social sciences: with Schmoller in economic sociology; Adolf Wagner, in social history; with Max Weber and the Ger-
manophile, von Treitschke. I gained ready admittance to two rather
exclusive seminars, and my horizon in the social sciences was broadened not only by teachers, but by students from France, Belgium,
Russia, Italy and Poland. I traveled, on foot and third-class railway,
to all parts of Germany and most of Central Europe. I got a bird's eye
glimpse of modern western culture at the turn of the century.

But of greater importance, was the opportunity which my *Wan-
derjahre* in Europe gave of looking at the world as a man and not
simply from a narrow racial and provincial outlook. This was primarily the result not so much of my study, as of my human companionship, unveiled by the accident of color. From the days of my later
youth to my boarding a Rhine passenger steamer at Rotterdam in
August, 1892, I had not regarded white folk as human in quite the
same way that I was. I had reached the habit of expecting color
prejudice so universally, that I found it even when it was not there.
So when I saw on this little steamer a Dutch lady with two grown
daughters and one of twelve, I proceeded to put as much space
between us as the small vessel allowed. But it did not allow much, and
the lady's innate breeding allowed less. Before we reached the end of
our trip, we were happy companions, laughing, eating and singing
together, talking English, French and German, visiting in couples, as

the steamer stopped, the lovely castled German towns, and acting like normal, well-bred human beings. I waved them all good-bye, in the solemn arched aisles of the Köln cathedral, with tears in my eyes.

So too in brave old Eisenach, beneath the shadow of Luther's Wartburg, I spent a happy holiday with French and English boys, and German girls, in a home where university training and German home-making left no room for American color prejudice, although one American woman did what she could to introduce it. She thought that I was far too popular with the German girls and secretly warned the house-mother. I was popular, but there was no danger in the American sense. I was quite wedded to my task in America. When blue-eyed Dora confessed her readiness to marry me *"gleich!"* I told her frankly and gravely that it would be unfair to himself and cruel to her for a colored man to take a white bride to America. She could not understand.

From this unhampered social intermingling with Europeans of education and manners, I emerged from the extremes of my racial provincialism. I became more human; learned the place in life of "Wine, Women, and Song"; I ceased to hate or suspect people simply because they belonged to one race or color; and above all I began to understand the real meaning of scientific research and the dim outline of methods of employing its technique and its results in the new social sciences for the settlement of the Negro problems in America.

James Baldwin was born in New York City in 1924. His long list
of works include *Go Tell It On the Mountain*; *Another Country*;
the essay collections *Notes of a Native Son* and *The Fire Next
Time*; and a play, *The Amen Corner*. Baldwin was the recipient
of numerous awards and honors, including a Guggenheim Fellowship. He died in Paris in 1987.

10

JAMES BALDWIN

From Notes of a Native Son

Stranger in the Village

(1953)

FROM ALL AVAILABLE evidence no black man had ever set foot in this tiny Swiss village before I came. I was told before arriving that I would probably be a "sight" for the village; I took this to mean that people of my complexion were rarely seen in Switzerland, and also that city people are always something of a "sight" outside of the city. It did not occur to me—possibly because I am an American—that there could be people anywhere who had never seen a Negro.

It is a fact that cannot be explained on the basis of the inaccessibility of the village. The village is very high, but it is only four hours from Milan and three hours from Lausanne. It is true that it is virtually unknown. Few people making plans for a holiday would elect to come here. On the other hand, the villagers are able, presumably, to come and go as they please—which they do: to another town at the foot of the mountain, with a population of approximately five thousand, the nearest place to see a movie or go to the bank. In the village there is no movie house, no bank, no library, no theater; very few radios, one jeep, one station wagon; and at the moment, one typewriter, mine, an invention which the woman next door to me here had never seen. There are about six hundred people living here, all Catholic—I conclude this from the fact that the Catholic church is open all year round, where as the Protestant chapel, set off on a hill a little removed from the village, is open only in the summertime when the tourists arrive. There are four or five hotels, all closed now, and four or five *bistros,* of which, however, only two do any business during the winter. These two do not do a great deal, for life in the village seems to end around nine or ten o'clock. There are a few stores, butcher, baker, *épicerie,* a hardware store, and a money-changer—who cannot change travelers' checks, but must send them down to the bank, an operation which takes two or three days. There is something called the *Ballet Haus,* closed in the winter and used for God knows what, certainly not ballet, during the summer. There seems to be only one schoolhouse in the village, and this for the quite young children; I suppose this to mean that their older brothers and sisters at some point descend from these mountains in order to complete their education—possibly, again, to the town just below. The landscape is absolutely forbidding, mountains towering on all four sides, ice and snow as far as the eye can reach. In this white wilderness, men and women and children move all day, carrying washing, wood, buckets of milk or water, sometimes skiing on Sunday afternoons. All week long boys and young men are to be seen shoveling snow off the rooftops, or dragging wood down from the forest in sleds.

The village's only real attraction, which explains the tourist season, is the hot spring water. A disquietingly high proportion of these tourists are cripples, or semi-cripples, who come year after year—from other parts of Switzerland, usually—to take the waters. This lends the village, at the height of the season, a rather terrifying air of sanctity, as though it were a lesser Lourdes. There is often something beautiful, there is always something awful, in the spectacle of a person who has lost one of his faculties, a faculty he never questioned until it was gone, and who struggles to recover it. Yet people remain people, on crutches or indeed on deathbeds; and wherever I passed, the first summer I was here, among the native villagers or among the lame, a wind passed with me—of astonishment, curiosity, amusement, and outrage. That first summer I stayed two weeks and never intended to return. But I did return in the winter, to work; the village offers, obviously, no distractions whatever and has the further advantage of being extremely cheap. Now it is winter again, a year later, and I am here again. Everyone in the village knows my name, though they scarcely ever use it, knows that I come from America—though, this, apparently, they will never really believe: black men come from Africa—and everyone knows that I am the friend of the son of a woman who was born here, and that I am staying in their chalet. But I remain as much a stranger today as I was the first day I arrived, and the children shout *Neger! Neger!* as I walk along the streets.

It must be admitted that in the beginning I was far too shocked to have any real reaction. In so far as I reacted at all, I reacted by trying to be pleasant—it being a great part of the American Negro's education (long before he goes to school) that he must make people "like" him. This smile-and-the-world-smiles-with-you routine worked about as well in this situation as it had in the situation for which it was designed, which is to say that it did not work at all. No one, after all, can be liked whose human weight and complexity cannot be, or has not been, admitted. My smile was simply another unheard-of phenomenon which allowed them to see my teeth—they did not, really, see my smile and I began to think that, should I take to snarling, no one would notice any difference. All of the physical characteristics of the Negro which had caused me, in America, a very different and almost forgotten pain were nothing less than miraculous—or infernal—in the eyes of the village people. Some thought my hair was the color of tar, that it had the texture of wire, or the texture of cotton. It was jocularly suggested that I might let it all grow long and make myself a winter coat. If I sat in the sun for more than five minutes some daring creature was certain to come along and gingerly put his fingers on my hair, as though he were afraid of an electric shock, or put his hand on my hand, astonished that the color did not rub off. In all of this, in which it must be conceded there was the charm of genuine wonder and in which there were certainly no element of intentional unkindness, there was yet no suggestion that I was human: I was simply a living wonder.

I knew that they did not mean to be unkind, and I know it now; it is necessary, nevertheless, for me to repeat this to myself each time that I walk out of the chalet. The children who shout *Neger!* have no way of knowing the echoes this sound raises in me. They are brimming with good humor and the more daring swell with pride when I stop to speak with them. Just the same, there are days when I cannot pause and smile, when I have no heart to play with them; when, indeed, I mutter sourly to myself, exactly as I muttered on the streets of a city these children have never seen, when I was no bigger than these children are now: *Your* mother *was a nigger.* Joyce is right about history being a nightmare—but it may be the nightmare from which no one can awaken. People are trapped in history and history is trapped in them.

There is a custom in the village—I am told it is repeated in many villages—of "buying" African natives for the purpose of converting them to Christianity. There stands in the church all year round a small box with a slot for money, decorated with a black figurine, and into this box the villagers drop their francs. During the *carnaval* which precedes Lent, two village children have their faces blackened—out of which bloodless darkness their blue eyes shine like ice—and fantastic horsehair wigs are placed on their blond heads; thus disguised, they solicit among the villagers for money for the missionaries in Africa. Between the box in the church and the blackened children, the village "bought" last year six or eight African natives. This was reported to me with pride by the wife of one of the *bistro* owners and I was careful to express astonishment and pleasure at the solicitude shown by the village for the souls of black folks. The *bistro* owner's wife beamed with a pleasure far more genuine than my own and seemed to feel that I might now breathe more easily concerning the souls of at least six of my kinsmen.

I tried not to think of these so lately baptized kinsmen, of the price paid for them, or the peculiar price they themselves would pay, and said nothing about my father, who having taken his own conversion too literally never, at bottom, forgave the white world (which he described as heathen) for having saddled him with a Christ in whom, to judge at least from their treatment of him, they themselves no longer believed. I thought of white men arriving for the first time in an African village, strangers there, as I am a stranger here, and tried to imagine the astounded populace touching their hair and marveling at the color of their skin. But there is a great difference between being the first white man to be seen by Africans and being the first black man to be seen by whites. The white man takes the astonishment as tribute, for he arrives to conquer and to convert the natives, whose inferiority in relation to himself is not even to be questioned; whereas I, without a thought of conquest, find myself among a people whose culture controls me, has even, in a sense, created me, people who have cost me more in anguish and rage than they will ever know, who yet do not even know of my existence. The astonishment with which I might have greeted them, should they have stumbled into my African village a few hundred years ago, might have rejoiced their hearts. But the astonishment with which they greet me today can only poison mine.

And this is so despite everything I may do to feel differently, despite my friendly conversations with the *bistro* owner's wife, despite their three-year-old son who has at last become my friend, despite the *saluts* and *bonsoirs*[1] which I exchange with people as I walk, despite the fact that I know that no individual can be taken to task for what history is doing, or has done. I say that the culture of these people controls me—but they can scarcely be held responsible for European culture. America comes out of Europe, but these people have never seen America, nor have most of them seen more of Europe than the hamlet at the foot of their mountain. Yet they move with an authority which I shall never have; and they regard me, quite rightly, not only as a stranger in their village but as a suspect latecomer, bearing no credentials, to everything they have—however unconsciously—inherited.

For this village, even were it incomparably more remote and incredibly more primitive, is the West, the West onto which I have been so strangely grafted. These people cannot be, from the point of view of power, strangers anywhere in the world; they have made the modern world, in effect, even if they do not know it. The most

[1]"Hellos" and "good evenings."

illiterate among them is related, in a way that I am not, to Dante, Shakespeare, Michelangelo, Aeschylus, Da Vinci, Rembrandt, and Racine; the cathedral at Chartres says something to them which it cannot say to me, as indeed would New York's Empire State Building, should anyone here ever see it. Out of their hymns and dances come Beethoven and Bach. Go back a few centuries and they are in their full glory—but I am in Africa, watching the conquerors arrive.

The rage of the disesteemed is personally fruitless, but it is also absolutely inevitable; this rage, so generally discounted, so little understood even among the people whose daily bread it is, is one of the things that makes history. Rage can only with difficulty, and never entirely, be brought under the domination of the intelligence and is therefore not susceptible to any arguments whatever. This is a fact which ordinary representatives of the *Herrenvolk*,[2] having never felt this rage and being unable to imagine, quite fail to understand. Also, rage cannot be hidden, it can only be dissembled. This dissembling deludes the thoughtless, and strengthens rage and adds, to rage, contempt. There are, no doubt, as many ways of coping with the resulting complex of tensions as there are black men in the world, but no black man can hope ever to be entirely liberated from this internal warfare—rage, dissembling, and contempt having inevitably accompanied his first realization of the power of white men. What is crucial here is that, since white men represent in the black man's world so heavy a weight, white men have for black men a reality which is far from being reciprocal; and hence all black men have toward all white men an attitude which is designed, really, either to rob the white man of the jewel of his naïveté, or else to make it cost him dear.

The black man insists, by whatever means he finds at his disposal, that the white man cease to regard him as an exotic rarity and recognize him as a human being. This is a very charged and difficult moment, for there is a great deal of will power involved in the white man's naïveté. Most people are not naturally reflective any more than they are naturally malicious, and the white man prefers to keep the black man at a certain human remove because it is easier for him thus

2Master race.

to preserve his simplicity and avoid being called to account for crimes committed by his forefathers, or his neighbors. He is inescapably aware, nevertheless, that he is in a better position in the world than black men are, nor can he quite put to death the suspicion that he is hated by black men therefore. He does not wish to be hated, neither does he wish to change places, and at this point in his uneasiness he can scarcely avoid having recourse to those legends which white men have created about black men, the most usual effect of which is that the white man finds himself enmeshed, so to speak, in his own language which describes hell, as well as the attributes which lead one to hell, as being as black as night.

Every legend, moreover, contains its residuum of truth, and the root function of language is to control the universe by describing it. It is of quite considerable significance that black men remain, in the imagination, and in overwhelming numbers in fact, beyond the disciplines of salvation; and this despite the fact that the West has been "buying" African natives for centuries. There is, I should hazard, an instantaneous necessity to be divorced from this so visibly unsaved stranger, in whose heart, moreover, one cannot guess what dreams of vengeance are being nourished; and, at the same time, there are few things on earth more attractive than the idea of the unspeakable liberty which is allowed the unredeemed. When, beneath the black mask, a human being begins to make himself felt one cannot escape a certain awful wonder as to what kind of human being it is. What one's imagination makes of other people is dictated, of course, by the laws of one's own personality and it is one of the ironies of black-white relations that, by means of what the white man imagines the black man to be, the black man is enabled to know who the white man is.

I have said, for example, that I am as much a stranger in this village today as I was the first summer I arrived, but this is not quite true. The villagers wonder less about the texture of my hair than they did then, and wonder rather more about me. And the fact that their wonder now exists on another level is reflected in their attitudes and in their eyes. There are the children who make those delightful, hilarious, sometimes astonishingly grave overtures of friendship in the unpredictable fashion of children; other children, having been taught that the devil is a black man, scream in genuine anguish as I approach. Some of the older women never pass without a friendly greeting, never pass, indeed, if it seems that they will be able to engage me in conversation; other women look down or look away or rather contemptuously smirk. Some of the men drink with me and suggest that I learn how to ski—partly, I gather, because they cannot imagine what I would look like on skis—and want to know if I am married, and ask questions about my *métier*. But some of the men have accused *le sale nègre*[3] —behind my back—of stealing wood and there is already in the eyes of some of them that peculiar, intent, paranoiac malevolence which one sometimes surprises in the eyes of American white men when, out walking with their Sunday girl, they see a Negro male approach.

There is a dreadful abyss between the streets of this village and the streets of the city in which I was born, between the children who shout *Neger!* today and those who shouted *Nigger!* yesterday—the abyss is experience, the American experience. The syllable hurled behind me today expresses, above all, wonder: I am a stranger here. But I am not a stranger in America and the same syllable riding on the American air expresses the war my presence has occasioned in the American soul.

For this village brings home to me this fact: that there was a day, and not really a very distant day, when Americans were scarcely Americans at all but discontented Europeans, facing a great unconquered continent and strolling, say, into a marketplace and seeing black men for the first time. The shock this spectacle afforded is suggested, surely, by the promptness with which they decided that these black men were not really men but cattle. It is true that the necessity on the part of the settlers of the New World of reconciling their moral assumptions with the fact—and the necessity—of slavery enhanced immensely the charm of this idea, and it is also true that this idea expresses, with a truly American bluntness, the attitude which to varying extents all masters have had toward all slaves.

[3]The dirty Negro.

But between all former slaves and slave-owners and the drama which begins for Americans over three hundred years ago at Jamestown, there are at least two differences to be observed. The American Negro slave could not suppose, for one thing, as slaves in past epochs had supposed and often done, that he would ever be able to wrest the power from his master's hands. This was a supposition which the modern era, which was to bring about such vast changes in the aims and dimensions of power, put to death; it only begins, in unprecedented fashion, and with dreadful implications, to be resurrected today. But even had this supposition persisted with undiminished force, the American Negro slave could not have used it to lend his condition dignity, for the reason that this supposition rests on another: that the slave in exile yet remains related to his past, has some means—if only in memory—of revering and sustaining the forms of his former life, is able, in short, to maintain his identity.

This was not the case with the American Negro slave. He is unique among the black men of the world in that his past was taken from him, almost literally, at one blow. One wonders what on earth the first slave found to say to the first dark child he bore. I am told that there are Haitians able to trace their ancestry back to African kings, but any American Negro wishing to go back so far will find his journey through time abruptly arrested by the signature on the bill of sale which served as the entrance paper for his ancestor. At the time—to say nothing of the circumstances—of the enslavement of the captive black man who was to become the American Negro, there was not the remotest possibility that he would ever take power from his master's hands. There was no reason to suppose that his situation would ever change, nor was there, shortly, anything to indicate that his situation had ever been different. It was his necessity, in the words of E. Franklin Frazier, to find a "motive for living under American culture or die." The identity of the American Negro comes out of this extreme situation, and the evolution of this identity was a source of the most intolerable anxiety in the minds and the lives of his masters.

For the history of the American Negro is unique also in this: that the question of his humanity, and of his rights therefore as a human being, became a burning one for several generations of Americans, so burning a question that it ultimately became one of those used to divide the nation. It is out of this argument that the venom of the epithet *Nigger!* is derived. It is an argument which Europe has never had, and hence Europe quite sincerely fails to understand how or why the argument arose in the first place, why its effects are frequently disastrous and always so unpredictable, why it refuses until today to be entirely settled. Europe's black possessions remained—and do remain—in Europe's colonies, at which remove they represented no threat whatever to European identity. If they posed any problem at all for the European conscience it was a problem which remained comfortingly abstract: in effect, the black man, as a *man*, did not exist for Europe. But in America, even as a slave, he was an inescapable part of the general social fabric and no American could escape having an attitude toward him. Americans attempt until today to make an abstraction of the Negro, but the very nature of these abstractions reveals the tremendous effect the presence of the Negro has had on the American character.

When one considers the history of the Negro in America it is of the greatest importance to recognize that the moral beliefs of a person, or a people, are never really as tenuous as life—which is not moral—very often causes them to appear; these create for them a frame of reference and a necessary hope, the hope being that when life has done its worst they will be enabled to rise above themselves and to triumph over life. Life would scarcely be bearable if this hope did not exist. Again, even when the worst has been said, to betray a belief is not by any means to have put oneself beyond its power; the betrayal of a belief is not the same thing as ceasing to believe. If this were not so there would be no moral standards in the world at all. Yet one must also recognize that morality is based on ideas and that all ideas are dangerous—dangerous because ideas can only lead to action and where the action leads no man can say. And dangerous in this respect: that confronted with the impossibility of remaining faithful to one's beliefs, and the equal impossibility of becoming free of them, one can be driven to the most inhuman excesses. The ideas on which American beliefs are based are not, though Americans often seem to think so, ideas which originated in America. They came out of Europe. And the establishment of democracy on the American continent was scarcely as radical a break with the past as was the necessity, which Americans faced, of broadening this concept to include black men.

This was, literally, a hard necessity. It was impossible, for one thing, for Americans to abandon their beliefs, not only because these beliefs alone seemed able to justify the sacrifices they had endured and the blood that they had spilled, but also because these beliefs afforded them their only bulwark against a moral chaos as absolute as the physical chaos of the continent it was their destiny to conquer. But in the situation in which Americans found themselves, these beliefs threatened an idea which, whether or not one likes to think so, is the very warp and woof of the heritage of the West, the idea of white supremacy.

Americans have made themselves notorious by the shrillness and the brutality with which they have insisted on this idea, but they did not invent it; and it has escaped the world's notice that those very excesses of which Americans have been guilty imply a certain, unprecedented uneasiness over the idea's life and power, if not, indeed, the idea's validity. The idea of white supremacy rests simply on the fact that white men are the creators of civilization (the present civilization, which is the only one that matters; all previous civilizations are simply "contributions" to our own) and are therefore civilization's guardians and defenders. Thus it was impossible for Americans to accept the black man as one of themselves, for to do so was to jeopardize their status as white men. But not so to accept him was to deny his human reality, his human weight and complexity, and the strain of denying the overwhelmingly undeniable forced Americans into rationalizations so fantastic that they approached the pathological.

At the root of the American Negro problem is the necessity of the American white man to find a way of living with the Negro in order to be able to live with himself. And the history of this problem can be reduced to the means used by Americans—lynch law and law, segregation and legal acceptance, terrorization and concession—either to come to terms with this necessity, or to find a way around it, or (most usually) to find a way of doing both these things at once. The resulting spectacle, at once foolish and dreadful, led someone to make the quite accurate observation that "the Negro-in-America is a form of insanity which overtakes white men."

In this long battle, a battle by no means finished, the unforeseeable effects of which will be felt by many future generations, the white man's motive was the protection of his identity; the black man was motivated by the need to establish an identity. And despite the terrorization which the Negro in America endured and endures sporadically until today, despite the cruel and totally inescapable ambivalence of his status in his country, the battle for his identity has long ago been won. He is not a visitor to the West, but a citizen there, an American; as American as the Americans who despise him, the Americans who fear him, the Americans who love him—the Americans who became less than themselves, or rose to be greater than themselves by virtue of the fact that the challenge he represented was inescapable. He is perhaps the only black man in the world whose relationship to white men is more terrible, more subtle, and more meaningful than the relationship of bitter possessed to uncertain possessors. His survival depended, and his development depends, on his ability to turn his peculiar status in the Western world to his own advantage and, it may be, to the very great advantage of that world. It remains for him to fashion out of his experience that which will give him sustenance, and a voice.

The cathedral at Chartres, I have said, says something to the people of this village which it cannot say to me; but it is important to understand that this cathedral says something to me which it cannot say to them. Perhaps they are struck by the power of the spires, the glory of the windows; but they have known God, after all, longer than I have known him, and in a different way, and I am terrified by the slippery bottomless well to be found in the crypt, down which heretics were hurled to death, and by the obscene, inescapable gargoyles jutting out of the stone and seeming to say that God and the devil can never be divorced. I doubt that the villagers think of the devil when they face a cathedral because they have never been identified with the devil. But I must accept the status which myth, if nothing else, gives me in the West before I can hope to change the myth.

Yet, if the American Negro has arrived at his identity by virtue of the absoluteness of his estrangement from his past, American white men still nourish the illusion that there is some means of recovering the European innocence, of returning to a state in which black men do not exist. This is one of the greatest errors Americans can make. The identity they fought so hard to protect has, by virtue of that battle, undergone a change: Americans are as unlike any other white people in the world as it is possible to be. I do not think, for example, that it is too much to suggest that the American vision of the world—which allows so little reality, generally speaking, for any of the darker forces in human life, which tends until today to paint moral issues in glaring black and white—owes a great deal to the battle waged by Americans to maintain between themselves and black men a human separation which could not be bridged. It is only now beginning to be borne in on us—very faintly, it must be admitted, very slowly, and very much against our will—that this vision of the world is danger-ously inaccurate, and perfectly useless. For it protects our moral high-mindedness at the terrible expense of weakening our grasp of reality. People who shut their eyes to reality simply invite their own destruction, and anyone who insists on remaining in a state of inno-cence long after that innocence is dead turns himself into a monster.

The time has come to realize that the interracial drama acted out on the American continent has not only created a new black man, it has created a new white man, too. No road whatever will lead Ameri-cans back to the simplicity of this European village where white men still have the luxury of looking on me as a stranger. I am not, really, a stranger any longer for any American alive. One of the things that distinguishes Americans from other people is that no other people has ever been so deeply involved in the lives of black men, and vice versa. This fact faced, with all its implications, it can be seen that the history of the American Negro problem is not merely shameful, it is also something of an achievement. For even when the worst has been said, it must also be added that the perpetual challenge posed by this problem was always, somehow, perpetually met. It is precisely this black-white experience which may prove of indispensable value to us in the world we face today. This world is white no longer, and it will never be white again.

Malcolm X (Malcolm Little, El-Hajj Malik El-Shabazz), Muslim and black separatist leader, was born in Omaha, Nebraska, in 1925. His conversion to Islam and his role in the black power movement are recounted in *The Autobiography of Malcolm X*. Malcolm X was assassinated in Harlem in 1965.

MALCOLM X

From The Autobiography of Malcolm X

Saved

(1964)

I DID WRITE to Elijah Muhammad. He lived in Chicago at that time, at 6116 South Michigan Avenue. At least twenty-five times I must have written that first one-page letter to him, over and over. I was trying to make it both legible and understandable. I practically couldn't read my handwriting myself; it shames even to remember it. My spelling and my grammar were as bad, if not worse. Anyway, as well as I could express it, I said I had been told about him by my brothers and sisters, and I apologized for my poor letter.

Mr. Muhammad sent me a typed reply. It had an all but electrical effect upon me to see the signature of the "Messenger of Allah." After he welcomed me into the "true knowledge," he gave me something to think about. The black prisoner, he said, symbolized white society's crime of keeping black men oppressed and deprived and ignorant, and unable to get decent jobs, turning them into criminals.

He told me to have courage. He even enclosed some money for me, a five-dollar bill. Mr. Muhammad sends money all over the country to prison inmates who write to him, probably to this day.

Regularly my family wrote to me, "Turn to Allah . . . pray to the East."

The hardest test I ever faced in my life was praying. You understand. My comprehending, my believing the teachings of Mr. Muhammad had only required my mind's saying to me, "That's right!" or "I never thought of that."

But bending my knees to pray—that *act*—well, that took me a week.

You know what my life had been. Picking a lock to rob someone's house was the only way my knees had ever been bent before.

I had to force myself to bend my knees. And waves of shame and embarrassment would force me back up.

For evil to bend its knees, admitting its guilt, to implore the forgiveness of God, is the hardest thing in the world. It's easy for me to see and to say that now. But then, when I was the personification of evil, I was going through it. Again, again, I would force myself back down into the praying-to-Allah posture. When finally I was able to make myself stay down—I didn't know what to say to Allah.

For the next years, I was the nearest thing to a hermit in the Norfolk Prison Colony. I never have been more busy in my life. I still marvel at how swiftly my previous life's thinking pattern slid away from me, like snow off a roof. It is as though someone else I knew of had lived by hustling and crime. I would be startled to catch myself thinking in a remote way of my earlier self as another person.

The things I felt, I was pitifully unable to express in the one-page letter that went every day to Mr. Elijah Muhammad. And I wrote at least one more daily letter, replying to one of my brothers and sisters. Every letter I received from them added something to my knowledge of the teachings of Mr. Muhammad. I would sit for long periods and study his photographs.

I've never been one for inaction. Everything I've ever felt strongly about, I've done something about. I guess that's why, unable to do anything else, I soon began writing to people I had known in the hustling world, such as Sammy the Pimp, John Hughes, the gambling house owner, the thief Jumpsteady, and several dope peddlers. I wrote them all about Allah and Islam and Mr. Elijah Muhammad. I had no idea where most of them lived. I addressed their letters in care of the Harlem or Roxbury bars and clubs where I'd known them.

I never got a single reply. The average hustler and criminal was too uneducated to write a letter. I have known many slick, sharp-looking hustlers, who would have you think they had an interest in Wall Street; privately, they would get someone else to read a letter if they received one. Besides, neither would I have replied to anyone writing me something as wild as "the white man is the devil."

What certainly went on the Harlem and Roxbury wires was that Detroit Red was going crazy in stir, or else he was trying some hype to shake up the warden's office.

During the years that I stayed in the Norfolk Prison Colony, never did any official directly say anything to me about those letters, although, of course, they all passed through the prison censorship. I'm sure, however, they monitored what I wrote to add to the files which every state and federal prison keeps on the conversion of Negro inmates by the teachings of Mr. Elijah Muhammad.

But at that time, I felt that the real reason was that the white man knew that he was the devil.

Later on, I even wrote to the Mayor of Boston, to the Governor of Massachusetts, and to Harry S. Truman. They never answered; they probably never even saw my letters. I handscratched to them how the white man's society was responsible for the black man's condition in this wilderness of North America.

It was because of my letters that I happened to stumble upon starting to acquire some kind of a homemade education.

I became increasingly frustrated at not being able to express what I wanted to convey in letters that I wrote, especially those to Mr. Elijah Muhammad. In the street, I had been the most articulate hustler out there—I had commanded attention when I said something. But now, trying to write simple English, I not only wasn't articulate, I wasn't even functional. How would I sound writing in slang, the way I would *say* it, something such as, "Look, daddy, let me pull your coat about a cat, Elijah Muhammad—"

Many who today hear me somewhere in person, or on television, or those who read something I've said, will think I went to school far beyond the eighth grade. This impression is due entirely to my prison studies.

It had really begun back in the Charlestown Prison, when Bimbi first made me feel envy of his stock of knowledge. Bimbi had always taken charge of any conversations he was in, and I had tried to emulate him. But every book I picked up had few sentences which didn't contain anywhere from one to nearly all of the words that might as well have been in Chinese. When I just skipped those words, of course, I really ended up with little idea of what the book said. So I had come to the Norfolk Prison Colony still going through only book-reading motions. Pretty soon, I would have quit even these motions, unless I had received the motivation that I did.

I saw that the best thing I could do was get hold of a dictionary—to study, to learn some words. I was lucky enough to reason also that I should try to improve my penmanship. It was sad. I couldn't even write in a straight line. It was both ideas together that moved me to request a dictionary along with some tablets and pencils from the Norfolk Prison Colony school.

I spent two days just riffling uncertainly through the dictionary pages. I'd never realized so many words existed! I didn't know *which* words I needed to learn. Finally, just to start some kind of action, I began copying.

In my slow, painstaking, ragged handwriting, I copied into my tablet everything printed on that first page, down to the punctuation marks.

I believe it took me a day. Then, aloud, I read back, to myself, everything I'd written on the tablet. Over and over, aloud, to myself, I read my own handwriting.

I woke up the next morning, thinking about those words—immensely proud to realize that not only had I written so much at one time, but I'd written words that I never knew were in the world. Moreover, with a little effort, I also could remember what many of these words meant. I reviewed the words whose meanings I didn't remember. Funny thing, from the dictionary first page right now, that "aardvark" springs to my mind. The dictionary had a picture of it, a long-tailed, long-eared, burrowing African mammal, which lives off termites caught by sticking out its tongue as an anteater does for ants.

I was so fascinated that I went on—I copied the dictionary's next page. And the same experience came when I studied that. With every succeeding page, I also learned of people and places and events from history. Actually the dictionary is like a miniature encyclopedia. Finally the dictionary's A section had filled a whole tablet—and I went on into the B's. That was the way I started copying what eventually became the entire dictionary. It went a lot faster after so much practice helped me to pick up handwriting speed. Between what I wrote in my tablet, and writing letters, during the rest of my time in prison I would guess I wrote a million words.

I suppose it was inevitable that as my word-base broadened, I could for the first time pick up a book and read and now begin to understand what the book was saying. Anyone who has read a great deal can imagine the new world that opened. Let me tell you something: from then until I left that prison, in every free moment I had, if I was not reading in the library, I was reading on my bunk. You couldn't have gotten me out of books with a wedge. Between Mr. Muhammad's teachings, my correspondence, my visitors—usually Ella and Reginald—and my reading of books, months passed without my even thinking about being imprisoned. In fact, up to then, I never had been so truly free in my life.

The Norfolk Prison Colony's library was in the school building. A variety of classes was taught there by instructors who came from such places as Harvard and Boston universities. The weekly debates between inmate teams were also held in the school building. You would be astonished to know how worked up convict debaters and audiences would get over subjects like "Should Babies Be Fed Milk?"

Available on the prison library's shelves were books on just about every general subject. Much of the big private collection that Parkhurst had willed to the prison was still in crates and boxes in the back of the library—thousands of old books. Some of them looked ancient: covers faded, old-time parchment-looking binding. Parkhurst, I've mentioned, seemed to have been principally interested in history and religion. He had the money and the special interest to have a lot of books that you wouldn't have in general circulation. Any college library would have been lucky to get that collection.

As you can imagine, especially in a prison where there was heavy emphasis on rehabilitation, an inmate was smiled upon if he demonstrated an unusually intense interest in books. There was a sizable number of well-read inmates, especially the popular debaters. Some were said by many to be practically walking encyclopedias. They were almost celebrities. No university would ask any student to devour literature as I did when this new world opened to me, of being able to read and *understand*.

I read more in my room than in the library itself. An inmate who was known to read a lot could check out more than the permitted maximum number of books. I preferred reading in the total isolation of my own room.

When I had progressed to really serious reading, every night at about ten P.M. I would be outraged with the "lights out." It always seemed to catch me right in the middle of something engrossing.

Fortunately, right outside my door was a corridor light that cast a glow into my room. The glow was enough to read by, once my eyes adjusted to it. So when "lights out" came, I would sit on the floor where I could continue reading in that glow.

At one-hour intervals the night guards paced past every room. Each time I heard the approaching footsteps, I jumped into bed and feigned sleep. And as soon as the guard passed, I got back out of bed onto the floor area of that light-glow, where I would read for another fifty-eight minutes—until the guard approached again. That went on until three or four every morning. Three or four hours of sleep a night was enough for me. Often in the years in the streets I had slept less than that.

The teachings of Mr. Muhammad stressed how history had been "whitened"—when white men had written history books, the black man simply had been left out. Mr. Muhammad couldn't have said anything that would have struck me much harder. I had never forgotten how when my class, me and all of those whites, had studied seventh-grade United States history back in Mason, the history of the Negro had been covered in one paragraph, and the teacher had gotten a big laugh with his joke, "Negroes' feet are so big that when they walk, they leave a hole in the ground."

This is one reason why Mr. Muhammad's teachings spread so

swiftly all over the United States, among *all* Negroes, whether or not they became followers of Mr. Muhammad. The teachings ring true—to every Negro. You can hardly show me a black adult in America—or a white one, for that matter—who knows from the history books anything like the truth about the black man's role. In my own case, once I heard of the "glorious history of the black man," I took special pains to hunt in the library for books that would inform me on details about black history.

I can remember accurately the very first set of books that really impressed me. I have since bought that set of books and I have it at home for my children to read as they grow up. It's called *Wonders of the World.* It's full of pictures of archeological finds, statues that depict, usually, non-European people.

I found books like Will Durant's *Story of Civilization.* I read H. G. Wells' *Outline of History. Souls of Black Folk* by W. E. B. DuBois gave me a glimpse into the black people's history before they came to this country. Carter G. Woodson's *Negro History* opened my eyes about black empires before the black slave was brought to the United States, and the early Negro struggles for freedom.

J. A. Rogers' three volumes of *Sex and Race* told about race-mixing before Christ's time; about Aesop being a black man who told fables; about Egypt's Pharaohs; about the great Coptic Christian Empires; about Ethiopia, the earth's oldest continuous black civilization, as China is the oldest continuous civilization.

Mr. Muhammad's teaching about how the white man had been created led me to *Findings in Genetics* by Gregor Mendel. (The dictionary's G section was where I had learned what "genetics" meant.) I really studied this book by the Austrian monk. Reading it over and over, especially certain sections, helped me to understand that if you started with a black man, a white man could be produced; but starting with a white man, you never could produce a black man—because the white chromosome is recessive. And since no one disputes that there was but one Original Man, the conclusion is clear.

During the last year or so, in the *New York Times,* Arnold Toynbee used the word "bleached" in describing the white man. (His words were: "White [i.e. bleached] human beings of North

European origin. . . .") Toynbee also referred to the European geographic area as only a peninsula of Asia. He said there is no such thing as Europe. And if you look at the globe, you will see for yourself that America is only an extension of Asia. (But at the same time Toynbee is among those who have helped to bleach history. He has written that Africa was the only continent that produced no history. He won't write that again. Every day now, the truth is coming to light.)

I never will forget how shocked I was when I began reading about slavery's total horror. It made such an impact upon me that it later became one of my favorite subjects when I became a minister of Mr. Muhammad's. The world's most monstrous crime, the sin and the blood on the white man's hands, are almost impossible to believe. Books like the one by Frederick Olmstead opened my eyes to the horrors suffered when the slave was landed in the United States. The European woman, Fannie Kimball, who had married a Southern white slaveowner, described how human beings were degraded. Of course I read *Uncle Tom's Cabin*. In fact, I believe that's the only novel I have ever read since I started serious reading.

Parkhurst's collection also contained some bound pamphlets of the Abolitionist Anti-Slavery Society of New England. I read descriptions of atrocities, saw those illustrations of black slave women tied up and flogged with whips; of black mothers watching their babies being dragged off, never to be seen by their mothers again; of dogs after slaves, and of the fugitive slave catchers, evil white men with whips and clubs and chains and guns. I read about the slave preacher Nat Turner, who put the fear of God into the white slavemaster. Nat Turner wasn't going around preaching pie-in-the-sky and "nonviolent" freedom for the black man. There in Virginia one night in 1831, Nat and seven other slaves started out at his master's home and through the night they went from one plantation "big house" to the next, killing, until by the next morning 57 white people were dead and Nat had about 70 slaves following him. White people, terrified for their lives, fled from their homes, locked themselves up in public buildings, hid in the woods, and some even left the state. A small army of soldiers took two months to catch and hang Nat Turner. Somewhere I have read where Nat Turner's example is said to have inspired John Brown to invade Virginia and attack Harpers Ferry nearly thirty years later, with thirteen white men and five Negroes.

I read Herodotus, "the father of History," or, rather, I read about him. And I read the histories of various nations, which opened my eyes gradually, then wider and wider, to how the whole world's white men had indeed acted like devils, pillaging and raping and bleeding and draining the whole world's non-white people. I remember, for instance, books such as Will Durant's *The Story of Oriental Civilization,* and Mahatma Gandhi's accounts of the struggle to drive the British out of India.

Book after book showed me how the white man had brought upon the world's black, brown, red, and yellow peoples every variety of the sufferings of exploitation. I saw how since the sixteenth century, the so-called "Christian trader" white man began to ply the seas in his lust for Asian and African empires, and plunder, and power. I read, I saw, how the white man never has gone among the non-white peoples bearing the Cross in the true manner and spirit of Christ's teachings—meek, humble, and Christ-like.

I perceived, as I read, how the collective white man had been actually nothing but a piratical opportunist who used Faustian machinations to make his own Christianity his initial wedge in criminal conquests. First, always "religiously," he branded "heathen" and "pagan" labels upon ancient non-white cultures and civilizations. The stage thus set, he then turned upon his non-white victims his weapons of war.

I read how, entering India—half a *billion* deeply religious brown people—the British white man, by 1759, through promises, trickery and manipulations, controlled much of India through Great Britain's East India Company. The parasitical British administration kept tentacling out to half of the sub-continent. In 1857, some of the desperate people of India finally mutinied—and, excepting the African slave trade, nowhere has history recorded any more unnecessary bestial and ruthless human carnage than the British suppression of the non-white Indian people.

Over 115 million African blacks—close to the 1930's population of the United States—were murdered or enslaved during the slave trade. And I read how when the slave market was glutted, the cannibalistic white powers of Europe next carved up, as their colonies, the richest areas of the black continent. And Europe's chancelleries for the next century played a chess game of naked exploitation and power from Cape Horn to Cairo.

Ten guards and the warden couldn't have torn me out of those books. Not even Elijah Muhammad could have been more eloquent than those books were in providing indisputable proof that the collective white man had acted like a devil in virtually every contact he had with the world's collective non-white man. I listen today to the radio, and watch television, and read the headlines about the collective white man's fear and tension concerning China. When the white man professes ignorance about why the Chinese hate him so, my mind can't help flashing back to what I read, there in prison, about how the blood forebears of this same white man raped China at a time when China was trusting and helpless. Those original white "Christian traders" sent into China millions of pounds of opium. By 1839, so many of the Chinese were addicts that China's desperate government destroyed twenty thousand chests of opium. The first Opium War was promptly declared by the white man. Imagine! Declaring *war* upon someone who objects to being narcotized! The Chinese were severely beaten, with Chinese-invented gunpowder.

The Treaty of Nanking made China pay the British white man for the destroyed opium: forced open China's major ports to British trade; forced China to abandon Hong Kong; fixed China's import tariffs so low that cheap British articles soon flooded in, maiming China's industrial development.

After a second Opium War, the Tientsin Treaties legalized the ravaging opium trade, legalized a British-French-American control of China's customs. China tried delaying that Treaty's ratification; Peking was looted and burned.

"Kill the foreign white devils!" was the 1901 Chinese war cry in the Boxer Rebellion. Losing again, this time the Chinese were driven from Peking's choicest areas. The vicious, arrogant white man put up the famous signs, "Chinese and dogs not allowed."

Red China after World War II closed its doors to the Western white world. Massive Chinese agricultural, scientific, and industrial efforts are described in a book that *Life* magazine recently published. Some observers inside Red China have reported that the world never has known such a hate-white campaign as is now going on in this non-white country where, present birth-rates continuing, in fifty more years Chinese will be half the earth's population. And it seems that some Chinese chickens will soon come home to roost, with China's recent successful nuclear tests.

Let us face reality. We can see in the United Nations a new world order being shaped, along color lines—an alliance among the nonwhite nations. America's U.N. Ambassador Adlai Stevenson complained not long ago that in the United Nations "a skin game" was being played. He was right. He was facing reality. A "skin game" *is* being played. But Ambassador Stevenson sounded like Jesse James accusing the marshal of carrying a gun. Because who in the world's history ever had played a worse "skin game" than the white man?

Mr. Muhammad, to whom I was writing daily, had no idea of what a new world had opened up to me through my efforts to document his teachings in books.

When I discovered philosophy, I tried to touch all the landmarks of philosophical development. Gradually, I read most of the old philosophers, Occidental and Oriental. The Oriental philosophers were the ones I came to prefer; finally, my impression was that most Occidental philosophy had largely been borrowed from the Oriental thinkers. Socrates, for instance, traveled in Egypt. Some sources even say that Socrates was initiated into some of the Egyptian mysteries. Obviously Socrates got some of his wisdom among the East's wise men.

I have often reflected upon the new vistas that reading opened to me. I knew right there in prison that reading had changed forever the course of my life. As I see it today, the ability to read awoke inside me some long dormant craving to be mentally alive. I certainly wasn't seeking any degree, the way a college confers a status symbol upon its students. My homemade education gave me, with every additional book that I read, a little bit more sensitivity to the deafness, dumbness, and blindness that was afflicting the black race in America. Not long ago, an English writer telephoned me from London, asking questions. One was, "What's your alma mater?" I told him, "Books." You will never catch me with a free fifteen minutes in which I'm not studying something I feel might be able to help the black man.

Yesterday I spoke in London, and both ways on the plane across the Atlantic I was studying a document about how the United Nations proposes to insure the human rights of the oppressed minorities of the world. The American black man is the world's most shameful case of minority oppression. What makes the black man think of himself as only an internal United States issue is just a catch-phrase, two words, "civil rights." How is the black man going to get "civil rights" before first he wins his *human* rights? If the American black man will start thinking about his *human* rights, and then start thinking of himself as part of one of the world's great peoples, he will see he has a case for the United Nations.

I can't think of a better case! Four hundred years of black blood and sweat invested here in America, and the white man still has the black man begging for what every immigrant fresh off the ship can take for granted the minute he walks down the gangplank.

But I'm digressing. I told the Englishman that my alma mater was books, a good library. Every time I catch a plane, I have with me a book that I want to read—and that's a lot of books these days. If I weren't out here every day battling the white man, I could spend the rest of my life reading, just satisfying my curiosity—because you can hardly mention anything I'm not curious about. I don't think anybody ever got more out of going to prison than I did. In fact, prison enabled me to study far more intensively than I would have if my life had gone differently and I had attended some college. I imagine that one of the biggest troubles with colleges is there are too many distractions, too much panty-raiding, fraternities, and boola-boola and all of that. Where else but in a prison could I have attacked my ignorance by being able to study intensely sometimes as much as fifteen hours a day?

Schopenhauer, Kant, Nietzsche, naturally, I read all of those. I don't respect them; I am just trying to remember some of those whose theories I soaked up in those years. These three, it's said, laid the groundwork on which the Fascist and Nazi philosophy was built. I don't respect them because it seems to me that most of their time was spent arguing about things that are not really important. They remind me of so many of the Negro "intellectuals," so-called, with whom I have come in contact—they are always arguing about something useless.

Spinoza impressed me for a while when I found out that he was black. A black Spanish Jew. The Jews excommunicated him because he advocated a pantheistic doctrine, something like the "allness of God," or "God in everything." The Jews read their burial services for Spinoza, meaning that he was dead as far as they were concerned; his family was run out of Spain, they ended up in Holland, I think.

I'll tell you something. The whole stream of Western philosophy has now wound up in a cul-de-sac. The white man has perpetrated upon himself, as well as upon the black man, so gigantic a fraud that he has put himself into a crack. He did it through his elaborate, neurotic necessity to hide the black man's true role in history.

And today the white man is faced head on with what is happening on the Black Continent, Africa. Look at the artifacts being discovered there, that are proving over and over again, how the black man had great, fine, sensitive civilizations before the white man was out of the caves. Below the Sahara, in the places where most of America's Negroes' foreparents were kidnapped, there is being unearthed some of the finest craftsmanship, sculpture and other objects, that has ever been seen by modern man. Some of these things now are on view in such places as New York City's Museum of Modern Art. Gold work of such fine tolerance and workmanship that it has no rival. Ancient objects produced by black hands . . . refined by those black hands with results that no human hand today can equal.

History has been so "whitened" by the white man that even the black professors have known little more than the most ignorant black man about the talents and rich civilizations and cultures of the black man of millenniums ago. I have lectured in Negro colleges and some of these brainwashed black Ph.D.'s, with their suspenders dragging the ground with degrees, have run to the white man's newspapers calling me a "black fanatic." Why, a lot of them are fifty years behind the times. If I were president of one of these black colleges, I'd hock the campus if I had to, to send a bunch of black students off digging in Africa for more, more and more proof of the black race's historical greatness. The white man now is in Africa digging and searching. An African elephant can't stumble without falling on some white man with a shovel. Practically every week, we read about some great new find from Africa's lost civilizations. All that's new is white science's attitude. The ancient civilizations of the black man have been buried on the Black Continent all the time.

Here is an example: a British anthropologist named Dr. Louis S. B. Leakey is displaying some fossil bones—a foot, part of a hand, some jaws, and skull fragments. On the basis of these, Dr. Leakey has said it's time to rewrite completely the history of man's origin.

This species of man lived 1,818,036 years before Christ. And these bones were found in Tanganyika. In the Black Continent.

It's a crime, the lie that has been told to generations of black men and white men both. Little innocent black children, born of parents who believed that their race had no history. Little black children seeing, before they could talk, that their parents considered themselves inferior. Innocent black children growing up, living out their lives, dying of old age—and all of their lives ashamed of being black. But the truth is pouring out of the bag now.

Two other areas of experience which have been extremely formative in my life since prison were first opened to me in the Norfolk Prison Colony. For one thing, I had my first experiences in opening the eyes of my brainwashed black brethren to some truths about the black race. And, the other: when I had read enough to know something, I began to enter the Prison Colony's weekly debating program—my baptism into public speaking.

I have to admit a sad, shameful fact. I had so loved being around the white man that in prison I really disliked how Negro convicts stuck together so much. But when Mr. Muhammad's teachings reversed my attitude toward my black brothers, in my guilt and shame I began to catch every chance I could to recruit for Mr. Muhammad.

You have to be careful, very careful, introducing the truth to the black man who has never previously heard the truth about himself, his own kind, and the white man. My brother Reginald had told me that all Muslims experienced this in their recruiting for Mr. Muhammad. The black brother is so brainwashed that he may even be repelled when he first hears the truth. Reginald advised that the truth had to be dropped only a little bit at a time. And you had to wait a while to let it sink in before advancing the next step.

I began first telling my black brother inmates about the glorious history of the black man—things they never had dreamed. I told them the horrible slavery-trade truths that they never knew. I would watch their faces when I told them about that, because the white man had completely erased the slaves' past, a Negro in America can never know his true family name, or even what tribe he was descended from: the Mandingos, the Wolof, the Serer, the Fula, the Fanti, the Ashanti, or others. I told them that some slaves brought from Africa spoke Arabic, and were Islamic in their religion. A lot of these black convicts still wouldn't believe it unless they could see that a white man had said it. So, often, I would read to these brothers selected passages from white men's books. I'd explain to them that the real truth was known to some white men, the scholars; but there had been a conspiracy down through the generations to keep the truth from black men.

I would keep close watch on how each one reacted. I always had to be careful. I never knew when some brainwashed black imp, some dyed-in-the-wool Uncle Tom, would nod at me and then go running to tell the white man. When one was ripe—and I could tell—then away from the rest, I'd drop it on him, what Mr. Muhammed taught: "The white man is the devil."

That would shock many of them—until they started thinking about it.

This is probably as big a single worry as the America prison system has today—the way the Muslim teachings, circulated among all Negroes in the country, are converting new Muslims among black men in prison, and black men are in prison in far greater numbers than their proportion in the population.

The reason is that among all Negroes the black convict is the most perfectly preconditioned to hear the words, "the white man is the devil."

You tell that to any Negro. Except for those relatively few "integration"-mad so-called "intellectuals," and those black men who are otherwise fat, happy, and deaf, dumb, and blinded, with their crumbs from the white man's rich table, you have struck a nerve center in the American black man. He may take a day to react, a month, a year; he may never respond, openly; but of one thing you can be sure—when he thinks about his own life, he is going to see where, to him, personally, the white man sure has acted like a devil.

And, as I say, above all Negroes, the black prisoner. Here is a black man caged behind bars, probably for years, put there by the white man. Usually the convict comes from among those bottom-of-the-pile Negroes, the Negroes who through their entire lives have been kicked about, treated like children—Negroes who never have met one white man who didn't either take something from them or do something to them.

You let this caged-up black man start thinking, the same way I did when I first heard Elijah Muhammad's teachings: let him start thinking how, with better breaks when he was young and ambitious he might have been a lawyer, a doctor, a scientist, anything. You let this caged-up black man start realizing, as I did, how from the first landing of the first slave ship, the millions of black men in America have been like sheep in a den of wolves. That's why black prisoners become Muslims so fast when Elijah Muhammad's teachings filter into their cages by way of other Muslim convicts. "The white man is the devil" is a perfect echo of that black convict's lifelong experience.

I've told how debating was a weekly event there at the Norfolk Prison Colony. My reading had my mind like steam under pressure. Some way, I had to start telling the white man about himself to his face. I decided I could do this by putting my name down to debate.

Standing up and speaking before an audience was a thing that throughout my previous life never would have crossed my mind. Out there in the streets, hustling, pushing dope, and robbing, I could have had the dreams from a pound of hashish and I'd never have dreamed anything so wild as that one day I would speak in coliseums and arenas, at the greatest American universities, and on radio and television programs, not to mention speaking all over Egypt and Africa and in England.

But I will tell you that, right there, in the prison, debating, speaking to a crowd, was as exhilarating to me as the discovery of knowledge through reading had been. Standing up there, the faces looking up at me, the things in my head coming out of my mouth, while my brain searched for the next best thing to follow what I was saying, and if I could sway them to my side by handling it right, then I had won the debate—once my feet got wet, I was gone on debating. Whichever side of the selected subject was assigned to me, I'd track down and study everything I could find on it. I'd put myself in my opponent's place and decide how I'd try to win if I had the other side; and then I'd figure a way to knock down those points. And if there was any way in the world, I'd work into my speech the devilishness of the white man.

"Compulsory Military Training—Or None?" That's one good chance I got unexpectedly, I remember. My opponent flailed the air about the Ethiopians throwing rocks and spears at Italian airplanes, "proving" that compulsory military training was needed. I said the Ethiopians' black flesh had been splattered against trees by bombs the Pope in Rome had blessed, and the Ethiopians would have thrown even their bare bodies at the airplanes because they had seen that they were fighting the devil incarnate.

They yelled "foul," that I'd made the subject a race issue. I said it wasn't race, it was a historical fact, that they ought to go and read Pierre van Paassen's *Days of Our Years,* and something not surprising to me, that book, right after the debate, disappeared from the prison library. It was right there in prison that I made up my mind to devote the rest of my life to telling the white man about himself—or die. In a debate about whether or not Homer had ever existed, I threw into those white faces the theory that Homer only symbolized how white Europeans kidnapped black Africans, then blinded them so that they could never get back to their own people. (Homer and Omar and *Moor,* you see, are related terms; it's like saying Peter, Pedro, and *petra,* all three of which mean rock.) These blinded Moors the Europeans taught to sing about the Europeans' glorious accomplishments. I made it clear that was the devilish white man's idea of kicks. Aesop's *Fables*—another case in point. "Aesop" was only the Greek name for an Ethiopian.

Another hot debate I remember I was in had to do with the identity of Shakespeare. No color was involved there; I just got intrigued over the Shakespearean dilemma. The King James translation of the Bible is considered the greatest piece of literature in English. Its language supposedly represents the ultimate in using the King's English. Well, Shakespeare's language and the Bible's language are one and the same. They say that from 1604 to 1611, King James got poets to translate, to write the Bible. Well, if Shakespeare existed, he was then the top poet around. But Shakespeare is nowhere reported connected with the Bible. If he existed, why didn't King James use him? And if he did use him, why is it one of the world's best kept secrets?

I know that many say that Francis Bacon was Shakespeare. If that is true, why would Bacon have kept it secret? Bacon wasn't royalty, when royalty sometimes used the *nom de plume* because it was "improper" for royalty to be artistic or theatrical. What would Bacon have had to lose? Bacon, in fact, would have had everything to gain.

In the prison debates I argued for the theory that King James himself was the real poet who used the *nom de plume* Shakespeare. King James was brilliant. He was the greatest king who ever sat on the British throne. Who else among royalty, in his time, would have had the giant talent to write Shakespeare's works? It was he who poetically "fixed" the Bible—which in itself and its present King James version has enslaved the world.

When my brother Reginald visited, I would talk to him about new evidence I found to document the Muslim teachings. In either volume 43 or 44 of The Harvard Classics, I read Milton's *Paradise Lost*. The devil, kicked out of Paradise, was trying to regain possession. He was using the forces of Europe, personified by the Popes, Charlemagne, Richard the Lionhearted, and other knights. I interpreted this to show that the Europeans were motivated and led by the devil, or the personification of the devil. So Milton and Mr. Elijah Muhammad were actually saying the same thing.

I couldn't believe it when Reginald began to speak ill of Elijah Muhammad. I can't specify the exact things he said. They were more in the nature of implications against Mr. Muhammad—the pitch of Reginald's voice, or the way that Reginald looked, rather than what he said.

It caught me totally unprepared. It threw me into a state of confusion. My blood brother, Reginald, in whom I had so much confidence, for whom I had so much respect, the one who had introduced me to the Nation of Islam. I couldn't believe it! And now Islam meant more to me than anything I ever had known in my life. Islam and Mr. Elijah Muhammad had changed my whole world.

Reginald, I learned, had been suspended from the Nation of Islam by Elijah Muhammad. He had not practiced moral restraint. After he had learned the truth, and had accepted the truth, and the Muslim laws, Reginald was still carrying on improper relations with the then secretary of the New York Temple. Some other Muslim who learned of it had made charges against Reginald to Mr. Muhammad in Chicago, and Mr. Muhammad had suspended Reginald.

When Reginald left, I was in torment. That night, finally, I wrote to Mr. Muhammad, trying to defend my brother, appealing for him. I told him what Reginald was to me, what my brother meant to me.

I put the letter into the box for the prison censor. Then all the rest of that night, I prayed to Allah. I don't think anyone ever prayed more sincerely to Allah. I prayed for some kind of relief from my confusion.

It was the next night, as I lay on my bed, I suddenly, with a start, became aware of a man sitting beside me in my chair. He had on a dark suit, I remember. I could see him as plainly as I see anyone I look at. He wasn't black, and he wasn't white. He was light-brown-skinned, an Asiatic cast of countenance, and he had oily black hair.

I looked right into his face.

I didn't get frightened. I knew I wasn't dreaming. I couldn't move, I didn't speak, and he didn't. I couldn't place him racially—other than that I knew he was a non-European. I had no idea whatsoever who he was. He just sat there. Then, suddenly as he had come, he was gone.

Soon, Mr. Muhammad sent me a reply about Reginald. He wrote, "If you once believed in the truth, and now you are beginning to doubt the truth, you didn't believe the truth in the first place. What could make you doubt the truth other than your own weak self?"

That struck me. Reginald was not leading the disciplined life of a Muslim. And I knew that Elijah Muhammad was right, and my blood brother was wrong. Because right is right, and wrong is wrong. Little did I then realize the day would come when Elijah Muhammad would be accused by his own sons as being guilty of the same acts of immorality that he judged Reginald and so many others for.

But at that time, all of the doubt and confusion in my mind was removed. All of the influence that my brother had wielded over me was broken. From that day on, as far as I am concerned, everything that my brother Reginald has done is wrong.

But Reginald kept visiting me. When he had been a Muslim, he had been immaculate in his attire. But now, he wore things like a T-shirt, shabby-looking trousers, and sneakers. I could see him on the way down. When he spoke, I heard him coldly. But I would listen. He was my blood brother.

Gradually, I saw the chastisement of Allah—what Christians would call "the curse"—come upon Reginald. Elijah Muhammad said that Allah was chastising Reginald—and that anyone who challenged Elijah Muhammad would be chastened by Allah. In Islam we were taught that as long as one didn't know the truth, he lived in darkness. But once the truth was accepted, and recognized, he lived in light, and whoever would then go against it would be punished by Allah.

Mr. Muhammad taught that the five-pointed star stands for justice, and also for the five senses of man. We were taught that Allah executes justice by working upon the five senses of those who rebel against His Messenger, or against His truth. We were taught that this was Allah's way of letting Muslims know His sufficiency to defend His Messenger against any and all opposition, as long as the Messenger himself didn't deviate from the path of truth. We were taught that

Allah turned the minds of any defectors into a turmoil. I thought truly that it was Allah doing this to my brother.

One letter, I think from my brother Philbert, told me that Reginald was with them in Detroit. I heard no more about Reginald until one day, weeks later, Ella visited me; she told me that Reginald was at her home in Roxbury, sleeping. Ella said she had heard a knock, she had gone to the door, and there was Reginald, looking terrible. Ella said she had asked, "Where did you come from?" And Reginald had told her he came from Detroit. She said she asked him, "How did you get here?" And he had told her, "I walked."

I believed he *had* walked. I believed in Elijah Muhammad, and he had convinced us that Allah's chastisement upon Reginald's mind had taken away Reginald's ability to gauge distance and time. There is a dimension of time with which we are not familiar here in the West. Elijah Muhammad said that under Allah's chastisement, the five senses of a man can be so deranged by those whose mental powers are greater than his that in five minutes his hair can turn snow white. Or he will walk nine hundred miles as he might walk five blocks.

In prison, since I had become a Muslim, I had grown a beard. When Reginald visited me, he nervously moved about in his chair; he told me that each hair of my beard was a snake. Everywhere, he saw snakes.

He next began to believe that he was the "Messenger of Allah." Reginald went around in the streets of Roxbury, Ella reported to me, telling people that he had some divine power. He graduated from this to saying that he was Allah.

He finally began saying he was *greater* than Allah.

Authorities picked up Reginald, and he was put into an institution. They couldn't find what was wrong. They had no way to understand Allah's chastisement. Reginald was released. Then he was picked up again, and was put into another institution.

Reginald is in an institution now. I know where, but I won't say. I would not want to cause him any more trouble than he has already had.

I believe, today, that it was written, it was meant, for Reginald to be used for one purpose only: as a bait, as a minnow to reach into that ocean of blackness where I was, to save me.

I cannot understand it any other way.

After Elijah Muhammad himself was later accused as a very immoral man, I came to believe that it wasn't a divine chastisement upon Reginald, but the pain he felt when his own family totally rejected him for Elijah Muhammad, and this hurt made Reginald turn insanely upon Elijah Muhammad.

It's impossible to dream, or to see, or to have a vision of someone whom you never have seen before—and to see him exactly as he is. To see someone, and to see him exactly as he looks, is to have a pre-vision.

I would later come to believe that my pre-vision was of Master W. D. Fard, the Messiah, the one whom Elijah Muhammad said had appointed him—Elijah Muhammad—as His Last Messenger to the black people of North America.

My last year in prison was spent back in the Charlestown Prison. Even among the white inmates, the word had filtered around. Some of those brainwashed black convicts talked too much. And I know that the censors had reported on my mail. The Norfolk Prison Colony officials had become upset. They used as a reason for my transfer that I refused to take some kind of shots, an inoculation or something.

The only thing that worried me was that I hadn't much time left before I would be eligible for parole-board consideration. But I reasoned that they might look at my representing and spreading Islam in another way: instead of keeping me in they might want to get me out.

I had come to prison with 20/20 vision. But when I got sent back to Charlestown, I had read so much by the lights-out glow in my room at the Norfolk Prison Colony that I had astigmatism and the first pair of the eyeglasses that I have worn ever since.

I had less maneuverability back in the much stricter Charlestown Prison. But I found that a lot of Negroes attended a Bible class, and I went there.

Conducting the class was a tall, blond, blue-eyed (a perfect "devil") Harvard Seminary student. He lectured, and then he starred in a question-and-answer session. I don't know which of us had read the Bible more, he or I, but I had to give him credit; he really was heavy on his religion. I puzzled and puzzled for a way to upset him, and to give those Negroes present something to think and talk about and circulate.

Finally, I put up my hand; he nodded. He had talked about Paul.

I stood up and asked, "What color was Paul?" And I kept talking, with pauses, "He had to be black . . . because he was a Hebrew . . . and the original Hebrews were black . . . weren't they?"

He had started flushing red. You know the way white people do. He said "Yes."

I wasn't through yet. "What color was Jesus . . . he was Hebrew, too . . . wasn't he?"

Both the Negro and the white convicts had sat bolt upright. I don't care how tough the convict, be he brainwashed black Christian, or a "devil" white Christian, neither of them is ready to hear anybody saying Jesus wasn't white. The instructor walked around. He shouldn't have felt bad. In all of the years since, I never have met any intelligent white man who would try to insist that Jesus was white. How could they? He said, "Jesus was brown."

I let him get away with that compromise.

Exactly as I had known it would, almost overnight the Charlestown convicts, black and white, began buzzing with the story. Wherever I went, I could feel the nodding. And anytime I got a chance to exchange words with a black brother in stripes, I'd say, "My man! You ever heard about somebody named Mr. Elijah Muhammad?"

Claude Brown, born in 1937, is best known for his autobiography, *Manchild in the Promised Land*. He also wrote *The Children of Harlem* and several plays, which were performed by the American Negro Theater Guild.

12

CLAUDE BROWN

From Manchild in the Promised Land

(1965)

IF ANYONE HAD asked me around the latter part of 1957 just what I thought had made the greatest impression on my generation in Harlem, I would have said, "Drugs." I don't think too many people would have contested this. About ten years earlier, in 1947, or just eight years earlier, in 1949, this wouldn't have been true.

In 1949, I would have answered that same question with the answer, "The knife." Perhaps all this could have been summed up in saying, "The bad mother-fucker." Throughout my childhood in Harlem, nothing was more strongly impressed upon me than the fact that you had to fight and that you should fight. Everybody would accept it if a person was scared to fight, but not if he was so scared that he didn't fight.

As I saw it in my childhood, most of the cats I swung with were more afraid of not fighting than they were of fighting. This was how it was supposed to be, because this was what we had come up under. The adults in the neighborhood practiced this. They lived by the concept that a man was supposed to fight. When two little boys got into a fight in the neighborhood, the men around would encourage them and egg them on. They'd never think about stopping the fight.

There were some little boys, like myself, who when we got into a fight—even though we weren't ten years old yet—all the young men, the street-corner cats, they would come out of the bars or the numbers joints or anyplace they were and watch. Somebody would say, "Little Sonny Boy is on the street fightin' again," and everybody had to see this.

Down on 146th Street, they'd put money on street fights. If there were two little boys on one block who were good with their hands, or one around the corner and one on Eighth Avenue, men on the corner would try and egg them into a fight.

I remember Big Bill, one of the street-corner hustlers before he went to jail for killing a bartender. When I was about seven or eight years old, I remember being on the street and Bill telling me one day, "Sonny Boy, I know you can kick this little boy's ass on 146th Street, and I'll give you a dollar to do it."

I knew I couldn't say no, couldn't be afraid. He was telling all these other men around there on the street that I could beat this boy's ass. There was another man, a numbers hustler, who said, "No. They ain't got no boy here on Eighth Avenue who could beat little Rip's ass on 146th Street."

Bill said, "Sonny Boy, can you do it?" And he'd already promised me the dollar.

I said, "Yeah." I was scared, because I'd seen Rip and heard of him.

He was a mean-looking little boy. He was real dark-skinned, had big lips and bulgy eyes, and looked like he was always mad. One time I had seen him go at somebody with a knife. A woman had taken the knife out of his hands, but she cut her hand getting it. I knew he would have messed up the cat if he could have held on to that knife.

He knew me too, and he had never messed with me. I remember one time he told me that he was going to kick my ass. I said, "Well, here it is. Start kickin'." He never did. I don't think he was too anxious to mess with me. I didn't want to mess with him either, but since Big Bill had given me this dollar and kept pushing me, I couldn't have said no. They would have said I was scared of him, and if that had gotten back to him, I know he would have messed with me.

I fought him for three days. I beat him one day, and he beat me the next day. On the third day, we fought three fights. I had a black eye, and he had a bloody lip. He had a bloody nose, and I had a bloody nose. By the end of the day, we had become good friends. Somebody took us to the candy store and bought us ice-cream cones.

Rip and I got real tight. If anybody messed with him and I heard about it, I wanted to fight them. And it was the same with him if anybody messed with me.

This was something that took place in all the poor colored neighborhoods throughout New York City. Every place I went, it was the same way, at least with the colored guys. You had to fight, and everybody respected people for fighting. I guess if you were used to it and were good at it, there was nothing else you could do. I guess that was why Turk became a fighter. He had fought so long and had been so preoccupied with fighting that he couldn't do anything else. He had to get this fighting out of his system.

With cats like Turk and many others who came up on the Harlem streets, the first day they came out of the house by themselves, at about five or six years old, the prizefight ring beckoned to them. It beckoned to them in the form of the cat around the corner who had the reputation or the cat who wanted to mess with your little brother or your little sister. If you went to school and somebody said, "I'm gon kick your ass if you don't bring me some money tomorrow to buy my lunch," it was the prizefight ring beckoning to you.

I remember they used to say on the streets, "Don't mess with a man's money, his woman, or his manhood." This was the thing when I was about twelve or thirteen. This was what the gang fights were all about. If somebody messed with your brother, you could just punch him in his mouth, and this was all right. But if anybody was to mess with your sister, you had to really fuck him up—break his leg or stab him in the eye with an ice pick, something vicious.

I suppose the main things were the women in the family and the money. This was something we learned very early. If you went to the store and lost some money or if you let somebody gorilla you out of some money that your mother or your father had given you, you got your ass beaten when you came back home. You couldn't go upstairs and say, "Well, Daddy, that big boy down there took the money that you gave me to buy some cigars." Shit, you didn't have any business letting anybody take your money. You got your ass whipped for that, and you were supposed to.

You were supposed to go to war about your money. Maybe this was why the cats on the corner were killing each other over a two-dollar crap game or a petty debt. People were always shooting, cutting, or killing somebody over three dollars.

I remember going to the store for my father on a Sunday morning. He'd given me a quarter to get him some chewing tobacco. I had to walk up to 149th Street, because no place else was open. I went up to this drugstore on 149th Street, and there were some cats standing around there. I was about eight, and they were about ten or eleven.

One of them said, "Hey, boy, come here," one of those things. I was scared to run, because I knew I wouldn't be able to outrun them all. I figured that if I acted kind of bad, they might not be so quick to mess with me. So I walked right up to them. One cat said, "You got any money?"

I said, "No, I ain't got no money."

I guess I shouldn't have said that. He kept looking at me real mean, trying to scare me. He said, "Jump up and down." I knew what this was all about, because I used to do it myself. If you jumped up and down and the cat who was shaking you down heard some change jingling, he was supposed to try to beat your ass and take the money.

I said, "No, man. I ain't jumpin' up and down."

He grabbed me by my collar. Somebody said, "He's got something in his hand." That was Dad's quarter. One cat grabbed my hand. I'd forgotten all about the guy who had my collar. I hit the boy who had my hand. Then the cat who had me by the collar started punching me in the jaw. I wasn't even thinking about him. I was still fighting the other cat to keep that quarter.

A woman came out a door and said, "You all stop beatin' that boy!"

I had a bloody nose; they'd kicked my ass good, but I didn't mind, because they hadn't taken my quarter. It wasn't the value of money. It couldn't have been. It was just that these things symbolized a man's manhood or principles. That's what Johnny Wilkes used to like to call it, a man's principles. You don't mess with a man's money; you don't mess with a man's woman; you don't mess with a man's family or his manhood—these were a man's principles, according to Johnny Wilkes.

Most girls in Harlem could fight pretty well themselves, and if other girls bothered them, they could take care of themselves. You couldn't let other cats bother your sisters. In the bebopping days in Harlem, if the girls had brothers who were scared to fight, everybody would mess with them and treat them like they wanted to. Cats would come up and say things like, "You better meet me up on the roof," or "You better meet me in the park."

It went deep. It went very deep—until drugs came. Fighting was the thing that people concentrated on. In our childhood, we all had to make our reputations in the neighborhood. Then we'd spend the rest of our lives living up to them. A man was respected on the basis of his reputation. The people in the neighborhood whom everybody looked up to were the cats who'd killed somebody. The little boys in the neighborhood whom the adults respected were the little boys who didn't let anybody mess with them.

Dad once saw me run away from a fight. He was looking out the window one day, and the Morris brothers were messing with me. I didn't think I could beat both of them, so I ran in the house. Dad was at the door when I got there. He said, "Where are you runnin' to, boy?"

I said, "Dad, these boys are out there, and they messin' with me."

He said, "Well, if you come in here, I'm gon mess with you too. You ain't got no business runnin' from nobody."

I said, "Yeah, Dad, I know that. But there's two of 'em, and they're both bigger than me. They can hit harder than I can hit."

Dad said, "You think they can hit harder than I can hit?"

I said, "No, Dad. I know they can't hit harder than you." I was wondering what was behind this remark, because I knew he wasn't going to go out there on the street and fight some boys for me. He wasn't going to fight anybody for me.

He said, "Well, damn right I can hit harder than they can. And if you come in here you got to get hit by me."

He stood on the side of the door and held on to the knob with one hand. I knew I couldn't go in there. If I went downstairs, the Morris brothers were going to kick my ass. I just stood there looking at Dad, and he stood there for a while looking at me and mumbling about me running from somebody like some little girl, all that kind of shit.

Dad had a complex about his size, I think. He was real short. Maybe that's why he played that bad mother-fucker part so strong. That's probably why he always had his knife. This was what used to scare me about him more than anything—the scar on the neck and his knife. I used to associate the two of them together.

Every night when Dad went to bed, he'd put his watch, his money, his wallet, and his knife under his pillow. When he got up, he would wind his watch, but he would take more time with his knife. He had a switchblade, and he would try it a couple of times. Sometimes he would oil it. He never went out without his knife. He never went to church, but I don't think Dad would have even gone to church without his knife. I guess it was because of that scar on his neck; he never was going to get caught without it again.

The Morris brothers were hollering, "Sonny, you ain't comin' down? Man, you better not come down here any more, 'cause I'm gon kick your ass."

They would take turns hollering up and telling me all this. Dad was standing there in the doorway, and I had a headache. I had a real bad headache, but I knew that wasn't going to help. Dad started telling me about running from somebody who was bigger than me. He said, "You'll probably be short all your life, and little too. But that don't mean you got to run from anybody. If you gon start runnin' this early, you better be good at it, 'cause you probably gon be runnin' all your life."

I just sat down there on the cold hallway tile, my head hurting.

Dad said, "Get up off that floor, boy."

Mama came to the door and said, "Boy, what's wrong with you?"

Dad said, "There ain't nothin' wrong with him. He just scared, that's all. That's what's wrong with him. The thing that's wrong is you try and pamper him too much. You stay away from that boy."

Mama said, "That boy looks like he sick. Don't be botherin' him now. What you gettin' ready to beat him for?"

Dad said, "Ain't nobody gettin' ready to beat him. I'm just gon beat him if he come in this house."

Mama came in the hallway and put her arms around me and said, "Come on in the house and lay down."

I went in and I laid down. I just got sicker until I went downstairs. They really did kick my ass. But it was all right. I didn't feel sick any more.

I remember one time I hit a boy in the face with a bottle of Pepsi-Cola. I did it because I knew the older cats on 146th Street were watching me. The boy had messed with Carole. He had taken her candy from her and thrown it on the ground.

I came up to him and said, "Man, what you mess with my sister for?"

All the older guys were saying, "That's that little boy who lives on Eighth Avenue. They call him Sonny Boy. We gon see somethin' good out here now."

There was a Pepsi-Cola truck there; they were unloading some crates. They were stacking up the crates to roll them inside. The boy who had hit Carole was kind of big and acted kind of mean. He had a stick in his hand, and he said, "Yeah, I did it, so what you gon do about it?"

I looked at him for a while, and he looked big. He was holding that stick like he meant to use it, so I snatched a Pepsi-Cola bottle and hit him right in the face. He grabbed his face and started crying. He fell down, and I started to hit him again, but the man who was unloading the Pepsi-Cola bottles grabbed me. He took the bottle away from me and shook me. He asked me if I was crazy or something.

All the guys on the corner started saying, "You better leave that boy alone," and "Let go of that kid." I guess he got kind of scared.

He was white, and here were all these mean-looking colored cats talking about "Let go that kid" and looking at him. They weren't asking him to let me go; they were telling him. He let me go.

Afterward, if I came by, they'd start saying, "Hey, Sonny Boy, how you doin'?" They'd ask me, "You kick anybody's ass today?" I knew that they admired me for this, and I knew that I had to keep on doing it. This was the reputation I was making, and I had to keep living up to it every day that I came out of the house. Every day, there was a greater demand on me. I couldn't beat the same little boys every day. They got bigger and bigger. I had to get more vicious as the cats got bigger. When the bigger guys started messing with you, you couldn't hit them or give them a black eye or a bloody nose. You had to get a bottle or a stick or a knife. All the other cats out there on the streets expected this of me, and they gave me encouragement.

When I was about ten years old, the Forty Thieves—part of the Buccaneers—adopted me. Danny and Butch and Kid were already in it. Johnny Wilkes was older than Butch, and Butch was older than Danny and Kid. Johnny was an old Buccaneer. He had to be. When he came out on the streets in the early forties, it must have been twice as hard as it was a few years later. Harlem became less vicious from year to year, and it was hard when I first started coming out of the house, in 1944 and 1945, and raising all kinds of hell. It was something terrible out there on the streets.

Being one of the older Buccaneers, Johnny took Butch, Danny, and Kid as his fellows. He adopted them. I guess he liked the fact that they all admired him. They adopted me because I was a thief. I don't know why or how I first started stealing. I remember it was Danny and Butch who were the first ones who took me up on the hill to the white stores and downtown. I had already started stealing in Harlem. It was before I started going to school, so it must have been about 1943. Danny used to steal money, and he used to take me to the show with him and buy me popcorn and potato chips. After a while, I stole money too. Stealing became something good. It was exciting. I don't know what made it so exciting, but I liked it. I liked stealing more than I liked fighting.

I didn't like fighting at first. But after a while, it got me a lot of praise and respect in the street. It was the fighting and the stealing that made me somebody. If I hadn't fought or stolen, I would have been just another kid in the street. I put bandages on cats, and people would ask, "Who did that?" The older cats didn't believe that a little boy had broke somebody's arm by hitting him with a pipe or had hit somebody in the face with a bottle or had hit somebody in the head with a door hinge and put that big patch on his head. They didn't believe things like this at first, but my name got around and they believed it.

I became the mascot of the Buccaneers. They adopted me, and they started teaching me things. At that time, they were just the street-corner hoodlums, the delinquents, the little teen-age gangsters of the future. They were outside of things, but they knew the people who were into things, all the older hustlers and the prostitutes, the bootleggers, the pimps, the numbers runners. They knew the professional thieves, the people who dealt the guns, the stickup artists, the people who sold reefers. I was learning how to make homemades and how to steal things and what reefers were. I was learning all the things that you needed to know in the streets. The main thing I was learning was our code.

We looked upon ourselves as the aristocracy of the community. We felt that we were the hippest people and that the other people didn't know anything. When I was in the street with these people, we all had to live for one another. We had to live in a way that we would be respected by one another. We couldn't let our friends think anything terrible of us, and we didn't want to think anything bad about our friends.

I think everybody, even the good boys who stayed in the house, started growing into this manly thing, a man's money, a man's family, a man's manhood. I felt so much older than most of the guys my age because I had been in it for a long time before they came out of the house. They were kids, and I felt like an old man. This was what made life easier on me in Harlem in the mid-fifties than it was for other cats my age, sixteen, seventeen, and eighteen. I had been through it. I didn't have to prove anything any more, because I'd been proving myself for years and years and years.

In a way, I used to feel sorry for the cats coming out of the house at sixteen and seventeen. I knew they were afraid. I'd always been afraid too, and I wasn't afraid of what they were afraid of. I wasn't afraid of not using drugs. I sort of knew that I wouldn't have to kill anybody.

I suppose I was luckier because, when I was young, I knew all the time that I couldn't get in but so much trouble. If I had killed somebody when I was twelve or thirteen, I knew I couldn't go to the chair; I knew they couldn't send me to Sing Sing or anyplace like that.

Then the manhood thing started getting next to cats through drugs. I saw it so many times. Young cats wanted to take drugs because they used to listen to the way the junkies talked, with a drag in their voice. I used to see some of the younger cats on the corner trying to imitate the junkie drag, that harsh "Yeah, man" sort of thing.

It was changing. By 1957 the fight thing had just about gone. A man didn't have to prove himself with his hands as much as he had before. By then, when I met cats who had just come out of jail, out of Woodburn, Sing Sing, Coxsackie, and I asked about somebody, they'd say, "Oh, yeah, man, I think I know the cat," and they would start describing him by features, his height, his voice, that sort of thing. But as late as 1953, if I asked somebody, "Do you know a cat by the name of K.B.?" The guy would say, "Yeah. He's left-handed, and he always fights with his left hand cocked back?"

This was something that was dying out. Now people would ask if you knew somebody by scars or the way he talked, something like that. The fighting thing didn't seem to be important any more. The only thing that seemed to matter now, to my generation in Harlem, was drugs. Everybody looked at it as if it were inevitable. If you asked about somebody, a cat would say, "Oh, man, he's still all right. He's doin' pretty good. He's not strung out yet."

I never got too involved with drugs, but it gave me a pretty painful moment. I was walking down Eighth Avenue, and I saw somebody across the street. It was a familiar shape and a familiar walk. My heart lit up.

The person looked like something was wrong with her, even though she was walking all right and still had her nice shape. It was Sugar. She was walking in the middle of the street.

I ran across the street and snatched her by the arm. I was happy. I knew she'd be happy to see me, because I hadn't seen her in a long time. I said, "Sugar, hey, baby, what you doin'? You tryin' to commit suicide or somethin'? Why don't you just go and take some sleeping pills? I think it would be less painful, and it would be easier on the street cleaners."

I expected her to grab me and hug me and be just as glad to see me, but she just looked around and said, "Oh, hi." Her face looked bad. She looked old, like somebody who'd been crying a long time because they had lost somebody, like a member of the family had died.

I said, "What's wrong, baby? What's the matter?"

She looked at me and said, "You don't know?"

"Uh-uh, uh-uh."

I looked at her, and she said, "Yeah, baby, that's the way it is. I've got a jones," and she dropped her head.

"Well, anyway, come on out of the street."

"I don't care. Claude, I just had a bad time. You know a nigger named Cary who lives on 148th Street?"

"I don't know him. Why?"

"He just beat me out of my last five dollars, and my jones is on me; it's on me something terrible. I feel so sick."

I was so hurt and stunned I just didn't know what to do. I said, "Come on, Sugar, let me take you someplace where I know you can get some help. Look, there's a man in East Harlem. His name is Reverend Eddie, and he's been doing a lot of good work with young drug addicts, and I think he could help you. He could get you into Metropolitan Hospital or Manhattan General, one of the places where they've started treating drug addicts. Come on, you got to get a cure, baby. This life is not for you."

I pulled on her, and she said, "Claude, Claude, I'm sick. There's only one thing you can do for me if you really want to help me. There's only one thing anybody can do for me right now, and that's loan me five dollars to get me some stuff, because I feel like I'm dyin'. Oh, Lord, I feel so bad."

I looked at her, and she was a part of my childhood. I just couldn't stand to see her suffer. I only had one five-dollar bill and some change. I said, "Look, baby, why don't you get off this thing? Because it's gonna be the same story tomorrow. You'll just be delaying it until another day."

"Look, Claude, I'll go anyplace with you, but I can't go now. In a little while, I'm gon be laying down in the street there holdin' my stomach and hopin' a car runs over me before the pains get any worse."

"Shit. Come on with me. I'm not gon give you another five dollars to go and give it to somebody and get bit again. Come on with me. Come on to 144th Street. I know somebody there who's got some drugs, and I understand it's pretty good. I'll get you some drugs and take care of that. Then we're gon see about doin' something for you."

"Okay. You get me high and I'll go anyplace with you after that. But first I want to go downtown. You could come with me, down around Times Square. I really appreciate this, and I'm gonna give you ten dollars."

"Shit. You gon give me ten dollars? Why don't you just go on and . . ."

"No, I ain't got the money now. I got to go down there and turn a trick. I'll give you ten dollars, or I'll give you twenty dollars if you need some money. I'll turn a few tricks for you tonight."

I wanted to hit her when she said that, because it meant she thought of me as somebody who might want her to turn a trick, somebody who would accept her turning a trick for him. But I knew that it wasn't so much me. This was what she'd been into, and she'd probably turned a whole lot of tricks. She probably thought of everybody that way now, as somebody who she could turn a trick for. I suppose that's all anybody had wanted from her for a long time.

I was hurt. I said, "Come on." I took her to Ruby's, on 144th

Street. Ruby was a chick I knew who was dealing drugs. I said, "Look, you can get high right here."

I told Ruby who Sugar was. I introduced Sugar to her. I told her I wanted to get Sugar high. Ruby said, "No! I'm surprised. Damn, Sonny, you sure waited a long time to start dabblin', didn't you?"

"No, baby, it's not for me; it's for Sugar."

She said, "Oh, yeah? She looks like she's having a bad way."

Ruby told us to sit down in the living room. She had a bent-up spoon that she cooked stuff in for the poison people. She cooked some for Sugar. While Sugar was waiting for her to cook it, I asked her, "Sugar, what's been happening? The last time I heard about you, you were dancing with a popular troupe, and you were doin' good."

"Yeah, I was dancin', but I haven't done any dancin' in a long time."

"I guess not. What happened? You were doin' so good. You had finished high school. I thought you were really gonna do things; you were a damn good girl." I asked her what had happened to the young cat that she had eyes for when I wanted her to be my woman, about five years before.

"Oh, that was just one of those childish flames. It burned itself out."

"Yeah? I heard you'd gotten married. Wasn't it to him?"

"No, it wasn't to him. He wasn't mature enough for anybody to marry."

"Well, what happened with the marriage?"

"It's a long story, Claude, but I guess I owe it to you."

"No, baby, you don't owe me a thing. Save it if that's the way you feel about it."

"No, I want to tell it to you anyway. I guess you're the one I've been waiting to tell it to . . . Do you remember a boy on 149th Street by the name of Melvin Jackson?"

"No, I don't know him."

"Anyway, he use to be in a lot of trouble, too, around the same time that you were raisin' all that hell. I think he was a year or two older than you. When you were at Warwick, he was at Coxsackie. He came out about a year after you did.

"He was a lonely sort of guy. He seemed to really need somebody. Claude, you know what I think? I think all my life, I'd been looking for somebody who needed somebody real bad, and who could need me. Who could need all of me and everything that I had to give him."

I said, "Yeah, baby, I think I know."

"We got married in '55. For about a year, we were happy. Marriage was good. I thought this was something that would last and last for a long time."

"Yeah."

"Claude, I hope you don't have anyplace to go tonight. The first thing I want to do after I get high is go down and turn a trick and get some money."

"Look, girl, stop saying that. Stop saying that before I beat your ass."

She looked at me and smiled and said, "Yeah, won't you do it? I think I'd like that, just for old time's sake." And she went on with telling me about the marriage.

"For the first year, we were happy. He was working and I was working. After about a year, he started going out nights and stayin' real late. He'd get up out of bed at one o'clock in the morning, go out, and come back about four or five. At first, I thought it was another woman or something like that. I thought it was for a long time, until I found out.

"At first he just started goin' out and stayin' for a few hours. After a while, he started goin' out at night or early in the morning and not comin' back for two and three days. I got worried. After a while, I couldn't work. I had a miscarriage about a month before he started staying out all night long. I was kind of sick. I was weak, and I would get worried and couldn't go to work in the morning.

"Once, when he came home, I asked him where he'd been. He just said, 'I had to go out, baby.' I knew he knew a whole lot of shady people, because he'd been in street life for a long time, most of his life. And he knew a whole lot of characters who I didn't want him to bring around the house and who he was respectful enough not to bring around.

"I didn't ask him too much about these people. I didn't try to butt into his business, because we just had this understanding. We never talked about it. That's just the way we understood each other.

"I knew him, and I knew he loved me. I think he loved me more than anybody ever loved me in all my life before. That's what made it so bad when he started staying out at night. All that love I had finally found, the love that I'd been seekin' so strongly all my life, was being threatened. It made me sick. I'd wake up in the morning, feel that he wasn't there, and I became so scared I felt like a little kid hidin' in the closet from monsters.

"My eyes just started pushin' the water out. Heat waves would swell up and come out of my eyes in tears. That's how I felt. It wasn't a thing of body with him. It wasn't a thing of this flesh stuff. He didn't even know that I had a body when I first met him. He didn't like me; he couldn't stand having me around. One day, he said something kind, and I realized that it wasn't just me that he disliked. It was everybody. And he was lonely. He needed somebody, and I knew that the somebody could've been me.

"I'd never felt so un-alone, you know, until I met this guy. I never felt as though I had anybody or anything but him. I would've lived with him or done anything he asked. I would've went out on the street corners and tricked for him if that was what he wanted me to do, because he became a part of me, and I wanted him just that badly.

"But he really loved me; he didn't expect anything out of me. That wasn't the worst part of it. I thought he was getting money from me to give to another woman, because sometimes he'd be going into my handbag in the middle of the night, and he'd take money out of it. Then he'd be gone. Maybe he'd come back later that night, or maybe he wouldn't come back until the next day or two days later. It scared me.

"Well, anyway, one night, he was layin' next to me, sleepin'. I should've suspected it, because I came up in Harlem, and I knew what was goin' on. I don't know, I guess I was so frightened about this other woman thing that I couldn't see the symptoms. He seemed to be almost losin' his nature. He would . . . you know how if a guy wakes up in the morning, and he's a young guy, he usually has a piss hard-on. But he'd be as soft as a rag all the time. I was wonderin' if it was just that he was gettin' tired of me. Maybe I was making him lose his nature, because he didn't want to be bothered with me any more. I just got so afraid of this . . . and I should've known. I should have known what it was.

"Anyway, he didn't eat. I became more afraid of this thing. I became afraid to ask him, 'What's wrong?' I wanted to say, 'What's wrong, Mel?' But I was scared. I was so afraid he might say, 'Look, I'm tired of you, and I got to get out of this thing.' I thought it was gonna come one day anyway. He was gonna tell me, 'Look, I got another woman, and I got to leave you.' But it was gettin' to be too much for me to keep quiet about, because when he woke up at night and started leavin', I would be awake most of these times. I'd be tellin' myself for a week, 'Look, I'm gonna ask him the next time.'

"But still I was scared; I was scared of losin' him. I'd already lost him in that love thing. He always was quiet, but now he was more quiet than he'd ever been. It seemed as though he didn't want to kiss me. If I played with him in the bed, he'd get mad, that sort of thing.

"One night, he got up, and I asked him. I said, 'Mel, turn on the light, please.' He had been nervous. I hadn't been sleepin' for over a week, because I use to lay awake just wonderin', Is he gonna go out tonight, or maybe he's gonna come back to me? Our sex life had been dwindling away to almost nothin'. I thought, Maybe tonight, maybe tonight he'll play with me. I kept hopin'.

"When he got up to dress, that night I asked him to turn on the light, he was real nervous. He just said, 'Bitch, go on to sleep, and don't bother me!'

"I was kind of hurt, because he'd never said anything like this to me. We were real sweet to each other. This was crazy. I could've never imagined him saying it to me. When he said that, I had to jump up and turn on the light. I had my scream all ready. I told you what I was gonna tell him about the other woman, and all that sort of thing.

"When I opened my mouth, I could taste the tears, and I heard myself talkin' to him in a real soft voice. I was sayin', 'Mel, please tell me where you goin'.'

"He said, 'Look, baby, go on to sleep, and don't worry about me. Try and forget me. Imagine that I never even lived, 'cause I think my life is ruined. I don't want to ruin yours. I'm goin' out tonight, and I'm not comin' back.'

"I said, 'Where're you goin'? Tell me something.'

"He got mad. He'd been gettin' irritable for a long time. He just snapped at me; he said, 'Shit, if you got to know, I'm goin' to my first love.'

"When he told me this, it stunned me. I felt as though I'd been hit in the face by a prizefighter. Everything was quiet. I was stunned, and I think he knew it. It was as though lightning had struck the house, and now all was silent.

"Then I said, 'Mel, I thought I was your first love.'

"He just said, 'No, baby, you're not my first love.' He said, 'Stuff is my first love.'

"I said, 'What do you mean "stuff"?'

"He said, 'You've heard of shit, haven't you, duji, heroin?'

"I wanted to cry. I wanted to cry. But it didn't make sense, because I was already cryin'. I didn't know what to do. I just said, 'Oh, no, no, it couldn't be.' He left."

When Sugar said that bit about "he left," she tried to smile. I felt uncomfortable. Then she said, "It seemed that I stood there in that dark room for hours with the word 'stuff' echoing in my mind. I knew but one thing in life for a whole week. All I knew was that I had to learn about stuff. I had to find out what it was that could make the man I loved love it more than he loved me. Well, Claude, baby, you can see I found out. Yeah . . . I really found out."

Ruby brought in the works; she had a makeshift syringe with a spike on the end of it. She was holding it upside down. I'd given her the five dollars when I first came in. She handed the spike to Sugar, and Sugar paid it no mind. She just rolled down her stocking and pinched her thigh. I saw the needle marks on her thigh.

She looked at me and smiled. She said, "Do you want to hold the flesh for me?"

I said, "Thanks for the offer," and smiled, but I just didn't want to help her get high. I watched as she hit herself with the spike, and I thought about the fact that just a few short years ago, to put my hand on those thighs would have given me more pleasure than anything else I was doing back in those days. I could never have imagined myself saying no to an offer to feel her thighs. Those were the same thighs that had all the needle marks on them.

I watched the syringe as the blood came up into the drugs that seemed like dirty water. It just filled up with blood, and as the blood and the drugs started its way down into the needle, I thought, This is our childhood. Our childhood had been covered with blood, as the drugs had been. Covered with blood and gone down into somewhere. I wondered where.

I wanted to say, "Sugar, I'm sorry for the time I didn't kiss you at the bus. I'm sorry for not telling people that you were my girl friend. I'm sorry for never telling you that I loved you and for never asking you to be my girl friend." I wanted to say, "I'm sorry for everything. I'm sorry for ever having hesitated to kiss you because of your buckteeth."

Sugar took the spike out, and she patted herself. She started scratching her arm and went into a nod. "That's some nice stuff," she said.

I got up, went over to where Sugar was sitting, bent over, and kissed her. She smiled and went into another nod.

That was the last time I saw her, nodding and climbing up on the duji cloud.

Eldridge Cleaver, born in Arkansas in 1935, is the author of *Soul on Ice* and *Soul on Fire.* He was the Minister of Information for the Black Panther Party for Self-Defense.

13

ELDRIDGE CLEAVER

From Soul on Ice

On Becoming

(1968)

Folsom Prison,
June 25th, 1965

NINETEEN FIFTY-FOUR, when I was eighteen years old, is held to be a crucial turning point in the history of the Afro-American—for the U.S.A. as a whole—the year segregation was outlawed by the U.S. Supreme Court. It was also a crucial year for me because on June 18th, 1954, I began serving a sentence in state prison for possession of marijuana.

The Supreme Court decision was only one month old when I entered prison, and I do not believe that I had even the vaguest idea of its importance or historical significance. But later, the acrimonious controversy ignited by the end of the separate-but-equal doctrine was to have a profound effect on me. This controversy awakened me to my position in America and I began to form a concept of what it meant to be black in white America.

Of course I'd always known that I was black, but I'd never really stopped to take stock of what I was involved in. I met life as an individual and took my chances. Prior to 1954, we lived in an atmosphere of novocain. Negroes found it necessary, in order to maintain whatever sanity they could, to remain somewhat aloof and detached from "the problem." We accepted indignities and the mechanics of the apparatus of oppression without reacting by sitting-in or holding mass demonstrations. Nurtured by the fires of the controversy over segregation, I was soon aflame with indignation over my newly discovered social status, and inwardly I turned away from America with horror, disgust and outrage.

In Soledad state prison, I fell in with a group of young blacks who, like myself, were in vociferous rebellion against what we perceived as a continuation of slavery on a higher plane. We cursed everything American—including baseball and hot dogs. All respect we may have had for politicians, preachers, lawyers, governors, Presidents, senators, congressmen was utterly destroyed as we watched them temporizing and compromising over right and wrong, over legality and illegality, over constitutionality and unconstitutionality. We knew that in the end what they were clashing over was us, what to do with the blacks, and whether or not to start treating us as human beings. I despised all of them.

The segregationists were condemned out of hand, without even listening to their lofty, finely woven arguments. The others I despised for wasting time in debates with the segregationists: why not just crush them, put them in prison—they were defying the law, weren't they? I defied the law and they put me in prison. So why not put those dirty mothers in prison too? I had gotten caught with a shopping bag full of marijuana, a shopping bag full of love—I was in love with the weed and I did not for one minute think that anything was wrong with getting high. I had been getting high for four or five years and was convinced, with the zeal of a crusader, that marijuana was superior to lush—yet the rulers of the land seemed all to be lushes. I could not see how they were more justified in drinking than I was in blowing the gage. I was a grasshopper, and it was natural that I felt myself to be unjustly imprisoned.

While all this was going on, our group was espousing atheism. Unsophisticated and not based on any philosophical rationale, our atheism was pragmatic. I had come to believe that there is no God; if there is, men do not know anything about him. Therefore, all religions were phony—which made all preachers and priests, in our eyes, fakers, including the ones scurrying around the prison who, curiously, could put in a good word for you with the Almighty Creator of the universe but could not get anything down with the warden or parole board—they could usher you through the Pearly Gates *after you were dead,* but not through the prison gate *while you were still alive and kicking.* Besides, men of the cloth who work in prison have an ineradicable stigma attached to them in the eyes of convicts because they escort condemned men into the gas chamber. Such men of God are powerful arguments in favor of atheism. Our atheism was a source of enormous pride to me. Later on, I bolstered our arguments by reading Thomas Paine and his devastating critique of Christianity in particular and organized religion in general.

Through reading I was amazed to discover how confused people were. I had thought that, out there beyond the horizon of my own ignorance, unanimity existed, that even though I myself didn't know what was happening in the universe, other people certainly did. Yet here I was discovering that the whole U.S.A. was in a chaos of disagreement over segregation/integration. In these circumstances I decided that the only safe thing for me to do was go for myself. It became clear that it was possible for me to take the initiative: instead of simply *reacting* I could *act.* I could unilaterally—whether anyone agreed with me or not—repudiate all allegiances, morals, values— even while continuing to exist within this society. My mind would be free and no power in the universe could force me to accept something if I didn't want to. But I would take my own sweet time. That, too, was a part of my new freedom. I would accept nothing until it was proved that it was good—for me. I became an extreme iconoclast. Any affirmative assertion made by anyone around me became a target for tirades of criticism and denunciation.

This little game got good to me and I got good at it. I attacked all forms of piety, loyalty, and sentiment: marriage, love, God, patriotism, the Constitution, the founding fathers, law, concepts of right-wrong-good-evil, all forms of ritualized and conventional behavior. As I pranced about, club in hand, seeking new idols to smash, I encountered really for the first time in my life, with any seriousness, The Ogre, rising up before me in a mist. I discovered, with alarm, that

The Ogre possessed a tremendous and dreadful power over me, and I didn't understand this power or why I was at its mercy. I tried to repudiate The Ogre, root it out of my heart as I had done God, Constitution, principles, morals, and values—but The Ogre had its claws buried in the core of my being and refused to let go. I fought frantically to be free, but The Ogre only mocked me and sank its claws deeper into my soul. I knew then that I had found an important key, that if I conquered The Ogre and broke its power over me I would be free. But I also knew that it was a race against time and that if I did not win I would certainly be broken and destroyed. I, a black man, confronted The Ogre—the white woman.

In prison, those things withheld from and denied to the prisoner become precisely what he wants most of all, of course. Because we were locked up in our cells before darkness fell, I used to lie awake at night racked by painful craving to take a leisurely stroll under the stars, or to go to the beach, to drive a car on a freeway, to grow a beard, or to make love to a woman.

Since I was not married conjugal visits would not have solved my problem. I therefore denounced the idea of conjugal visits as inherently unfair; single prisoners needed and deserved *action* just as married prisoners did. I advocated establishing a system under Civil Service whereby salaried women would minister to the needs of those prisoners who maintained a record of good behavior. If a married prisoner preferred his own wife, that would be his right. Since California was not about to inaugurate either conjugal visits or the Civil Service, one could advocate either with equal enthusiasm and with the same result: nothing.

This may appear ridiculous to some people. But it was very real to me and as urgent as the need to breathe, because I was in my bull stage and lack of access to females was absolutely a form of torture. I suffered. My mistress at the time of my arrest, the beautiful and lonely wife of a serviceman stationed overseas, died unexpectedly three weeks after I entered prison; and the rigid, dehumanized rules governing correspondence between prisoners and free people prevented me from corresponding with other young ladies I knew. It left me without any contact with females except those in my family.

In the process of enduring my confinement, I decided to get myself a pin-up girl to paste on the wall of my cell. I would fall in love with her and lavish my affections upon her. She, a symbolic representative of the forbidden tribe of women, would sustain me until I was free. Out of the center of *Esquire,* I married a voluptuous bride. Our marriage went along swell for a time: no quarrels, no complaints. And then, one evening when I came in from school, I was shocked and enraged to find that the guard had entered my cell, ripped my sugar from the wall, torn her into little pieces, and left the pieces floating in the commode: it was like seeing a dead body floating in a lake. Giving her a proper burial, I flushed the commode. As the saying goes, I sent her to Long Beach. But I was genuinely beside myself with anger: almost every cell, excepting those of the homosexuals, had a pin-up girl on the wall and the guards didn't bother them. Why, I asked the guard the next day, had he singled me out for special treatment?

"Don't you know we have a rule against pasting up pictures on the walls?" he asked me.

"Later for the rules," I said. "You know as well as I do that that rule is not enforced."

"Tell you what," he said, smiling at me (the smile put me on my guard), "I'll compromise with you: get yourself a colored girl for a pin-up—no white women—and I'll let it stay up. Is that a deal?"

I was more embarrassed than shocked. He was laughing in my face. I called him two or three dirty names and walked away. I can still recall his big moon-face, grinning at me over yellow teeth. The disturbing part about the whole incident was that a terrible feeling of guilt came over me as I realized that I had chosen the picture of the white girl over the available pictures of black girls. I tried to rationalize it away, but I was fascinated by the truth involved. Why hadn't I thought about it in this light before? So I took hold of the question and began to inquire into my feelings. Was it true, did I really prefer white girls over black? The conclusion was clear and inescapable: I did. I decided to check out my friends on this point and it was easy to determine, from listening to their general conversation, that the white woman occupied a peculiarly prominent place in all of our frames of reference. With what I have learned since then, this all seems terribly elementary now. But at the time, it was a tremendously intriguing adventure of discovery.

One afternoon, when a large group of Negroes was on the prison yard shooting the breeze, I grabbed the floor and posed the question: which did they prefer, white women or black? Some said Japanese women were their favorite, others said Chinese, some said European women, others said Mexican women—they all stated a preference, and they generally freely admitted their dislike for black women.

"I don't want nothing black but a Cadillac," said one.

"If money was black I wouldn't want none of it," put in another.

A short little stud, who was a very good lightweight boxer with a little man's complex that made him love to box heavyweights, jumped to his feet. He had a yellowish complexion and we called him Butterfly.

"All you niggers are sick!" Butterfly spat out. "I don't like no stinking white woman. My grandma is a white woman and I don't even like her!"

But it just so happened that Butterfly's crime partner was in the crowd, and after Butterfly had his say, his crime partner said, "Aw, sit down and quit that lying, lil o' chump. What about that gray girl in San Jose who had your nose wide open? Did you like her, or were you just running after her with your tongue hanging out of your head because you hated her?"

Partly because he was embarrassed and partly because his crime partner was a heavyweight, Butterfly flew into him. And before we could separate them and disperse, so the guard would not know who had been fighting, Butterfly bloodied his crime partner's nose. Butterfly got away but, because of the blood, his crime partner got caught. I ate dinner with Butterfly that evening and questioned him sharply about his attitude toward white women. And after an initial evasiveness he admitted that the white woman bugged him too. "It's a sickness," he said. "All our lives we've had the white woman dangled before our eyes like a carrot on a stick before a donkey: look but don't touch." (In 1958, after I had gone out on parole and was returned to San Quentin as a parole violater with a new charge, Butterfly was still there. He had become a Black Muslim and was chiefly responsible for teaching me the Black Muslim philosophy. Upon his release from San

Quentin, Butterfly joined the Los Angeles Mosque, advanced rapidly through the ranks, and is now a full-fledged minister of one of Elijah Muhammad's mosques in another city. He successfully completed his parole, got married—to a very black girl—and is doing fine.)

From our discussion, which began that evening and has never yet ended, we went on to notice how thoroughly, as a matter of course, a black growing up in America is indoctrinated with the white race's standard of beauty. Not that the whites made a conscious, calculated effort to do this, we thought, but since they constituted the majority the whites brainwashed the blacks by the very processes the whites employed to indoctrinate themselves with their own group standards. It intensified my frustrations to know that I was indoctrinated to see the white woman as more beautiful and desirable than my own black woman. It drove me into books seeking light on the subject. In Richard Wright's *Native Son,* I found Bigger Thomas and a keen insight into the problem.

My interest in this area persisted undiminished and then, in 1955, an event took place in Mississippi which turned me inside out: Emmett Till, a young Negro down from Chicago on a visit, was murdered, allegedly for flirting with a white woman. He had been shot, his head crushed from repeated blows with a blunt instrument, and his badly decomposed body was recovered from the river with a heavy weight on it. I was, of course, angry over the whole bit, but one day I saw in a magazine a picture of the white woman with whom Emmett Till was said to have flirted. While looking at the picture, I felt that little tension in the center of my chest I experience when a woman appeals to me. I was disgusted and angry with myself. Here was a woman who had caused the death of a black, possibly because, when he looked at her, he also felt the same tensions of lust and desire in his chest—and probably for the same general reasons that I felt them. It was all unacceptable to me. I looked at the picture again and again, and in spite of everything and against my will and the hate I felt for the woman and all that she represented, she appealed to me. I flew into a rage at myself, at America, at white women, at the history that had placed those tensions of lust and desire in my chest.

Two days later I had a "nervous breakdown." For several days

I ranted and raved against the white race, against white women in particular, against white America in general. When I came to myself, I was locked in a padded cell with not even the vaguest memory of how I got there. All I could recall was an eternity of pacing back and forth in the cell, preaching to the unhearing walls.

I had several sessions with a psychiatrist. His conclusion was that I hated my mother. How he arrived at this conclusion I'll never know, because he knew nothing about my mother; and when he'd ask me questions I would answer him with absurd lies. What revolted me about him was that he had heard me denouncing the whites, yet each time he interviewed me he deliberately guided the conversation back to my family life, to my childhood. That in itself was all right, but he deliberately blocked all my attempts to bring out the racial question, and he made it clear that he was not interested in my attitude toward whites. This was a Pandora's box he did not care to open. After I ceased my diatribes against the whites, I was let out of the hospital, back into the general inmate population just as if nothing had happened. I continued to brood over these events and over the dynamics of race relations in America.

During this period I was concentrating my reading in the field of economics. Having previously dabbled in the theories and writings of Rousseau, Thomas Paine, and Voltaire, I had added a little polish to my iconoclastic stance, without, however, bothering too much to understand their affirmative positions. In economics, because everybody seemed to find it necessary to attack and condemn Karl Marx in their writings, I sought out his books, and although he kept me with a headache, I took him for my authority. I was not prepared to understand him, but I was able to see in him a thoroughgoing critique and condemnation of capitalism. It was like taking medicine for me to find that, indeed, American capitalism deserved all the hatred and contempt that I felt for it in my heart. This had a positive, stabilizing effect upon me—to an extent because I was not about to become stable—and it diverted me from my previous preoccupation: morbid broodings on the black man and the white woman. Pursuing my readings into the history of socialism, I read, with very little understanding, some of the passionate, exhortatory writings of Lenin; and

I fell in love with Bakunin and Nechayev's *Catechism of the Revolutionist*—the principles of which, along with some of Machiavelli's advice, I sought to incorporate into my own behavior. I took the *Catechism* for my bible and, standing on a one-man platform that had nothing to do with the reconstruction of society, I began consciously incorporating these principles into my daily life, to employ tactics of ruthlessness in my dealings with everyone with whom I came into contact. And I began to look at white America through these new eyes.

Somehow I arrived at the conclusion that, as a matter of principle, it was of paramount importance for me to have an antagonistic, ruthless attitude toward white women. The term *outlaw* appealed to me and at the time my parole date was drawing near, I considered myself to be mentally free—I was an "outlaw." I had stepped outside of the white man's law, which I repudiated with scorn and self-satisfaction. I became a law unto myself—my own legislature, my own supreme court, my own executive. At the moment I walked out of the prison gate, my feelings toward white women in general could be summed up in the following lines:

TO A WHITE GIRL

I love you
Because you're white,
Not because you're charming
Or bright.
Your whiteness
Is a silky thread
Snaking through my thoughts
In redhot patterns
Of lust and desire.

I hate you
Because you're white.
Your white meat
Is nightmare food.
White is
The skin of Evil.
You're my Moby Dick,

White Witch,
Symbol of the rope and hanging tree,
Of the burning cross.
Loving you thus
And hating you so,
My heart is torn in two.
Crucified.

I became a rapist. To refine my technique and *modus operandi,* I started out by practicing on black girls in the ghetto—in the black ghetto where dark and vicious deeds appear not as aberrations or deviations from the norm, but as part of the sufficiency of the Evil of a day—and when I considered myself smooth enough, I crossed the tracks and sought out white prey. I did this consciously, deliberately, willfully, methodically—though looking back I see that I was in a frantic, wild, and completely abandoned frame of mind.

Rape was an insurrectionary act. It delighted me that I was defying and trampling upon the white man's law, upon his system of values, and that I was defiling his women—and this point, I believe, was the most satisfying to me because I was very resentful over the historical fact of how the white man has used the black woman. I felt I was getting revenge. From the site of the act of rape, consternation spreads outwardly in concentric circles. I wanted to send waves of consternation throughout the white race. Recently, I came upon a quotation from one of LeRoi Jones's poems, taken from his book *The Dead Lecturer:*

A cult of death need of the simple striking arm under the street lamp. The cutters from under their rented earth. Come up, black dada nihilismus. Rape the white girls. Rape their fathers. Cut the mothers' throats.

I have lived those lines and I know that if I had not been apprehended I would have slit some white throats. There are, of course, many young blacks out there right now who are slitting white throats and raping the white girl. They are not doing this because they read LeRoi Jones's poetry, as some of his critics seem to believe. Rather, LeRoi is expressing the funky facts of life.

After I returned to prison, I took a long look at myself and, for the first time in my life, admitted that I was wrong, that I had gone astray—astray not so much from the white man's law as from being human, civilized—for I could not approve the act of rape. Even though I had some insight into my own motivations, I did not feel justified. I lost my self-respect. My pride as a man dissolved and my whole fragile moral structure seemed to collapse, completely shattered.

That is why I started to write. To save myself.

I realized that no one could save me but myself. The prison authorities were both uninterested and unable to help me. I had to seek out the truth and unravel the snarled web of my motivations. I had to find out who I am and what I want to be, what type of man I should be, and what I could do to become the best of which I was capable. I understood that what had happened to me had also happened to countless other blacks and it would happen to many, many more.

I learned that I had been taking the easy way out, running away from problems. I also learned that it is easier to do evil than it is to do good. And I have been terribly impressed by the youth of America, black and white. I am proud of them.because they have reaffirmed my faith in humanity. I have come to feel what must be love for the young people of America and I want to be part of the good and greatness that they want for all people. From my prison cell, I have watched America slowly coming awake. It is not fully awake yet, but there is soul in the air and everywhere I see beauty. I have watched the sit-ins, the freedom rides, the Mississippi Blood Summers, demonstrations all over the country, the F.S.M. movement, the teach-ins, and the mounting protest over Lyndon Strangelove's foreign policy—all of this, the thousands of little details, show me it is time to straighten up and fly right. That is why I decided to concentrate on my writings and efforts in this area. We are a very sick country—I, perhaps, am sicker than most. But I accept that. I told you in the beginning that I am extremist by nature—so it is only right that I should be extremely sick.

I was very familiar with the Eldridge who came to prison, but that Eldridge no longer exists. And the one I am now is in some ways a stranger to me. You may find this difficult to understand but it is very easy for one in prison to lose his sense of self. And if he has been undergoing all kinds of extreme, involved, and unregulated changes, then he ends up not knowing who he is. Take the point of being attractive to women. You can easily see how a man can lose his arrogance or certainty on that point while in prison! When he's in the free world, he gets constant feedback on how he looks from the number of female heads he turns when he walks down the street. In prison he gets only hatestares and sour frowns. Years and years of bitter looks. Individuality is not nourished in prison, neither by the officials nor by the convicts. It is a deep hole out of which to climb.

What must be done, I believe, is that all these problems—particularly the sickness between the white woman and the black man—must be brought out into the open, dealt with and resolved. I know that the black man's sick attitude toward the white woman is a revolutionary sickness: it keeps him perpetually out of harmony with the system that is oppressing him. Many whites flatter themselves with the idea that the Negro male's lust and desire for the white dream girl is purely an esthetic attraction, but nothing could be further from the truth. His motivation is often of such a bloody, hateful, bitter, and malignant nature that whites would really be hard pressed to find it flattering. I have discussed these points with prisoners who were convicted of rape, and their motivations are very plain. But they are very reluctant to discuss these things with white men who, by and large, make up the prison staffs. I believe that in the experience of these men lies the knowledge and wisdom that must be utilized to help other youngsters who are heading in the same direction. I think all of us, the entire nation, will be better off if we bring it all out front. A lot of people's feelings will be hurt, but that is the price that must be paid.

It may be that I can harm myself by speaking frankly and directly, but I do not care about that at all. Of course I want to get out of prison, badly, but I shall get out some day. I am more concerned with what I am going to be after I get out. I know that by following the course which I have charted I will find my salvation. If I had followed the path laid down for me by the officials, I'd undoubtedly have long since been out of prison—but I'd be less of a man. I'd be weaker and less certain of where I want to go, what I want to do, and how to go about it.

The price of hating other human beings is loving oneself less.

Maya Angelou was born in Saint Louis, Missouri, in 1928. She has trained and performed as a dancer and actress, on both stage and screen. Her writings include *Gather Together in My Name, Singin & Swingin & Gettin Merry Like Christmas,* and *Shaker Why Don't You Sing;* and *I Know Why the Caged Bird Sings.* She has received a Tony nomination for her acting and numerous awards and honorary degrees for her literary achievements. Currently, Maya Angelou is a professor at Wake Forest University in North Carolina.

14

MAYA ANGELOU

From I Know Why the Caged Bird Sings

(1968)

RECENTLY A WHITE woman from Texas, who would quickly describe herself as a liberal, asked me about my hometown. When I told her that in Stamps my grandmother had owned the only Negro general merchandise store since the turn of the century, she exclaimed, "Why, you were a debutante." Ridiculous and even ludicrous. But Negro girls in small Southern towns, whether poverty-stricken or just munching along on a few of life's necessities, were given as extensive and irrelevant preparations for adulthood as rich white girls shown in magazines. Admittedly the training was not the same. While white girls learned to waltz and sit gracefully with a tea cup balanced on their knees, we were lagging behind, learning the mid-Victorian values with very little money to indulge them. (Come and see Edna Lomax spending the money she made picking cotton on five balls of ecru tatting thread. Her fingers are bound to snag the work and she'll have to repeat the stitches time and time again. But she knows that when she buys the thread.)

We were required to embroider and I had trunkfuls of colorful dishtowels, pillowcases, runners and handkerchiefs to my credit. I mastered the art of crocheting and tatting, and there was a lifetime's supply of dainty doilies that would never be used in sacheted dresser drawers. It went without saying that all girls could iron and wash, but the finer touches around the home, like setting a table with real silver, baking roasts and cooking vegetables without meat, had to be learned elsewhere. Usually at the source of those habits. During my tenth year, a white woman's kitchen became my finishing school.

Mrs. Viola Cullinan was a plump woman who lived in a three-bedroom house somewhere behind the post office. She was singularly unattractive until she smiled, and then the lines around her eyes and mouth which made her look perpetually dirty disappeared, and her face looked like the mask of an impish elf. She usually rested her smile until late afternoon when her women friends dropped in and Miss Glory, the cook, served them cold drinks on the closed-in porch.

The exactness of her house was inhuman. This glass went here and only here. That cup had its place and it was an act of impudent rebellion to place it anywhere else. At twelve o'clock the table was set. At 12:15 Mrs. Cullinan sat down to dinner (whether her husband had arrived or not). At 12:16 Miss Glory brought out the food.

It took me a week to learn the difference between a salad plate, a bread plate and a dessert plate.

Mrs. Cullinan kept up the tradition of her wealthy parents. She was from Virginia. Miss Glory, who was a descendant of slaves that had worked for the Cullinans, told me her history. She had married beneath her (according to Miss Glory). Her husband's family hadn't had their money very long and what they had "didn't 'mount to much."

As ugly as she was, I thought privately, she was lucky to get a husband above or beneath her station. But Miss Glory wouldn't let me say a thing against her mistress. She was very patient with me, however, over the housework. She explained the dishware, silverware and servants' bells. The large round bowl in which soup was served wasn't a soup bowl, it was a tureen. There were goblets, sherbet glasses, ice-cream glasses, wine glasses, green glass coffee cups with matching saucers, and water glasses. I had a glass to drink from, and it sat with Miss Glory's on a separate shelf from the others. Soup spoons, gravy boat, butter knives, salad forks and carving platter were additions to my vocabulary and in fact almost represented a new language. I was fascinated with the novelty, with the fluttering Mrs. Cullinan and her Alice-in-Wonderland house.

Her husband remains, in my memory, undefined. I lumped him with all the other white men that I had ever seen and tried not to see.

On our way home one evening, Miss Glory told me that Mrs. Cullinan couldn't have children. She said that she was too delicate-boned. It was hard to imagine bones at all under those layers of fat. Miss Glory went on to say that the doctor had taken out all her lady organs. I reasoned that a pig's organs included the lungs, heart and liver, so if Mrs. Cullinan was walking around without those essentials, it explained why she drank alcohol out of unmarked bottles. She was keeping herself embalmed.

When I spoke to Bailey about it, he agreed that I was right, but he also informed me that Mr. Cullinan had two daughters by a colored lady and that I knew them very well. He added that the girls were the spitting image of their father. I was unable to remember what he looked like, although I had just left him a few hours before, but I thought of the Coleman girls. They were very light-skinned and cer-tainly didn't look very much like their mother (no one ever mentioned Mr. Coleman).

My pity for Mrs. Cullinan preceded me the next morning like the Cheshire cat's smile. Those girls, who could have been her daughters, were beautiful. They didn't have to straighten their hair. Even when they were caught in the rain, their braids still hung down straight like tamed snakes. Their mouths were pouty little cupid's bows. Mrs. Cullinan didn't know what she missed. Or maybe she did. Poor Mrs. Cullinan.

For weeks after, I arrived early, left late and tried very hard to make up for her barrenness. If she had had her own children, she wouldn't have had to ask me to run a thousand errands from her back door to the back door of her friends. Poor old Mrs. Cullinan.

Then one evening Miss Glory told me to serve the ladies on the porch. After I set the tray down and turned toward the kitchen, one of the women asked, "What's your name, girl?" It was the speckled-faced one. Mrs. Cullinan said, "She doesn't talk much. Her name's Margaret."

"Is she dumb?"

"No. As I understand it, she can talk when she wants to but she's usually quiet as a little mouse. Aren't you, Margaret?"

I smiled at her. Poor thing. No organs and couldn't even pronounce my name correctly.

"She's a sweet little thing, though."

"Well, that may be, but the name's too long. I'd never bother myself. I'd call her Mary if I was you."

I fumed into the kitchen. That horrible woman would never have the chance to call me Mary because if I was starving I'd never work for her. I decided I wouldn't pee on her if her heart was on fire. Giggles drifted in off the porch and into Miss Glory's pots. I wondered what they could be laughing about.

Whitefolks were so strange. Could they be talking about me? Everybody knew that they stuck together better than the Negroes did. It was possible that Mrs. Cullinan had friends in St. Louis who heard about a girl from Stamps being in court and wrote to tell her. Maybe she knew about Mr. Freeman.

My lunch was in my mouth a second time and I went outside and relieved myself on the bed of four-o'clocks. Miss Glory thought I might be coming down with something and told me to go on home, that Momma would give me some herb tea, and she'd explain to her mistress.

I realized how foolish I was being before I reached the pond. Of course Mrs. Cullinan didn't know. Otherwise she wouldn't have given me the two nice dresses that Momma cut down, and she certainly wouldn't have called me a "sweet little thing." My stomach felt fine, and I didn't mention anything to Momma.

That evening I decided to write a poem on being white, fat, old and without children. It was going to be a tragic ballad. I would have to watch her carefully to capture the essence of her loneliness and pain.

The very next day, she called me by the wrong name. Miss Glory and I were washing up the lunch dishes when Mrs. Cullinan came to the doorway. "Mary?"

Miss Glory asked, "Who?"

Mrs. Cullinan, sagging a little, knew and I knew. "I want Mary to go down to Mrs. Randall's and take her some soup. She's not been feeling well for a few days."

Miss Glory's face was a wonder to see. "You mean Margaret, ma'am. Her name's Margaret."

"That's too long. She's Mary from now on. Heat that soup from last night and put it in the china tureen and, Mary, I want you to carry it carefully."

Every person I knew had a hellish horror of being "called out of his name." It was a dangerous practice to call a Negro anything that could be loosely construed as insulting because of the centuries of their having been called niggers, jigs, dinges, blackbirds, crows, boots and spooks.

Miss Glory had a fleeting second of feeling sorry for me. Then as she handed me the hot tureen she said, "Don't mind, don't pay that no mind. Sticks and stones may break your bones, but words . . . You know, I been working for her for twenty years."

She held the back door open for me. "Twenty years. I wasn't much older than you. My name used to be Hallelujah. That's what Ma named me, but my mistress give me 'Glory,' and it stuck. I likes it better too."

I was in the little path that ran behind the houses when Miss Glory shouted, "It's shorter too."

For a few seconds it was a tossup over whether I would laugh (imagine being named Hallelujah) or cry (imagine letting some white woman rename you for her convenience). My anger saved me from either outburst. I had to quit the job, but the problem was going to be how to do it. Momma wouldn't allow me to quit for just any reason.

"She's a peach. That woman is a real peach." Mrs. Randall's maid was talking as she took the soup from me, and I wondered what her name used to be and what she answered to now.

For a week I looked into Mrs. Cullinan's face as she called me Mary. She ignored my coming late and leaving early. Miss Glory was a little annoyed because I had begun to leave egg yolk on the dishes and wasn't putting much heart in polishing the silver. I hoped that she would complain to our boss, but she didn't.

Then Bailey solved my dilemma. He had me describe the contents of the cupboard and the particular plates she liked best. Her favorite piece was a casserole shaped like a fish and the green glass coffee cups. I kept his instructions in mind, so on the next day when Miss Glory was hanging out clothes and I had again been told to serve the old biddies on the porch, I dropped the empty serving tray. When I heard Mrs. Cullinan scream, "Mary!" I picked up the casserole and two of the green glass cups in readiness. As she rounded the kitchen door I let them fall on the tiled floor.

I could never absolutely describe to Bailey what happened next, because each time I got to the part where she fell on the floor and screwed up her ugly face to cry, we burst out laughing. She actually wobbled around on the floor and picked up shards of the cups and cried, "Oh, Momma. Oh, dear Gawd. It's Momma's china from Virginia. Oh, Momma, I sorry."

Miss Glory came running in from the yard and the women from the porch crowded around. Miss Glory was almost as broken up as her mistress. "You mean to say she broke our Virginia dishes? What we gone do?"

Mrs. Cullinan cried louder, "That clumsy nigger. Clumsy little black nigger."

Old speckled-face leaned down and asked, "Who did it, Viola? Was it Mary? Who did it?"

Everything was happening so fast I can't remember whether her action preceded her words, but I know that Mrs. Cullinan said, "Her name's Margaret, goddamn it, her name's Margaret." And she threw a wedge of the broken plate at me. It could have been the hysteria which put her aim off, but the flying crockery caught Miss Glory right over her ear and she started screaming.

I left the front door wide open so all the neighbors could hear.

Mrs. Cullinan was right about one thing. My name wasn't Mary.

The last inch of space was filled, yet people continued to wedge themselves along the walls of the Store. Uncle Willie had turned the radio up to its last notch so that youngsters on the porch wouldn't miss a word. Women sat on kitchen chairs, dining-room chairs, stools and upturned wooden boxes. Small children and babies perched on every lap available and men leaned on the shelves or on each other.

The apprehensive mood was shot through with shafts of gaiety, as a black sky is streaked with lightning.

"I ain't worried 'bout this fight. Joe's gonna whip that cracker like it's open season."

"He gone whip him till that white boy call him Momma."

At last the talking was finished and the string-along songs about razor blades were over and the fight began.

"A quick jab to the head." In the Store the crowd grunted. "A left to the head and a right and another left." One of the listeners cackled like a hen and was quieted.

"They're in a clench, Louis is trying to fight his way out."

Some bitter comedian on the porch said, "That white man don't mind hugging that niggah now, I betcha."

"The referee is moving in to break them up, but Louis finally pushed the contender away and it's an uppercut to the chin. The contender is hanging on, now he's backing away. Louis catches him with a short left to the jaw."

A tide of murmuring assent poured out the doors and into the yard.

"Another left and another left. Louis is saving that mighty right . . ." The mutter in the Store had grown into a baby roar and it was pierced by the clang of a bell and the announcer's "That's the bell for round three, ladies and gentlemen."

As I pushed my way into the Store I wondered if the announcer gave any thought to the fact that he was addressing as "ladies and gentlemen" all the Negroes around the world who sat sweating and praying, glued to their "master's voice."

There were only a few calls for R.C. Colas, Dr Peppers, and Hire's root beer. The real festivities would begin after the fight. Then even the old Christian ladies who taught their children and tried themselves to practice turning the other cheek would buy soft drinks, and if the Brown Bomber's victory was a particularly bloody one they would order peanut patties and Baby Ruths also.

Bailey and I lay the coins on top of the cash register. Uncle Willie didn't allow us to ring up sales during a fight. It was too noisy and might shake up the atmosphere. When the gong rang for the next round we pushed through the near-sacred quiet to the herd of children outside.

"He's got Louis against the ropes and now it's a left to the body and a right to the ribs. Another right to the body, it looks like it was low . . . Yes, ladies and gentlemen, the referee is signaling but the contender keeps raining the blows on Louis. It's another to the body, and it looks like Louis is going down."

My race groaned. It was our people falling. It was another lynching, yet another Black man hanging on a tree. One more woman ambushed and raped. A Black boy whipped and maimed. It was hounds on the trail of a man running through slimy swamps. It was a white woman slapping her maid for being forgetful.

The men in the Store stood away from the walls and at attention. Women greedily clutched the babes on their laps while on the porch the shufflings and smiles, flirtings and pinching of a few minutes before were gone. This might be the end of the world. If Joe lost we were back in slavery and beyond help. It would all be true, the accusations that we were lower types of human beings. Only a little higher than the apes. True that we were stupid and ugly and lazy and dirty and, unlucky and worst of all, that God Himself hated us and ordained us to be hewers of wood and drawers of water, forever and ever, world without end.

We didn't breathe. We didn't hope. We waited.

"He's off the ropes, ladies and gentlemen. He's moving towards the center of the ring." There was no time to be relieved. The worst might still happen.

"And now it looks like Joe is mad. He's caught Carnera with a left hook to the head and a right to the head. It's a left jab to the body and another left to the head. There's a left cross and a right to the head. The contender's right eye is bleeding and he can't seem to keep his block up. Louis is penetrating every block. The referee is moving in, but Louis sends a left to the body and it's the uppercut to the chin and the contender is dropping. He's on the canvas, ladies and gentlemen."

Babies slid to the floor as women stood up and men leaned toward the radio.

"Here's the referee. He's counting. One, two, three, four, five, six, seven . . . Is the contender trying to get up again?"

All the men in the store shouted, "NO."

"—eight, nine, ten." There were a few sounds from the audience, but they seemed to be holding themselves in against tremendous pressure.

"The fight is all over, ladies and gentlemen. Let's get the microphone over to the referee . . . Here he is. He's got the Brown Bomber's hand, he's holding it up . . . Here he is . . ."

Then the voice, husky and familiar, came to wash over us—"The winnah, and still heavyweight champeen of the world . . . Joe Louis."

Champion of the world. A Black boy. Some Black mother's son. He was the strongest man in the world. People drank Coca-Colas like ambrosia and ate candy bars like Christmas. Some of the men went behind the Store and poured white lightning in their soft-drink bottles, and a few of the bigger boys followed them. Those who were not chased away came back blowing their breath in front of themselves like proud smokers.

It would take an hour or more before the people would leave the Store and head for home. Those who lived too far had made arrangements to stay in town. It wouldn't do for a Black man and his family to be caught on a lonely country road on a night when Joe Louis had proved that we were the strongest people in the world.

Angela Davis, author and activist, was born in Birmingham, Alabama, in 1944. She taught at UCLA despite efforts to oust her for being Communist. Angela Davis was the vice-presidential candidate of the Communist party in 1980. Her writings include *Angela Davis: An Autobiography; Women, Race and Class;* and *Women, Culture, & Politics.*

15

ANGELA DAVIS

From Angela Davis:
An Autobiography

(1974)

LIFE IN JAIL was arranged and controlled from above in accordance with pragmatic principles of the worst order. Just enough activities were provided to distract the prisoners from any prolonged reflection upon their wretched condition. The point was to fill up the day with meaningless activities, empty diversions.

As a result, a whole network of institutions was there to absorb the energies of the prisoners. Commissary, needless to say, was an important aspect of survival in captivity. Three days out of the week women awaiting trial visited this small store to purchase the little things that made life slightly less intolerable. Mondays and Wednesdays, there was a three-dollar limit on what we could buy; on Fridays we could spend one dollar more. The coveted articles on sale were such things as cigarettes, cosmetics, primitive writing materials— pencils (but no pens) and lined pads, and stamps; knitting and crocheting paraphernalia; and foodstuffs such as cookies, candies, sugar, instant coffee and hot chocolate. Unless you were pregnant, the only available source of real milk was the commissary.

The centrality of commissary emerges from the deprivation which is such an important element of official control and authority. In jail, you learn that nothing can be taken for granted; the normal need-fulfillment process is shattered. You cannot assume that even your most basic needs will be satisfied. There are always strings attached. If you conduct yourself in such a way as to provoke an officer to place you in lockup, you lose your commissary privileges. If you happen not to have cigarettes, you must simply do without. The threat of withdrawing commissary privileges is a powerful negative stimulus.

Another method used to fill time was the church services each Sunday morning. Out of curiosity, I went down to the chapel on the first Sunday I spent in the main population. I was surprised at the number of prisoners in attendance. But soon I realized that many of the women had ulterior motives unrelated to any serious religious feelings. It was one of the two consistent meeting places where women from one part of the jail could see and converse with their friends from other floors.

The other weekly meeting place was the movies—that is, if the projector was not broken. Not even the curiosity that attracted me to the church services could make me attend one of these insipid Hollywood movies. Needless to say, it was a favorite trysting place of homosexual couples.

For those who enjoyed reading, the library would have been a saving grace had it not been for the fact that the vast majority of the books were mysteries, romances and just plain bad literature whose sole function was to create emotional paths of escape. During my days of solitary confinement, after Margaret had persuaded the warden that I should have access to reading material, I spent a few sessions alone in the library. Within a short time I had combed the entire place, turning up only a few books which held the slightest interest: A book on the Chinese Revolution by Edgar Snow, the autobiography of W. E. B. DuBois and a book on communism written by an astonishingly objective little-known author.

After my discovery of these books, my thoughts kept wandering back to their enigmatic presence. And suddenly it hit me: they had probably been read by Elizabeth Gurley Flynn, Claudia Jones or one of the other Communist leaders who had been persecuted under the Smith Act during the McCarthy era. I myself had been told that if

I received any books during my time there, I would have to donate them to the library—which was a pleasure, considering the state of that so-called place of learning. As I turned the pages of those books, I felt honored to be following in the tradition of some of this country's most outstanding heroines: Communist women leaders, especially the Black Communist Claudia Jones.

If you wanted books which were not in the library, they had to be mailed directly from the publisher. I decided to have as many books sent to me as possible, so as to provide, for succeeding prisoners, literature that was more interesting, more relevant, more serious than the trash on the shelves of the library. Apparently, the jailers saw through my scheme, especially when ten copies of George Jackson's *Soledad Brother* came in, for they harshly informed me that none of my books were to leave my hands. They would follow me to whichever jail I went.

The few remaining jail institutions were even more limited. There were short exercise periods on the roof of the building. This, I admit, was my favorite activity, and as long as the weather permitted, I looked forward with great pleasure to our volleyball games atop the jail. On the roof, in enclosed rooms, there were also arts and crafts, dancing, and games such as cards and Scrabble. With this, the range of activities behind the walls was practically complete. It was amazing, however, how much time could be consumed in these things, most of which contributed not in the least to the educational, cultural or social development of the prisoners. The main purpose of these pastimes was to encourage, in a subtle way, obedience and submissiveness.

Jails and prisons are designed to break human beings, to convert the population into specimens in a zoo—obedient to our keepers, but dangerous to each other. In response, imprisoned men and women will invent and continually invoke various and sundry defenses. Consequently, two layers of existence can be encountered within almost every jail or prison. The first layer consists of the routines and behavior prescribed by the governing penal hierarchy. The second layer is the prisoner culture itself: the rules and standards of behavior that come from and are defined by the captives in order to shield themselves from the open or covert terror designed to break their spirits.

In an elemental way, this culture is one of resistance, but a resistance of desperation. It is, therefore, incapable of striking a significant blow against the system. All its elements are based on an assumption that the prison system will continue to survive. Precisely for this reason, the system does not move to crush it. (In fact, it sometimes happens that there is an under-the-table encouragement of the prisoners' subculture.) I was continually astonished by the infinite details of the social regions which the women in the House of Detention considered their exclusive domain. This culture was contemptuously closed to the keepers. I sometimes wandered innocently through the doors and found myself thoroughly disoriented. A telling example happened on my second day in population. A sister asked me, "What did you think of my grandfather? He said he saw you this morning." I was sure I had misheard her question, but when she repeated it, I told her she must be mistaken, because I had no idea who her grandfather was. Besides, I hadn't had any visitors that day. But the joke was on me. I was in a foreign country and hadn't learned the language. I discovered from her that a woman prisoner who had come by my cell earlier in the day was the "grandfather" to whom she was referring. Because she didn't seem eager to answer any questions, I contained my curiosity until I found someone who could explain to me what the hell was going on.

A woman a few cells down gave me a fascinating description of a whole system through which the women could adopt their jail friends as relatives. I was bewildered and awed by the way in which the vast majority of the jail population had neatly organized itself into generations of families: mothers/wives, fathers/husbands, sons and daughters, even aunts, uncles, grandmothers and grandfathers. The family system served as a defense against the fact of being no more than a number. It humanized the environment and allowed an identification with others within a familiar framework.

In spite of its strong element of escapism and fantasy, the family system could solve certain immediate problems. Family duties and responsibilities were a way in which sharing was institutionalized. Parents were expected to provide for their children, particularly the young ones, if they could not afford "luxury items" from commissary.

Like filial relationships outside, some sons and daughters had, or developed, ulterior motives. Quite a few of them joined certain families because the material benefits were greater there.

What struck me most about this family system was the homosexuality at its core. But while there was certainly an overabundance of homosexual relationships within this improvised kinship structure, it was nevertheless not closed to "straight" women. There were straight daughters and husbandless, i.e., straight, mothers.

I recall with fondness a young woman of sixteen, with a very intense beauty, who told me plainly and simply one day that she was going to consider me her mother. Although I shared my commissary with her (and others as well) when she didn't have enough money in her account, she never once asked me for anything. She was quiet, serious and very curious about the Black Liberation movement. My obligations to her seemed to consist primarily of carrying on discussions with her about the movement. Housed with the "adolescents" in another corridor on my floor, she always managed with a calm firmness to persuade the officers to let her into my corridor.

Since the majority of the prisoners seemed to be at least casually involved in the family structure, there had to be a great number of lesbians throughout the jail. Homosexuality is bound to occur on a relatively large scale in any place of sexually segregated confinement. I knew this before I was arrested. I was not prepared, however, for the shock of seeing it so thoroughly entrenched in jail life. There were the masculine and feminine role-playing women; the former, the butches, were called "he." During the entire six weeks I spent on the seventh floor, I could not bring myself to refer to any woman with a masculine pronoun, although some of them, if they hadn't been wearing the mandatory dresses, would never have been taken for women.

Many of them—both the butches and the femmes—had obviously decided to take up homosexuality during their jail terms in order to make that time a little more exciting, in order to forget the squalor and degradation around them. When they returned to the streets they would rejoin their men and quickly forget their jail husbands and wives.

An important part of the family system was the marriages. Some of them were extremely elaborate—with invitations, a formal cere-mony, and some third person acting as the "minister." The "bride" would prepare for the occasion as if for a real wedding.

With all the marriages, the seeking of trysting places, the schem-ing which went on by one woman to catch another, the conflicts and jealousies—with all this—homosexuality emerged as one of the cen-ters around which life in the House of Detention revolved. Certainly, it was a way to counteract some of the pain of jail life; but objectively, it served to perpetuate all the bad things about the House of Deten-tion. "The Gay Life" was all-consuming; it prevented many of the women from developing their personal dissatisfaction with the condi-tions around them into a political dissatisfaction, because the homo-sexual fantasy life provided an easy and attractive channel for escape.

One of the corridors on the fourth floor, where the psychiatric bloc was located, was reserved for women with heavy heroin habits. When I caught glimpses of them during my trips to the elevator, I was struck by their physical deterioration. Their bodies were marred with leprous-like sores. These were the abscesses caused by dirty needles. Others had needle tracks all over their legs and arms and, because these veins had collapsed, they had begun to inject the drug into the veins in their necks.

The most tragic sight of all was the very young addicts, many of whom could have been no more than fourteen, despite the age they had given the police. Most of them had absolutely no intention of staying off the drug once they returned to the streets. To me, it was beyond comprehension that they could witness the most sordid effects of heroin while they were in jail and not be provoked to reconsider their own flirtations with the drug—flirtations that frequently became full-scale addiction.

Sometimes women with very heavy habits were brought in and left to kick alone in their cells. They would scream in agony all night long and not a single officer would help them. One evening an ema-ciated young woman was placed in the cell across from mine. By the time we were supposed to lock in for the night, she was doubled over, her whole face distorted in anguish. She needed medical help fast, but no doctor was forthcoming. Sisters in my corridor began to tell stories of women who had been in similar conditions and, left alone in their cells to kick, had died during the night. We decided that we would refuse to lock in unless she received medical attention immediately. Only after we took this stand did a doctor come to examine her and take her to the hospital.

There were many other occasions when we were forced to intervene in order to ensure medical help for one of our ill sisters. The most horrifying case of all was that of a woman on our corridor who began to complain one weekend about severe pains in her chest. On Monday morning at sick call, she saw one of the elderly white doctors, who told her that her problem was psychosomatic—the result of sitting around all day doing nothing. The doctor's advice to her was to "get a job." (If you were awaiting trial, as this sister was, you didn't even get the five or ten cents an hour that the sentenced prisoners received.)

The sister's pains grew worse over the next days, and finally we decided that we would have to issue a collective threat in order to force the jailers to get her the medical attention she needed. We refused to lock in until a competent doctor examined her. That day she didn't return to the cell; we later discovered that they had found tumors in her breasts and had rushed her to a hospital for tests and a possible mastectomy, if the tumors were found to be malignant.

The negligence toward the prisoners' health was also reflected in the daily routine of the jail. If pregnant women could not afford to buy a carton of milk on the three days we went to commissary, the only way they could supplement the three skimpy glasses of milk they received at mealtimes would be through our scheming. After I began to have problems with my eyes (a court injunction had allowed an outside doctor to examine me), a special diet, including milk, was prescribed for me. On numerous occasions, I smuggled my milk to a pregnant sister.

The first two weeks went by torturously slowly. I had the feeling that I had been in jail for a very long time. However, as soon as the jail routine began to inexorably impose itself, the days flowed imperceptibly into one another, and there seemed to be little difference between three days and three weeks.

At six o'clock each morning, the dim lights went on and the gates were unlocked for breakfast. Eight o'clock was the first lock-in of the day, and it lasted as long as it took to count prisoners and silverware to make sure a person or a spoon was not missing. Cleaning, doctor's rounds, mail time and commissary on Monday, Wednesday and Friday. Then lunch and silver count, followed by the 3 P.M. lock-in and count. Depending on the day of the week, afternoons were for roof exercises, the library or, once in a while, a movie. Dinner, silver count, visits, 8 P.M. lock-in and count and all lights out at nine.

I was fortunate to have Margaret's almost daily visits. John came as often as he could, and I received frequent visits from the lawyers working with Margaret on the suits around the jail conditions. They were Haywood Burns, the Director of the National Conference of Black Lawyers, and two members of the organization, Harold Washington and Napoleon Williams. We discussed the progress of the jail suit and the legal fight to prevent my extradition. John and Margaret were prepared to appeal the New York decision to return me to California all the way up through the appellate courts to the U.S. Supreme Court.

Those who had family or friends eagerly awaited the moment, after dinner, when the officer distributed the visit slips to the small crowd gathered behind the bars at the end of each corridor. Evening visits never lasted longer than twenty minutes; nevertheless they broke up the monotony of the days.

Once my lawyers had pressured the jail bureaucracy to let me have the regular evening visits—shortly after I was released from solitary—I had visitors practically every night. Whenever my sister Fania, Franklin and Kendra Alexander, Bettina Aptheker and other friends and comrades were in town, they came in to see me. Exactly twenty minutes after the beginning of a visit, I could expect to hear the loud announcement that time was up; it usually took just about that long to get into a serious conversation.

I always looked forward to Charlene Mitchell's visits. She was a close friend and member of the Political Committee (the leadership body) of the Communist Party. In the 1968 Presidential elections, she was our Party's candidate for President. Charlene had had a lot to do with my decision to join the Party, and over the last years my friendship with her had taught me a great deal about what it means to be a Communist. When the FBI pursuit began, without a hint of hesitation, she had placed herself in jeopardy in order to save my life. It was always frustrating to talk to her through the faulty telephones, and I was always painfully aware of the glass and wall which separated us. It would have meant so much to have simply been able to embrace her—or even to squeeze her hand.

One evening, I had an exciting visit with Henry Winston, the chairman of the Communist Party. Winnie, as our comrades affectionately called him, was born in Mississippi and, being both Black and a Communist, he had been an important target of the raging anti-communism of the forties and fifties. Close to ten years of prison, during which a brain tumor remained untreated, had left him almost totally blind. I had never seen him in person before his visit to the House of D. From the other side of the clouded pane, he greeted me with a very gentle voice, and I felt he could see me with far greater perceptiveness than someone with perfect eyesight. He wanted to know about my health, the jail food and how I was being treated by the officers. He assured me that the Party was totally committed to the fight for my freedom and that he, personally, would do whatever was necessary to ensure victory.

I thought about my family all the time. Not a day passed when I did not worry about how my mother, who was still in Birmingham, was standing up to the whole ordeal. Despite my desire to see her, I told Margaret not to encourage her to make the trip to New York. She is such a sensitive person that I was afraid that she might not be able to bear the strain of seeing her daughter behind bars in a filthy, mouse-ridden jail. I was very reluctant to subject her to the frustration of a twenty-minute visit through telephones, concrete and the tiny, dirty window.

Mother was determined to see me, regardless of the conditions. When she told us she was coming to New York, Margaret worked for days to arrange for a "special visit"—in the social worker's office.

Finally, when Margaret told the jailers that my mother had broken her foot and would find it difficult to stand during the visit, they agreed to the special visit.

Experience had taught me to be skeptical about everything. I didn't really believe that Mother would be allowed in the interior of the jail until the moment she actually arrived. She came walking in on crutches that morning, her foot still in a cast. When she put her arms around me, I could feel the tension throughout her body. For her benefit, I tried to appear especially cheerful. In an effort to conceal my thinness, I had worn the largest of the four jail-issued dresses. Even under normal circumstances, she gets upset when I lose a couple of pounds; during my fast I had lost fifteen pounds. Though she tried to appear in high spirits, I could tell from the deep furrows in her forehead that she was deeply disturbed. We talked about the family—Daddy, who was still at home; Benny, whose wife, Sylvia, and child I had not yet seen, and Fania, who was now a few months pregnant. Although she did not say it, I felt that my father was taking the whole thing rather hard, and I told her to tell him there was nothing to worry about—it was just a matter of time. Whenever I said something as optimistic as this, I am sure she must have been thinking about the gas chamber in California. So I kept telling her that there wasn't a doubt in my mind that I would soon be free—out there with her.

It was good that the New York Committee to Free Angela Davis had organized several events in which they invited Mother to participate. I knew it would hearten her to see that there were many people concerned about my fate. Several of the sympathetic officers attended a reception in her honor. This was particularly important, for she could see that even among those who were supposed to be my jailers there were women who wanted to join the mass movement against repression.

In addition to these officially sanctioned visits, I received numerous "street visits." Though illegal, this was a well-established custom among the prisoners. Friends would simply shout up to the jail windows from the street below. One evening after lock-in, several women from the Harlem Black Women to Free Angela Davis gathered on Greenwich Avenue to inform me about the activities they had planned on my behalf. I saw a policeman walk over to one of them and obviously issue a warning; when she continued to call up to me, he grabbed her and dragged her away.

Once I felt settled in the main population, my thoughts naturally turned toward the possibility of collective political activity in jail. Many people are unaware of the fact that jail and prison are two entirely different institutions. People in prison have already been convicted. Jails are primarily for pretrial confinement, holding places until prisoners are either convicted or found innocent. More than half of the jail population have never been convicted of anything, yet they languish in these cells. Because the bail system is inherently biased in the favor of the relatively well-off, jails are disproportionately inhabited by the poor, who cannot afford the fee. The O.R. program—which allows one to be released without posting bond, on one's own recognizance—is heavily tainted with racism. At least ninety-five percent of the women in the House of D. were either Black or Puerto Rican.

The biggest problem jail prisoners face is how to get out on bail. The political issue, therefore, is how accused men and women can benefit equally from the so-called presumption of innocence by being free until proven guilty. I assumed that this was the issue around which we could most effectively organize sisters in the House of D.—and, in fact, this is what we later did.

Originally the jailers had insisted that I had been placed in solitary confinement for my own protection—the women on the corridor would be hostile toward me, they said, because of my Communist politics. It was all a lie. The women were hospitable from the first moment, and they were loving and protective. Nothing illustrated this more clearly than the demonstration staged by the sixth-floor women in front of my solitary cell and the hunger strike which began to spread throughout the jail in solidarity with my action. Throughout my stay I received numerous written messages of support from the sisters. (Any written communication between prisoners is illegal; these notes are called "kites" because of the shape they are folded in for easy concealment.)

On the seventh floor, only a few days had gone by when the sisters wanted to talk about the movement—and this was on their own initiative, without the least prodding from me. We talked about racism and how it is not just the attitude that Black people are inferior. Racism, in the first place, is a weapon used by the wealthy to increase the profits they bring in—by paying Black workers less for their work. We talked about the way racism confuses white workers, who often forget that they are being exploited by a boss and instead vent their frustrations on people of color. On the corridor and in the recreation room, we had numerous discussions on the meaning of communism; the sisters were especially interested in hearing about my experiences in Cuba in 1969—a trip which had proved to me what socialism can do to eradicate racism.

One evening, after lock-up, a loud question broke the silence. It came from a sister who was reading a book I had lent her.

"Angela, what does 'imperialism' mean?"

I called out, "The ruling class of one country conquers the people of another in order to rob them of their land, their resources and to exploit their labor."

Another voice shouted, "You mean treating people in other countries the way Black people are treated here?"

This prompted an intense discussion that bounced through the cells, from my corridor to the one across the hall and back again.

Although I had ten copies of *Soledad Brother,* George's letters from prison, in my box in the library, not a single one was allowed on the corridor. Some of the friendly officers, however, smuggled a number of copies in from the outside. These became the most valuable pieces of contraband in the jail. They were always in demand and were widely read. When I wrote George of the enthusiastic reception of his book among the sisters there, it gave him pleasure to know that they were learning to relate to the movement through studying his individual political evolution. But there was one question that disturbed him: how were the sisters responding to the attitude toward Black women manifested in some of his early letters? In the past he had seen Black women as often acting as a deterrent to the involvement of Black men in the struggle. He had since discovered that this generalization was wrong, and was deeply concerned that the other women in the jail be informed of this.

Needless to say, there were reprisals for our activities. One sister was especially hard hit. Harriet had been in the House of D. many times before and knew her way through the crevices of this jail far better than many of the officers. I had first met her during my stint in solitary. Her job in the laundry room allowed her to travel throughout the jail, and she was the only prisoner permitted to enter my cell. When she came, she always brought something with her—when I told her my pencil would not stay sharp, she brought me a contraband ballpoint pen.

Harriet had known Joan Bird and Afeni Shakur of the New York Panther 21 while they were in the House of D. She was intensely interested in becoming a part of the movement for the liberation of her people. Later, when I was moved to the seventh floor, she came each day on her laundry missions and brought "kites" and news from the other floors.

As the weeks passed, the jailers began to grow wary of the solidarity welding us all together, and security became visibly tighter. Harriet was ordered to keep away from my cell and from the other women in that corridor. They assigned another woman to bring the laundry to the floor.

Until this moment, Harriet had had relatively decent relationships with the officers, even with the higher-ups. She had one of the most enviable jobs, for it meant she could go anywhere in the eleven-floor jail without explicit permission. After she was prohibited from being on our floor, she proudly threw this "privilege" right back into the jailers' faces. She quit her job and refused to talk, except with hostility, to the officers who were responsible for the order. Many did not understand why Harriet took such a drastic way out—and, considering the structures of imprisonment, this was unequivocally drastic. She got the word to me that this incident involved fundamental and principled issues, on which she would never accept a compromise.

A real togetherness was developing. I was anxious to strengthen this sense of community, and I knew it needed more than books and discussions to thrive. In order to keep it alive, I invited the sisters to join me in exercising in the corridors. Exercising was an indispensable requirement for my own survival in jail. Often I could not fall asleep unless I exercised to the point of exhaustion.

After a few days of doing calisthenics together, we added some simple karate movements. One of the women who also knew a little karate helped out with the instruction. It was not long before rumors were flying through official jail circles that I was teaching karate to the women in preparation for a confrontation with the jailers. They ordered it stopped, but we found a way to do it anyhow. Once the calisthenic phase of the exercises was over, a woman kept watch at the gate while we punched and kicked our way down the length of the corridor.

As my stay in the House of Detention was drawing to a close, a number of women's groups in New York began to organize a bail fund for the women inside the House of Detention. There were women who spent months in jail simply because they didn't have fifty dollars to make their bail. As this work was being accomplished outside, there was organizing going on within. The problem was to prevent the bail fund from becoming just another service organization to provide bail for women inside, much the same way as lawyers are provided by Legal Aid. We came up with an ideal solution: the women who would receive funds from the organization outside were to be elected collectively by the women in each corridor. When a woman was elected to be a beneficiary, she would not only have her bail paid, but would have responsibilities to the bail fund as well. Once out on the streets, she would have to work with the fund, helping to raise money; making whatever political contributions she could to the development of the organization.

Audre Lorde, poet and author, was born in New York City in 1934. She has written several highly acclaimed books of poetry and essays, including *Zami: A New Spelling of My Name*, *Sister Outsider*, and *A Burst of Light*. Currently, she is the Thomas Hunter Professor of English at Hunter College, City University of New York.

16

AUDRE LORDE

From Zami: A New Spelling of My Name

(1982)

WHEN I WAS five years old and still legally blind, I started school in a sight-conservation class in the local public school on 135th Street and Lenox Avenue. On the corner was a blue wooden booth where white women gave away free milk to Black mothers with children. I used to long for some Hearst Free Milk Fund milk, in those cute little bottles with their red and white tops, but my mother never allowed me to have any, because she said it was charity, which was bad and demeaning, and besides the milk was warm and might make me sick.

The school was right across the avenue from the Catholic school where my two older sisters went, and this public school had been used as a threat against them for as long as I could remember. If they didn't behave and get good marks in schoolwork and deportment, they could be "transferred." A "transfer" carried the same dire implications as "deportation" came to imply decades later.

Of course everybody knew that public school kids did nothing but "fight," and you could get "beaten up" every day after school, instead of being marched out of the schoolhouse door in two neat rows like little robots, silent but safe and unattacked, to the corner where the mothers waited.

But the Catholic school had no kindergarten, and certainly not one for blind children.

Despite my nearsightedness, or maybe because of it, I learned to read at the same time I learned to talk, which was only about a year or so before I started school. Perhaps *learn* isn't the right word to use for my beginning to talk, because to this day I don't know if I didn't talk earlier because I didn't know how, or if I didn't talk because I had nothing to say that I would be allowed to say without punishment. Self-preservation starts very early in West Indian families.

I learned how to read from Mrs. Augusta Baker, the children's librarian at the old 135th Street branch library, which has just recently been torn down to make way for a new library building to house the Schomburg Collection on African-American History and Culture. If that was the only good deed that lady ever did in her life, may she rest in peace. Because that deed saved my life, if not sooner, then later, when sometimes the only thing I had to hold on to was knowing I could read, and that that could get me through.

My mother was pinching my ear off one bright afternoon, while I lay spreadeagled on the floor of the Children's Room like a furious little brown toad, screaming bloody murder and embarrassing my mother to death. I know it must have been spring or early fall, because without the protection of a heavy coat, I can still feel the stinging soreness in the flesh of my upper arm. There, where my mother's sharp fingers had already tried to pinch me into silence. To escape those inexorable fingers I had hurled myself to the floor, roaring with pain as I could see them advancing toward my ears again. We were waiting to pick up my two older sisters from story hour, held upstairs on another floor of the dry-smelling quiet library. My shrieks pierced the reverential stillness.

Suddenly, I looked up, and there was a library lady standing over me. My mother's hands had dropped to her sides. From the floor where I was lying, Mrs. Baker seemed like yet another mile-high woman about to do me in. She had immense, light, hooded eyes and a very quiet voice that said, not damnation for my noise, but "Would you like to hear a story, little girl?"

Part of my fury was because I had not been allowed to go to that secret feast called story hour since I was too young, and now here was this strange lady offering me my own story.

I didn't dare to look at my mother, half-afraid she might say no, I was too bad for stories. Still bewildered by this sudden change of events, I climbed up upon the stool which Mrs. Baker pulled over for me, and gave her my full attention. This was a new experience for me and I was insatiably curious.

Mrs. Baker read me *Madeline,* and *Horton Hatches the Egg,* both of which rhymed and had huge lovely pictures which I could see from behind my newly acquired eyeglasses, fastened around the back of my rambunctious head by a black elastic band running from earpiece to earpiece. She also read me another storybook about a bear named Herbert who ate up an entire family, one by one, starting with the parents. By the time she had finished that one, I was sold on reading for the rest of my life.

I took the books from Mrs. Baker's hands after she was finished reading, and traced the large black letters with my fingers, while I peered again at the beautiful bright colors of the pictures. Right then I decided I was going to find out how to do that myself. I pointed to the black marks which I could now distinguish as separate letters, different from my sisters' more grown-up books, whose smaller print made the pages only one grey blur for me. I said, quite loudly, for whoever was listening to hear, "I want to read."

My mother's surprised relief outweighed whatever annoyance she was still feeling at what she called my whelpish carryings-on. From the background where she had been hovering while Mrs. Baker read, my mother moved forward quickly, mollified and impressed. I had spoken. She scooped me up from the low stool, and to my surprise, kissed me, right in front of everybody in the library, including Mrs. Baker.

This was an unprecedented and unusual display of affection in public, the cause of which I did not comprehend. But it was a warm and happy feeling. For once, obviously, I had done something right.

My mother set me back upon the stool and turned to Mrs. Baker, smiling.

"Will wonders never cease to perform!" Her excitement startled me back into cautious silence.

Not only had I been sitting still for longer than my mother would have thought possible, and sitting quietly. I had also spoken rather than screamed, something that my mother, after four years and a lot of worry, had despaired that I would ever do. Even one intelligible word was a very rare event for me. And although the doctors at the clinic had clipped the little membrane under my tongue so I was no longer tongue-tied, and had assured my mother that I was not retarded, she still had her terrors and her doubts. She was genuinely happy for any possible alternative to what she was afraid might be a dumb child. The ear-pinching was forgotten. My mother accepted the alphabet and picture books Mrs. Baker gave her for me, and I was on my way.

I sat at the kitchen table with my mother, tracing letters and calling their names. Soon she taught me how to say the alphabet forwards and backwards as it was done in Grenada. Although she had never gone beyond the seventh grade, she had been put in charge of teaching the first grade children their letters during her last year at Mr. Taylor's School in Grenville. She told me stories about his strictness as she taught me how to print my name.

I did not like the tail of the Y hanging down below the line in Audrey, and would always forget to put it on, which used to disturb my mother greatly. I used to love the evenness of AUDRELORDE at four years of age, but I remembered to put on the Y because it pleased my mother, and because, as she always insisted to me, that was the way it had to be because that was the way it was. No deviation was allowed from her interpretations of correct.

So by the time I arrived at the sight-conservation kindergarten, braided, scrubbed, and bespectacled, I was able to read large-print books and write my name with a regular pencil. Then came my first rude awakening about school. Ability had nothing to do with expectation.

There were only seven or eight of us little Black children in a big classroom, all with various serious deficiencies of sight. Some of us were cross-eyed, some of us were nearsighted, and one little girl had a patch over one of her eyes.

We were given special short wide notebooks to write in, with very widely spaced lines on yellow paper. They looked like my sister's music notebooks. We were also given thick black crayons to write with. Now you don't grow up fat, Black, nearly blind, and ambidextrous in a West Indian household, particularly my parents' household, and survive without being or becoming fairly rigid fairly fast. And having been roundly spanked on several occasions for having made that mistake at home, I knew quite well that crayons were not what you wrote with, and music books were definitely not what you wrote in.

I raised my hand. When the teacher asked me what I wanted, I asked for some regular paper to write on and a pencil. That was my undoing. "We don't have any pencils here," I was told.

Our first task was to copy down the first letter of our names in those notebooks with our black crayons. Our teacher went around the room and wrote the required letter into each one of our notebooks. When she came around to me, she printed a large A in the upper left corner of the first page of my notebook, and handed me the crayon.

"I can't," I said, knowing full well that what you do with black crayons is scribble on the wall and get your backass beaten, or color around the edges of pictures, but not write. To write, you needed a pencil. "I can't!" I said, terrified, and started to cry.

"Imagine that, a big girl like you. Such a shame, I'll have to tell your mother that you won't even try. And such a big girl like you!"

And it was true. Although young, I was the biggest child by far in the whole class, a fact that had not escaped the attention of the little boy who sat behind me, and who was already whispering "fatty, fatty!" whenever the teacher's back was turned.

"Now just try, dear. I'm sure you can try to print your A. Mother will be so pleased to see that at least you tried." She patted my stiff braids and turned to the next desk.

Well, of course, she had said the magic words, because I would have walked over rice on my knees to please Mother. I took her nasty old soft smudgy crayon and pretended that it was a nice neat pencil with a fine point, elegantly sharpened that morning outside the bathroom door by my father, with the little penknife that he always carried around in his bathrobe pocket.

I bent my head down close to the desk that smelled like old spittle and rubber erasers, and on that ridiculous yellow paper with those laughably wide spaces I printed my best AUDRE. I had never been too good at keeping between straight lines no matter what their width, so it slanted down across the page something like this: A

                                                          U

                                                              D

                                                                  R

                                                                      E

The notebooks were short and there was no more room for anything else on that page. So I turned the page over, and wrote again, earnestly and laboriously, biting my lip, L

                          O

                              R

                                  D

                                      E

half-showing off, half-eager to please.

By this time, Miss Teacher had returned to the front of the room.

"Now when you're finished drawing your letter, children," she said, "Just raise your hand high." And her voice smiled a big smile. It is surprising to me that I can still hear her voice but I can't see her face, and I don't know whether she was Black or white. I can remember the way she smelled, but not the color of her hand upon my desk.

Well, when I heard that, my hand flew up in the air, wagging frantically. There was one thing my sisters had warned me about school in great detail: you must never talk in school unless you raised your hand. So I raised my hand, anxious to be recognized. I could imagine what teacher would say to my mother when she came to fetch me home at noon. My mother would know that her warning to me to "be good" had in truth been heeded.

Miss Teacher came down the aisle and stood beside my desk,

looking down at my book. All of a sudden the air around her hand beside my notebook grew very still and frightening.

"Well I never!" Her voice was sharp. "I thought I told you to draw this letter? You don't even want to try and do as you are told. Now I want you to turn that page over and draw your letter like everyone . . ." and turning to the next page, she saw my second name sprawled down across the page.

There was a moment of icy silence, and I knew I had done something terribly wrong. But this time, I had no idea what it could be that would get her so angry, certainly not being proud of writing my name.

She broke the silence with a wicked edge to her voice. "I see," she said. "I see we have a young lady who does not want to do as she is told. We will have to tell her mother about that." And the rest of the class snickered, as the teacher tore the page out of my notebook.

"Now I am going to give you one more chance," she said, as she printed another fierce A at the head of the new page. "Now you copy that letter exactly the way it is, and the rest of the class will have to wait for you." She placed the crayon squarely back into my fingers.

By this time I had no idea at all what this lady wanted from me, and so I cried and cried for the rest of the morning until my mother came to fetch me home at noon. I cried on the street while we stopped to pick up my sisters, and for most of the way home, until my mother threatened to box my ears for me if I didn't stop embarrassing her on the street.

That afternoon, after Phyllis and Helen were back in school, and I was helping her dust, I told my mother how they had given me crayons to write with and how the teacher didn't want me to write my name. When my father came home that evening, the two of them went into counsel. It was decided that my mother would speak to the teacher the next morning when she brought me to school, in order to find out what I had done wrong. This decision was passed on to me, ominously, because of course I must have done something wrong to have made Miss Teacher so angry with me.

The next morning at school, the teacher told my mother that she did not think that I was ready yet for kindergarten, because I couldn't follow directions, and I wouldn't do as I was told.

My mother knew very well I could follow directions, because she herself had spent a good deal of effort and arm-power making it very painful for me whenever I did not follow directions. And she also believed that a large part of the function of school was to make me learn how to do what I was told to do. In her private opinion, if this school could not do that, then it was not much of a school and she was going to find a school that could. In other words, my mother had made up her mind that school was where I belonged.

That same morning, she took me off across the street to the Catholic school, where she persuaded the nuns to put me into the first grade, since I could read already, and write my name on regular paper with a real pencil. If I sat in the first row I could see the blackboard. My mother also told the nuns that unlike my two sisters, who were models of deportment, I was very unruly, and that they should spank me whenever I needed it. Mother Josepha, the principal, agreed, and I started school.

My first grade teacher was named Sister Mary of Perpetual Help, and she was a disciplinarian of the first order, right after my mother's own heart. A week after I started school she sent a note home to my mother asking her not to dress me in so many layers of clothing because then I couldn't feel the strap on my behind when I was punished.

Sister Mary of Perpetual Help ran the first grade with an iron hand in the shape of a cross. She couldn't have been more than eighteen. She was big, and blond, I think, since we never got to see the nuns' hair in those days. But her eyebrows were blonde, and she was supposed to be totally dedicated, like all the other Sisters of the Blessed Sacrament, to caring for the Colored and Indian children of America. Caring for was not always caring about. And it always felt like Sister MPH hated either teaching or little children.

She had divided up the class into two groups, the Fairies and the Brownies. In this day of heightened sensitivity to racism and color usage, I don't have to tell you which were the good students and which were the baddies. I always wound up in the Brownies, because either I talked too much, or I broke my glasses, or I perpetrated some other awful infraction of the endless rules of good behavior.

But for two glorious times that year, I made it into the Fairies for brief periods of time. One was put into the Brownies if one misbehaved, or couldn't learn to read. I had learned to read already, but I couldn't tell my numbers. Whenever Sister MPH would call a few of us up to the front of the room for our reading lesson, she would say, "All right, children, now turn to page six in your readers," or, "Turn to page nineteen, please, and begin at the top of the page."

Well, I didn't know what page to turn to, and I was ashamed of not being able to read my numbers, so when my turn came to read I couldn't, because I didn't have the right place. After the prompting of a few words, she would go on to the next reader, and soon I wound up in the Brownies.

This was around the second month of school, in October. My new seatmate was Alvin, and he was the worst boy in the whole class. His clothes were dirty and he smelled unwashed, and rumor had it he had once called Sister MPH a bad name, but that couldn't have been possible because he would have been suspended permanently from school.

Alvin used to browbeat me into lending him my pencil to draw endless pictures of airplanes dropping huge penile bombs. He would always promise to give me the pictures when he was finished. But of course, whenever he was finished, he would decide that the picture was too good for a girl, so he would have to keep it, and make me another. Yet I never stopped hoping for one of them, because he drew airplanes very well.

He also would scratch his head and shake out the dandruff onto our joint spelling book or reader, and then tell me the flakes of dandruff were dead lice. I believed him in this, also, and was constantly terrified of catching cooties. But Alvin and I worked out our own system together for reading. He couldn't read, but he knew all his numbers, and I could read words, but I couldn't find the right page.

The Brownies were never called up to the front of the room; we had to read in anonymity from our double seats, where we scrunched over at the edges, ordinarily, to leave room in the middle for our two guardian angels to sit. But whenever we had to share a book our guardian angels had to jump around us and sit on the outside edge of our seats. Therefore, Alvin would show me the right pages to turn to when Sister called them out, and I would whisper the right words to him whenever it came his turn to read. Inside of a week after we devised this scheme of things, we had gotten out of the Brownies together. Since we shared a reader, we always went up together to read with the Fairies, so we had a really good thing going there for a while.

But Alvin began to get sick around Thanksgiving, and was absent a lot, and he didn't come back to school at all after Christmas. I used to miss his dive-bomber pictures, but most of all I missed his page numbers. After a few times of being called up by myself and not being able to read, I landed back in the Brownies again.

Years later I found out that Alvin had died of tuberculosis over Christmas, and that was why we all had been X-rayed in the auditorium after Mass on the first day back to school from Christmas vacation.

I spent a few more weeks in the Brownies with my mouth almost shut during reading lesson, unless the day's story fell on page eight, or ten, or twenty, which were the three numbers I knew.

Then, over one weekend, we had our first writing assignment. We were to look in our parents' newspaper and cut out words we knew the meaning of, and make them into simple sentences. We could only use one "the." It felt like an easy task, since I was already reading the comics by this time.

On Sunday morning after church, when I usually did my homework, I noticed an ad for White Rose Salada Tea on the back of the *New York Times Magazine* which my father was reading at the time. It had the most gorgeous white rose on a red background, and I decided I must have that rose for my picture—our sentences were to be illustrated. I searched through the paper until I found an "I," and then a "like," which I dutifully clipped out along with my rose, and the words "White," "Rose," "Salada," and "Tea." I knew the brand-name well because it was my mother's favorite tea.

On Monday morning, we all stood our sentence papers up on the chalk-channels, leaning them against the blackboards. And there among the twenty odd "The boy ran," "it was cold," was "I like White Rose Salada Tea" and my beautiful white rose on a red background.

That was too much coming from a Brownie. Sister Mary of PH frowned.

"This was to be our own work, children," she said. "Who helped you with your sentence, Audre?" I told her I had done it alone.

"Our guardian angels weep when we don't tell the truth, Audre. I want a note from your mother tomorrow telling me that you are sorry for lying to the baby Jesus."

I told the story at home, and the next day I brought a note from my father saying that the sentence had indeed been my own work. Triumphantly, I gathered up my books and moved back over to the Fairies.

The thing that I remember best about being in the first grade was how uncomfortable it was, always having to leave room for my guardian angel on those tiny seats, and moving back and forth across the room from Brownies to Fairies and back again.

This time I stayed in the Fairies for a long time, because I finally started to recognize my numbers. I stayed there until the day I broke my glasses. I had taken them off to clean them in the bathroom and they slipped out of my hand. I was never to do that, and so I was in disgrace. My eyeglasses came from the eye clinic of the medical center, and it took three days to get a new pair made. We could not afford to buy more than one pair at a time, nor did it occur to my parents that such an extravagance might be necessary. I was almost sightless without them, but my punishment for having broken them was that I had to go to school anyway, even though I could see nothing. My sisters delivered me to my classroom with a note from my mother saying I had broken my glasses despite the fact they were tied to me by the strip of elastic.

I was never supposed to take my glasses off except just before getting into bed, but I was endlessly curious about these magical circles of glass that were rapidly becoming a part of me, transforming my universe, and remaining movable. I was always trying to examine them with my naked, nearsighted eyes, usually dropping them in the process.

Since I could not see at all to do any work from the blackboard, Sister Mary of PH made me sit in the back of the room on the window seat with a dunce cap on. She had the rest of the class offer up a prayer for my poor mother who had such a naughty girl who broke her glasses and caused her parents such needless extra expense to replace them. She also had them offer up a special prayer for me to stop being such a wicked-hearted child.

I amused myself by counting the rainbows of color that danced like a halo around the lamp on Sister Mary of PH's desk, watching the starburst patterns of light that the incandescent light bulb became without my glasses. But I missed them, and not being able to see. I never once gave a thought to the days when I believed that bulbs were starburst patterns of color, because that was what all light looked like to me.

It must have been close to summer by this time. As I sat with the dunce cap on, I can remember the sun pouring through the classroom window hot upon my back, as the rest of the class dutifully intoned their Hail Marys for my soul, and I played secret games with the distorted rainbows of light, until Sister noticed and made me stop blinking my eyes so fast.

How I Became a Poet

"Wherever the bird with no feet flew she found trees with no limbs."

When the strongest words for what I have to offer come out of me sounding like words I remember from my mother's mouth, then I either have to reassess the meaning of everything I have to say now, or re-examine the worth of her old words.

My mother had a special and secret relationship with words, taken for granted as language because it was always there. I did not speak until I was four. When I was three, the dazzling world of strange lights and fascinating shapes which I inhabited resolved itself in mundane definitions, and I learned another nature of things as seen through eyeglasses. This perception of things was less colorful and confusing but much more comfortable than the one native to my nearsighted and unevenly focused eyes.

I remember trundling along Lenox Avenue with my mother, on our way to school to pick up Phyllis and Helen for lunch. It was late spring because my legs felt light and real, unencumbered by bulky snowpants. I dawdled along the fence around the public playground, inside of which grew one stunted plane tree. Enthralled, I stared up at the sudden revelation of each single and particular leaf of green, precisely shaped and laced about with unmixed light. Before my glasses, I had known trees as tall brown pillars ending in fat puffy swirls of paling greens, much like the pictures of them I perused in my sisters' storybooks from which I learned so much of my visual world.

But out of my mother's mouth a world of comment came cascading when she felt at ease or in her element, full of picaresque constructions and surreal scenes.

We were never dressed too lightly, but rather "in next kin to nothing." *Neck skin to nothing?* Impassable and impossible distances were measured by the distance "from Hog to Kick 'em Jenny." *Hog? Kick 'em Jenny?* Who knew until I was sane and grown a poet with a mouthful of stars, that these were two little reefs in the Grenadines, between Grenada and Carriacou.

The euphemisms of body were equally puzzling, if no less colorful. A mild reprimand was accompanied not by a slap on the behind, but a "smack on the backass," or on the "bamsy." You sat on your "bam-bam," but anything between your hip-bones and upper thighs was consigned to the "lower-region," a word I always imagined to have french origins, as in "Don't forget to wash your *l'oregión* before you go to bed." For more clinical and precise descriptions, there was always "between your legs"—whispered.

The sensual content of life was masked and cryptic, but attended in well-coded phrases. Somehow all the cousins knew that Uncle Cyril couldn't lift heavy things because of his "bam-bam-coo," and the lowered voice in which this hernia was spoken of warned us that it had something to do with "down there." And on the infrequent but magical occasions when mother performed her delicious laying on of hands for a crick in the neck or a pulled muscle, she didn't massage your backbone, she "raised your zandalee."

I never caught cold, but "got co-hum, co-hum," and then everything turned "cro-bo-so," topsy-turvy, or at least, a bit askew.

I am a reflection of my mother's secret poetry as well as of her hidden angers.

Sitting between my mother's spread legs, her strong knees gripping my shoulders tightly like some well-attended drum, my head in her lap, while she brushed and combed and oiled and braided. I feel my mother's strong, rough hands all up in my unruly hair, while I'm squirming around on a low stool or on a folded towel on the floor, my rebellious shoulders hunched and jerking against the inexorable sharp-toothed comb. After each springy portion is combed and braided, she pats it tenderly and proceeds to the next.

I hear the interjection of *sotto voce* admonitions that punctuated whatever discussion she and my father were having.

"Hold your back up, now! Deenie, keep still! Put your head so!" Scratch, scratch. "When last you wash your hair? Look the dandruff!" Scratch, scratch, the comb's truth setting my own teeth on edge. Yet, these were some of the moments I missed most sorely when our real wars began.

I remember the warm mother smell caught between her legs, and the intimacy of our physical touching nestled inside of the anxiety/ pain like a nutmeg nestled inside its covering of mace.

The radio, the scratching comb, the smell of petroleum jelly, the grip of her knees and my stinging scalp all fall into—*the rhythms of a litany, the rituals of Black women combing their daughters' hair.*

Saturday morning. The one morning of the week my mother does not leap from bed to prepare me and my sisters for school or church. I wake in the cot in their bedroom, knowing only it is one of those lucky days when she is still in bed, and alone. My father is in the kitchen. The sound of pots and the slightly off-smell of frying bacon mixes with the smell of percolating Bokar coffee.

The click of her wedding ring against the wooden headboard. She is awake. I get up and go over and crawl into my mother's bed. Her smile. Her glycerine-flannel smell. The warmth. She reclines upon her back and side, one arm extended, the other flung across her forehead. A hot-water bottle wrapped in body-temperature flannel, which she used to quiet her gall-bladder pains during the night. Her large soft breasts beneath the buttoned flannel of her nightgown. Below, the rounded swell of her stomach, silent and inviting touch.

I crawl against her, playing with the enflanneled, warm, rubber bag, pummeling it, tossing it, sliding it down the roundness of her stomach to the warm sheet between the bend of her elbow and the curve of her waist below her breasts, flopping sideward inside the printed cloth. Under the covers, the morning smells soft and sunny and full of promise.

I frolic with the liquid-filled water bottle, patting and rubbing its firm giving softness. I shake it slowly, rocking it back and forth, lost in sudden tenderness, at the same time gently rubbing against my mother's quiet body. Warm milky smells of morning surround us.

Feeling the smooth deep firmness of her breasts against my shoulders, my pajama'd back, sometimes, more daringly, against my ears and the sides of my cheeks. Tossing, tumbling, the soft gurgle of the water within its rubber casing. Sometimes the thin sound of her ring against the bedstead as she moves her hand up over my head. Her arm comes down across me, holding me to her for a moment, then quiets my frisking.

"All right, now."

I nuzzle against her sweetness, pretending not to hear.

"All right, now, I said; stop it. It's time to get up from this bed. Look lively, and mind you spill that water."

Before I can say anything she is gone in a great deliberate heave. The purposeful whip of her chenille robe over her warm flannel gown and the bed already growing cold beside me.

"Wherever the bird with no feet flew she found trees with no limbs."

Roger Wilkins was born in Kansas City, Missouri, in 1932. Wilkins won a Pulitzer Prize for his Watergate editorials while working for the *Washington Post.* He is the author of *A Man's Life: An Autobiography* and *Quiet Riots: Race and Poverty in the United States,* and is the Robinson Distinguished Professor at George Mason University.

17

ROGER WILKINS

From A Man's Life

(1982)

THERE HAD NEVER been any question about it—I would go to college. Even when I was a child in Kansas City, it was assumed that I would go—as my parents and their sisters and brother had gone—to the University of Minnesota. My parents talked about it because of segregation. In the thirties Negroes were barred from the University of Missouri, and Negro parents of even very young children did not then foresee a time when things would be different. But under decisions of the Supreme Court—then still contorting itself to carry out the separate-but-equal façade mandated by the late-nineteenth-century decision in *Plessy* v. *Ferguson*—states that barred Negroes from state-supported schools were required to provide them equal educational opportunities. So, Negro parents could send their children to a comparable public university where there was no segregation and pay only the expenses they would have paid if the child could have gone to the local state or university. The student's state government was required to pay the difference.

From the time I was about four, I heard my parents talk about how I would go to Minnesota under such a plan.

So, when the time to go to college actually came, I was simply fulfilling a lifelong expectation and doing just what all my white friends were doing. Only, instead of Minnesota, I decided on the University of Michigan because it had the best football team in the nation. No reason to look any further!

I didn't think of Michigan as a white school, explicitly. Of course it was white—I thought all good things in this society were—but I knew it was also integrated. Yet, in those days you knew that even the most liberal institutions would do foolish and insulting things to you if you were a Negro. Michigan was no different. Though the university did not ask for racial designations on application forms—state law forbade it—in its housing application, Michigan required a photograph of each applicant. Sure enough, when I showed up at Hayden House in the East Quadrangle, both my roommates were Negroes just like me. Except they weren't just like me. They were both older than I was, and we had very little in common. The information elicited by the application form about reading habits and "other interests" had clearly been subsumed by the commonality of the color of our skins. There were, of course, no Negro floors, suites or wings of dormitories, just Negro rooms spotted at random, but with a delicate eye for balance. Throughout the dormitory, that was the pattern of integration at Michigan in 1949, and we all fell into it and held pretty much to it throughout our college years.

Beyond our room, I was beginning to perceive an even more rigid social structure. In 1949 white people and black people didn't often mix at any level of society, and the society was mirrored in the patterns of student life sanctioned and promoted by the university. There were about 20,000 students on that postwar Michigan campus and about 150 or so of us were Negroes. We lived together in the rooms assigned to us in the dormitories or we lived in rooming houses in the Negro sections of Ann Arbor that were kept by Negro couples to supplement their basic incomes. There were no integrated fraternities or sororities, and there were no apartments near the campus. There was no overt racial friction, but there was no interracial socializing either.

But I was lucky. Hayden House was one of the four houses in the new section of the East Quad. About two hundred boys lived in each one of the houses. And in that group of eight hundred boys, in addition to my roommates, there were about eight other Negroes. Six of them were sophomores and had, during their freshman year, formed a warm protective circle, which they found easy to expand to accept three new freshmen, excluding my roommates.

I wanted to be a journalist, a strange pursuit for us then, but that's what my father and uncle had been, and writing and reading were what I liked. But my choice of profession was no stranger than that of another Negro student, who was going to be a forester, and it was a lot less strange than that of the stiff loner from the West Quad who was going to be an actor. We all knew that he was crazy, partly because he never mixed with anybody and partly because everybody knew there were no decent acting jobs for Negroes anyway. Even after we had seen him in a few campus plays, we still thought he was crazy. His name was James Earl Jones.

Our group was a large enough critical mass that none of us was ever lonely. It was enough to tempt a fainthearted scholar to plunge wholeheartedly into the wonders of idle male companionship. For me, it was wonderful. It was the first time in five years that I had been with Negroes and submerged in interests and values we shared. I was square and awkward, and they recognized it, but they didn't try to hurt me with it. They weren't cruel. "Ready to scarf, man?" Conwell Carrington asked one day.

"What?" I replied.

"Scarf, man, you ready to scarf?" he repeated.

"What?" I asked again.

"Aw, nigger," Conwell said, "cmon. Let's go eat."

And then there was a girl. When I would head across the campus to Spanish class in the first semester every Monday, Wednesday and Friday at two, I would pass a tall, slim, brown-skinned girl with dancing eyes and a lush lower lip. After a while, I found out who she was—Ollie Mae Sanders, a freshman from Saginaw, Michigan. One day I asked her to go to the movies with me, and after a while I kissed her, and after that we were going steady. That was about as good as it ever got. I had my girl and I had my Negro friends and I usually went to class and sometimes studied.

Anytime I was between classes, or when I was cutting, I could go over to the cafeteria of the Women's League. There would be hundreds of students in there and the jukebox would be playing all the tunes the blacks had played by monopolizing the box. I could find the brothers and sisters easy, because their heads would be bobbing up and down above all the rest to the sounds of Ella Fitzgerald singing "A Tisket A Tasket"—except when some white jerk would slip in a nickel and play Johnny Ray whining away over some little cloud.

And we'd go to sports events to root on two levels: for Michigan and for the Negroes—any Negroes. Though there was a fair smattering of Negroes on football teams throughout the Big Ten, there was only *one* on any *basketball* team in the whole league—Bill Garrett of Indiana. I can see him now, tall, graceful, pigeon-toed and fast. Garrett was good and we always rooted for him to score thirty points and for Michigan to win by one. But it rarely happened that way. Garrett always got his share but Indiana usually won.

Although I got along well with the white boys in college, I was too aware of our differences to ever be completely comfortable. Take the thing about nappy hair. It started when I was a little boy, two or three years old, and my grandmother would put Vaseline on it just before bedtime. Then she would have me sit on the floor with my shoulders at her knees and she would brush it a hundred times on each side. She would put a cut-off stocking, tied at the top to form a cap, on my head and twist it tight. I would go to bed then and sleep with it on and in the morning my hair would be flat on my head, parted near the center. And though my hair still wasn't straight, it had no tight little woolly balls in it. My grandmother always stressed the importance of "training" my hair.

I used stocking caps for years after that, as did millions of other Negro males around the country. Often you could see men walking in the streets with their stocking caps showing just below the brims of their hats. Nobody ever had to tell me not to wear a stocking cap in public, of course, because I was too ashamed to do it. The whole practice had less to do with neatness than denying the natural properties of my hair and showing people—white people particularly—that I wasn't a woolly head, like the raggedy blacks they seemed so to despise. Even though I would never wear the cap in public the tightness of the cap would leave an indentation—a line across my forehead and around the back of my hairline every morning. I never did manage to master that problem.

One night at college, Robinson, an unpleasant white boy from the room next door, came barging in without knocking. I had been sitting there studying, with a stocking cap on my head. My roommates looked up at him with the minimal interest they generally displayed in anything other than their books, but I was mortified. Robinson was the first white person who had ever seen me with a stocking cap on, and I didn't know what to do. Should I snatch it off or leave it on? I was paralyzed with shame, so I left it on.

Still, I probably thought less about white people those first two years of college than at any other time in my life, before or since. They had their lives and we had ours, and though I would sometimes feel wistful after football games when I knew they were going back to parties at big fraternity houses, what they did or thought was of surprisingly little interest to me in the comfortable cocoon we Negro students had constructed for ourselves.

That is not to say there wasn't civil-rights activity on the campus. There was, but it was mainly carried on by white people. The burning issue for the Student Legislature that year was a resolution it had passed that would have banned any fraternity or sorority that had not—after a seven-year grace period—gotten rid of the discrimination clause in its charter. But that wasn't something the Negroes had pushed; none of us was on S.L., as the student government was called.

Ultimately, though, I was moved enough by my sense of S.L.'s power and by my own need to add a few layers of prestige to my still slender persona, that I ran for it in the second semester of my sophomore year.

That was not long after Ollie broke off our romance to go back with some football player at Michigan State whom she had dated in high school. I had lost my girlfriend, and I lost the election, though not by much. The next semester, I ran again and won, to become the only Negro in the student government. Shortly after that, I was appointed chairman of, naturally, the Human Relations Committee.

During that year we reviewed the issue of Greek-letter discrimination and I made an embarrassed and stiff speech about how difficult it was to be a Negro in America. It was my first civil-rights speech, and I was enormously self-conscious, talking about my embarrassing difference in front of all those people. Nevertheless, I managed to bring it off, and some people told me that that had been a moving moment in S.L. history. After that I put myself up for vice-president of the organization, and though I lost I was elected to one of the lesser, but still coveted, positions in the "cabinet."

Suddenly, I was the Negro politician on campus—a job that had a good deal more weight with the white students on campus than with my Negro brothers and sisters, who simply viewed it, I think, as another one of my eccentricities—and I began slowly to develop some sense of the world outside our comfortable Negro cocoon. Around this time I read a book called *But We Were Born Free* and became a civil libertarian as Joe McCarthy's name began to hit the headlines more and more frequently.

On campus, life was more urgent. Eve Tyler came to Michigan as a freshman from Cleveland at the beginning of my junior year. I met her when five of us were cruising one night in John Edwards' Oldsmobile convertible looking over the new crop of freshmen girls. This night, during their first or second night on campus, we offered five girls a ride home from some event for freshmen women at the Women's League. I was in the back seat, and the girls piled on top of us. I couldn't see any of them. All of us talked upper-class shit to them and the girl on my lap just laughed and laughed.

Later, when we talked about them, someone said, "That girl Eve, who was sitting on your lap, goddamn, she's fine."

"I couldn't see her," I said.

"Well she's really fine and you oughta see her momma," a third guy said. "She's outta sight, pink and blow."

"Pink and blow" meant light skin and hair that would move when the wind blew like a white girl's—automatically fine. Eve's mother indeed turned out to be pink and blow, but not really as good-looking, I thought, as her browner daughter. Eve knew something of the ways of Negro life in the city, but she was "straight from the home environment," as she put it, and her ways were almost as square as mine.

Eve and her roommate, Suane Milton, the daughter of a prominent doctor in Detroit, were, by a lot of people's reckoning, the prettiest Negro girls on campus, and before the year was out, they became, by far, the most popular. You had to call them weeks in advance for weekend dates, so my roommate John Loomis and I saw this as a challenge, since we elected ourselves the most desirable Negro boys on campus. We thought it would be great fun to launch a campaign to shut out every other Negro male on campus; so, we devised an ingenious strategy: coffee dates in the middle of the week for the hour before their ten-thirty curfew at the dorm and coded song requests for them on the most popular disc jockey show in town after that.

"Now the Divine Sarah Vaughn," the jock would say, "for the girls in 4 from the boys in 5."

The digits in their room number added up to 4; those in ours to 5. They thought it was sweet, and we thought it was clever—our campaign succeeded, and five years later they married us on successive weekends in June.

I rarely read newspapers in those days, except for the sports page of the *Michigan Daily,* but even the most isolated environment and my own fierce egocentricity couldn't altogether avoid the fact that Communism was an issue across the country and that Joe McCarthy was abroad in the land. I hadn't taken him all that seriously when he first became famous—I was only annoyed that he shared the name of the great man who had presided on the New York Yankee bench in the years when my baseball fantasies were formed.

There had been talk of Communism in my family, of course, and my mother was against it and thought those relatives who had flirted with it foolish. My Uncle Roy, a staunch believer in the American Constitution and its promise of legally accomplished equality, was against it too.

Moreover, Joe Stalin had given Communism a bad name. Despotic dictatorships—those of Hitler, Mussolini and Tojo—had constituted the dark side of my earliest political sensibilities formed by war movies, newsreels and stories about the Holocaust. So it wasn't hard to shift the points of my political compass after the war to the despotic and crazy mass-murderer Stalin and all he stood for and led. No analysis was necessary; Russia was an evil competitor, Stalin was a tyrant, so Communism was bad. And right-wingers and many of those who owned America had somehow contrived to pin that stench on almost all efforts at change in this country. So it was best to be careful.

One man who did not choose to be careful was an instructor named Seymour who had taught me Spanish in freshman year. I wasn't very good at Spanish, but there was something very loving about Seymour as he attempted gently and politely to persuade us to learn the material he presented so patiently every Monday, Wednesday and Friday at two. It was also charming to take Spanish from a man who spoke with a Brooklyn accent.

So, a couple of years later, when Seymour was dismissed with two other low-level faculty members for refusing to testify before the House Un-American Activities Committee, I was stunned and angry. By that time the evil in Joe McCarthy's methods had become apparent even to me. Though Seymour's problem had come at the hands of a House Committee and not McCarthy's, the smell was the same. And besides, through conversations with my parents and their friends, it was clear to me that a Congressman named Richard Nixon had given that committee a bad name too.

So the Human Relations Committee of the Student Legislature proposed to the whole student body a condemnation of the firings, because they abused academic freedom. Though I don't think the resolution was my idea originally, as chairman of the committee, I presented it to the full body with a short, but eloquent—I thought—speech about freedom, decency and the nature of a university. There was enthusiasm for the proposal and it passed handily.

The next day the *Daily* ran the story on the front page with a huge headline. Shortly after that, staccato bursts of criticism were fired at the Student Legislature from the University administration, the Board of Regents and some prominent alumni. The overt message was that student organizations shouldn't concern themselves with "off campus" issues—the Un-American Activities Committee hearings had been held in Detroit—but the clearest message was that these kids were crazy and couldn't be trusted. And from then on there was a gradual whittling away by the administration of the powers and prerogatives of the Student Legislature. It was an instructive lesson in power politics and the mood of America in the early fifties, and it marked the dawning of my political adulthood.

Mom was a liberal Democrat, and to the extent that I had any politics, I adopted hers. The summer vacation after the Student Legislature's venture into the realm of adult politics, I watched, enraptured, the televised battles of the Taft and the Eisenhower forces at the Republican National Convention, and I was thrilled at the eloquence of Adlai E. Stevenson's acceptance speech when the Democrats nominated him. I was working the four-to-midnight shift that summer at the American Seating Company's west-side factory taking metal stadium and theater seat parts out of an oven that baked the paint on them. I hated the job, because it was hot and I was always burning my arms on the fiery metal I had to handle. So I stayed glued to the television at home during the conventions until the last minute before dashing off to punch in on time. At the end of the shift I'd race like a madman to be at the head of the punch-out line and then drive like fury to get home, hoping that the convention would still be on.

In the Republican fight, I preferred Dwight D. Eisenhower to Robert A. Taft of Ohio, simply because I was against Taft and the rich, selfish conservatism I thought he represented, not because I liked Ike. I was twenty at the time, and Franklin Roosevelt had been President thirteen of those years. Truman had occupied the rest. I had loved Roosevelt as a black child of the Depression would, and my family had come to a grudging approval of Truman—so, naturally, I had too. I had never understood the general adulation of Eisenhower, and I figured he wasn't qualified to be President. What, after all, could a general know about running the country? He had known a segregated life in the Army and I figured that didn't argue well for the quest for racial justice. President Eisenhower! The phrase didn't even sit right in my mouth.

But Stevenson! He was a different story. I didn't need any clues from my family to admire him. He was my kind of white man. His speech was elegant, and he was suave and urbane. I could sit and listen to him talk all day—nothing rough, all grace, no trace of the South in his tones. The best of the Northern liberal tradition, I thought, a man who could be trusted to follow the best instincts of the Constitution and lead Negroes, at least Negroes like me, to equality.

Early in the morning on Labor Day, my old high-school friend Rich Kippen and I went downtown to Campau Square to watch Stevenson launch his campaign for the Presidency. He was smaller than I had expected, and the speech was a disappointment, but there were flashes of eloquence. That was enough for me. Though it was a dull, overcast day, I had seen my political beacon.

A couple of nights later, on my last night at the summer factory job, a white coworker persuaded me to do something special to celebrate the end of our summer labors. Like me, he was a student—a small sandy-haired junior from Michigan State. We had become friends mainly because of the general disdain in which student summer workers were held by the regular employees of the plant—a disdain which our four years of college enabled us to return in kind.

That night he suggested we go down to Commerce Street to buy ourselves some pussy. Though Pop had told me that the women who worked down there—all Negroes—didn't accept colored patronage, I figured maybe they'd take the two of us. He didn't have a car, so I drove and when we got to Commerce Street, I cruised slowly up and down a couple of times while we selected the house we wanted. Neither of us had been to such a place before, so we finally settled on the one that looked least ominous.

We got out of the car and I locked it carefully. Then we went up the steps and onto the porch. I felt apprehensive, but I hoped that my light-yellow Windbreaker with the University of Michigan seal on it made me look sophisticated and a little older. An old Negro woman opened the door and, shuffling in old slippers, led us through a dim hallway to a room with cracked linoleum, two moth-eaten couches, three or four straight-back wooden chairs and a big red Coca-Cola cooler.

"Wait in here," the old woman said. "If you want some beer, it's fifty cents apiece."

We both went to the cooler and pulled cans of beer from the crushed ice and gave the woman our money. She put it in a pocket of her old shapeless dress and disappeared. We sat down, worked on our beer and waited.

Finally, a younger Negro woman came out and motioned for my friend to follow her. I got up, took another beer and laid another fifty cents on the rim of the cooler.

Suddenly from the other side of walls that were very thin, I heard springs squeaking and wood knocking. The noise lasted a very short time and stopped as suddenly as it had started. Then I heard voices.

"Now you get your friend and go. We don't serve colored in here."

"He's not my friend," I heard my friend say. "I never saw him before in my life."

"Oh," the woman said. "I thought he was with you. You came up on the porch with him."

"No, he's not with me."

They came out of the door then and the woman looked at me. My friend headed toward the door without a glance in my direction.

"You have to go," she said. "We don't serve colored in here."

Embarrassed, but also relieved, I shrugged, stood up and left with as much dignity as a man can muster when he's being put out of a whorehouse. We walked down the steps and out to the car, my friend several steps ahead of me. I walked around to the driver's side, unlocked the door and got in. After I had started the engine, my friend rapped on the passenger window. I rolled it down about three inches.

"What do you want?" I asked.

"Come on," he said, "I know you're mad, but I can explain."

"Fuck you," I said.

"You can't just leave me here," he pleaded. "It's dark and probably not safe."

"Never saw you before in my life," I replied, and then I drove off.

★★★

There was nothing more to do after that summer but to go back to school, be president of my class and graduate. I had become president of the class almost by chance. One day I had suggested to my friend Crawford Young, who was to be editor of the *Michigan Daily* in our senior year, that he run for class president.

"No," he said, "I've got too much to do running the *Daily*. You run for president and I'll run for vice-president and we'll get Sid to run for treasurer. Sid Klaus was another editor on the *Daily* and a lovely guy. We sought him out, and he agreed.

Campaigning at Michigan consisted of putting up posters with your picture on them and going around to the houses where a lot of students lived and making little speeches at dinnertime. I did that and I won—to become only the second Negro ever to preside over the largest class at Michigan, literature, science and the arts. Val Johnson, a handsome, smooth-striding quarter-miler had been the first, in 1949, the year before I came to Michigan.

That resulted in my being tapped for Michigamua, the most prestigious honor society for men at Michigan. Crawford Young belonged to it, as did Howard Willens, the president of the Student Legislature, David Brown, the chairman of the Joint Judiciary Council, and Tim Green, the captain of the football team. There were about twenty of us in "The Tribe." I was close to, but not at the core of the group. I wasn't sufficiently self-confident. They accepted their positions of leadership with pride, but also with a natural ease born of belonging in a society. I had never belonged, and I was more grateful than natural. Moreover, I had learned that white America didn't like pushy Negroes, and I was always careful. I didn't want to offend white people.

After graduation, my immediate future seemed uncertain. Eisenhower had won the election and pledged that he would go to Korea to end the apparently endless stalemate there. One option was to join the Air Force and I volunteered to take the tests, reputed to be very hard, for Air Force Flight training. The recruiters looked at my credentials and I was soon given a railroad ticket to Chanute Air Force

Base in Rantoul, Illinois. I got there on a Thursday with ninety-nine other hopefuls for three days of testing.

The first day was the mental exam with a minimum of language and a maximum of math. The next morning before the physical, fifty candidates were sent home. That day we had physicals, and that night forty-four more guys got their ticket home. We six survivors of that ordeal were ecstatic. Though we had been together only two days, it seemed like months; we were old comrades, survivors, in a dreary and hostile place. We knew we would make it, because the third day of testing, by all accounts, was the fun day. It tested hand and eye coordination and the ability to manipulate a simple Link Trainer. We were filled with fantasies of pounding North Korean hills in our F 104s and blowing MIGs out of the sky.

And I was the lucky one. Only five candidates could be tested at a time, and since my name came last on the alphabetical list of six, I got extra sleep. The others had to be at the testing lab at six-thirty. I was due an hour later.

On Saturday morning, the others rose, dressed and left tossing a few rude remarks over their shoulders at me as I pulled up the bed covers for one last nap. I woke up with a start at seven-twenty in the now-empty barracks room we had occupied that night. I leaped out of bed, threw on my clothes and raced out toward the testing lab. When I got inside, panting, the large clock on the wall read 7:32. I found the sergeant in charge, told him what my name was and that I was there for the physical coordination tests.

"You're too late," he said. "We're closed."

"But I'm only two minutes late," I said.

The sergeant, a big red-faced man with sandy hair, gave me a hard look and repeated, "You're too late."

"Well, when will you be open again? When's the next time I can take the tests?" I asked, expecting that he'd set a time later in the day.

"Next Wednesday, six-thirty in the morning," he said coldly.

"Wednesday!" I exclaimed. "But I've got nothing to do on this base until then."

Another pause, another cold stare—it was now 7:34, and he snapped.

"Next test is Wednesday." Then he turned, muttered "nigger" just loudly enough for one to hear and walked rapidly to the door, opened it, passed through quickly and closed it firmly behind him.

I walked back to the barracks disconsolate. There was absolutely nothing to do on that base. I was an outsider and knew no one. My buddies would be heading north to Chicago on the eleven o'clock train. The days until Wednesday stretched ahead of me, empty. The next group of candidates wouldn't arrive until Sunday night, but I wouldn't be one of them. I was alone, and the sergeant had called me a nigger.

Despite the prospect of utter boredom, I'd have stayed but for the sergeant's last word. Instead, I took the eleven o'clock train with my friends and brooded about being drafted into the infantry and about Eve's being at Michigan for two more years without me. I didn't know what the hell to do with my life. I chose the usual Roger Wilkins way for those days—lying and expediency. I told my parents that I had been made night blind by an accident I had had in the Bissel Carpet Sweeper factory some summers before, when a lathe strap broke and hit me in the eye. Hell, you couldn't tell your parents that you weren't going out to defend America against Communism in a jet fighter because you had overslept.

And I wanted to be a writer. Oh Jesus, did I want to be a writer! That's what Daddy had done. I once told Rich Kippen in high school, when we were both writing for the *Creston Echo*, that my main ambition in life was to write a perfect paragraph. But they weren't hiring Negroes on papers of general circulation in those days and to go back to doing what my father had done twelve years before didn't advance the ball one inch. So I did what lots of other aimless people with A.B. degrees in political science did, I opted for law school—at Michigan. That would, at least, keep the vultures away from Eve!

Marita Golden was born in Washington D.C., in 1950. She was educated at American and Columbia universities in journalism and communications. Her articles have appeared in the *New York Times*, the *Washington Post*, and *Africa Magazine*, among other publications. She is the author of the autobiographical *Migrations of the Heart*, the novel *A Woman's Place*, and, most recently, the novel *Long Distance Life*.

18

MARITA GOLDEN

From Migrations of the Heart:
An Autobiography

(1983)

WHEN THE KNOWLEDGE CAME, its taste was sweet, bitter, eye-opening. A drug pulsing hot lead fire and ice through our veins. As clenched fists became the stars giving light to our night, the sound of "brother," "sister," our anthem, tumbled through full, determined lips. Turned the curse into a sacrament. Brow-beating, insistent, unforgiving, we took the offensive and for a moment turned white hatred into fear that drained blood from the face.

The tremors from the riots that convulsed the city had shuddered outward, piercing the solid certainty of the surrounding white world with bulging veins of doubt. Washington's private colleges hastily inaugurated scholarship programs for black high school students. A salve that absorbed the sting of the burn but left the wound startlingly clear.

I entered American University in the fall of 1968 as a Frederick Douglass Scholarship student, one of twenty-five from the inner city. The school sat nestled, almost hidden, in the comfortable upper reaches of northwest Washington, surrounded by embassies, cathedrals and the manicured, sprawling lawns of the city's upper class. To enter this world I caught the bus downtown and boarded it with black women domestic workers who rode to the end of the line to clean house for young and middle-aged white matrons. They gazed proudly at me, nodding at the books in my lap, slapping me on the back with a smile. In answer to the concern arching my brow, they told me with pursed, silent lips, "It's alright. It really is. I'd a done something else if I could've. Maybe been a teacher or something like that. But that was so long ago it don't even matter no more. So now you do it for me. But mostly do it for you." I accepted their encouragement and hated America for never allowing them to be selfish or greedy, to feel the steel-hard bite of ambition that could snatch their sleep at night or straighten their spines into a dare. They had parlayed their anger, brilliantly shaped it into a soft armor of survival.

The spirit of those women sat with me in every class I took at A.U. Once it was called "Jew U," because hordes rejected by Columbia or Temple or N.Y.U. were accepted there. Their affluence, measured in shiny sports cars and perfect-fit clothes, was a vulgar parody. Overhearing their conversations, I imagined their homes—cluttered with gadgets and objects, kept orderly and clean by thrice-weekly cleaning women. So much comfort, so little grace. Listening to them, I felt as though I were choking and would run to open space for air.

But my teachers, I almost forgave them for being white. I learned from all of them. The best ones combined intelligence with wit and polished it to gleaming with caring and concern. I was curious, and impatient with dullness and stupidity, so the reading lists that brought tears of frustration to the eyes of some comforted me. For it was books that, one luminous summer I shall always remember, made me want to be Harriet Tubman instead of Tuesday Weld.

The summer before entering American University I had joined the fold of a group of Howard University students. Their uniforms were dashikis and blue jeans, and wildly unkempt, brazen Afros. Charter members of SNCC, they had conceived and carried out the week-long shutdown of Howard that spring. With their anger turned into calloused hands, they brusquely stripped the lady of her white gloves and formal speech. Teeth now cut, they took on the South, where they registered black voters. One of them slapped a white

sheriff and lived to weave that act into the epic poem he saw his life
to be.

I went to their parties, held in crumbling, once glorious apartments that surrounded the Howard campus. The infrared darkness
hid the copies of *Liberator, Soulbrook,* and *Black World* stacked in
piles underfoot. Malcolm X's eyes were spears aimed at us from
posters peeling from the wall. When the throb of Sly's *Stand!* or James
Brown's "Say It Loud (I'm Black and I'm Proud)" was only a memory
frosting the air, we formed a circle and snake danced around the
room, hands clapping, feet stomping, singing "Beep Beep Bang Bang
Umgawah Black Power." They taught me the new language, how to
roll the words on my tongue. How to drain meanings from the sound
of each syllable that no one would ever forget. Power. Revolution. We
were prepared for war but would witness only skirmishes that left us
bloodied nevertheless.

I fell in love with one of them. He was a twenty-two-year-old
guerrilla/singer/songwriter/black poet/revolutionary. Beneath the
dingy, wrinkled sheets of his hardly-ever-slept-in bed, tongue sticky
wet promising in my ear, he called me his African queen. He bought
a .22 caliber handgun the day he discovered his phone was tapped and
handled it like a water pistol. Quieting my demands for time with him,
he reminded me that dates were what white girls wanted and, anyway,
there was no place for socializing in the midst of a revolution.

"Is there a place for love?" I asked, watching him hurriedly pull
on his shorts, wondering why his body turned corpse cold when I
cradled him in the moments after his frantic release.

"Only of black people as a whole. Not as individuals," he answered in the voice a man uses with a woman he secretly hates. Then
he smiled sadly, cupping my chin as though the realization awakened
an ache within him. At eighteen I could not suspect how wantonly
cruel his answer was. So I reached onto the platter for it. Swallowed
it whole without tasting. It landed, heavy and rebellious, in the pit of
my stomach.

Since there would be no love in our revolution, I turned to
hate. It was easy enough to do. The Drum and Spear Bookstore

was opened that summer by several members of the group. Its shelves stocked a whole range of books on black and African studies, and they finished the stories my father had begun. I learned of slave revolts, W. E. B. DuBois, black inventors, Carter G. Woodson, Reconstruction, Jean Toomer, Timbuktu, the precarious existence of freed slaves, Duke Ellington, Nat Turner, Bessie Smith. Page after page put flesh and blood on the bones of the past my father had kindled for me in spurts, which was our own carefully guarded secret. This was all mine. This wealth. This panorama of genius and endurance. And *they* had kept it from me. Now I knew why. Invincibility swelled my mind into a hard, gleaming muscle. And for an uneasy, tortured time I surrendered to hate. Because of two thousand lynchings and four little girls bombed in a Birmingham church. Because they told me I was a slave but never said that once I'd been a king. I became a true believer. I wrote a biweekly column for the *Eagle,* the campus newspaper, in which I spread the gospel of black consciousness, sat on a committee to implement a black studies program at A.U., tutored black high school students and wrote bristling black poetry that sizzled on the page. I was simultaneously driven and inspired. Dizzy with a confidence I'd grown up believing brown girls never knew.

And we never suffered a moment of doubt, bludgeoning critics into silence with our smug lack of humility. We knew, for example, that what's *on* your head is as important as what's *in* it.

The natural was sprouting everywhere—dark sunflowers filling a vacant field. No one could see my anger. But they could see my hair. See that I was no longer a Negro girl. That I had chosen to become a black woman.

My mother, nursed in the folds of a town that once christened its black babies Lee, after Robert E., and Jackson, after Stonewall, raised me on a dangerous generation's old belief. Because of my dark brown complexion, she warned me against wearing browns or yellows and reds, assuring me they would turn on me like an ugly secret revealed. And every summer I was admonished not to play in the sun, " 'cause you gonna have to get a light husband anyway, for the sake of your children."

My mother would never acknowledge or even suspect her self-denial. It gripped her all the tighter for the carelessness of her vision. Ground into my pores, this was the same skin through which I breathed. The eye through which I saw myself.

Up until I was eighteen, however, every other Saturday I had entered a state of grace. Holding down a rugged corner of 14th and T, on a block given over to funeral parlors, ragged, unpretentious barber shops and fried chicken carry-outs, the La Femme Beauty Salon was part haven, part refuge for the women who packed its small rooms on Saturday mornings. Over the click of steaming curlers, they testified, embellishing the fabric of their lives, stretching it into a more agreeable form and shape. When it was full, the shop sheltered, holding the smoky odor of straightening combs thrust into jars of grease and applied with unflinching belief to coarse hair. Special attention was paid to "the kitchen," the hairline at the nape of the neck that harbored the most stubborn patches of hair curled into tiny balls of opposition. Pushing my ear back, the beautician would warn, "Now you gonna have to hold still 'cause I can't be responsible for what this hot comb might do."

Between customers, twirling in her chair, white-stockinged legs crossed, my beautician lamented to the hairdresser in the next stall, "I sure hope that Gloria Johnson don't come in here asking for me today. I swear 'fore God her hair is this long." She snapped her fingers to indicate the length. Contempt riding her words, she lit a cigarette and finished, "Barely enough to wash, let alone press and curl."

Despite those years—perhaps because of them—the day I looked in the mirror at my natural was the first day I ever liked what I saw. "There is everything," I thought. Nappy, defiant, my hair was a small cap tapering around my head. Without apology, my nose claimed the center of my face. Because of the bangs I'd always worn, I'd never noticed my brows, thick and velvety. My eyes were small diamonds. Perfectly cut. This was not the face I had always known. It was the face I refused to believe I had.

I did not sojourn alone. My best friend, Wanda, was there. Two dark girls seeing themselves in the other. Don't explain. Had always been there. Waiting. Even before our minds wove together, strong-fingered hands clasped. Amidst the intellectual din, the emotional clutter ringing in the halls of Western High School, we had found one another. Imagination bound us stronger than love. Within its limitless borders we launched ships and love affairs, discovered lost worlds, made buildings and babies, found husbands, wrote letters and Broadway plays. We made ourselves up every day. And because we dreamed of everything, we vowed to rule no possibility out of our lives.

In high school we read Sartre. In college we tossed him aside and reached for Mao and Che Guevara. Summer afternoons were spent stretched on her bed reading Don Lee and Gwendolyn Brooks. Together. Silent. We could read each other's minds. Spellbound listening to Coltrane's "My Favorite Things" over and over, each time a sacrament. Sweating, groaning, we raised the banner of blackness and, after the staff was firmly planted, became part of the women we would always be. And uh-huh, she would be an actress. I, a writer. A hundred loves, it seemed, unreturned, misunderstood.

Me: Jive nigguhs, all they do is rap. What's wrong with the brothers?
Wanda: Askin, "Sistuh, can you *love* a black man?"
Me: Hey, brother, can you *understand* a black woman?
Us: Laughter so close to tears it hurt.

I lay in the debris of a ruined love affair. Her voice, indignant, terrified in the face of my passion, my tears, charged, "Marita, you give too much."

"And you don't give at all," I slap back, hard. "You take them into your *bed* but never into your *heart.*" She, the small bird chirping, afraid no one listens. Cautious. Fevered. The squirrel storing nuts of doubt. Love floods the rooms of her mind and she fills buckets with it, tossing the treasure out open windows. I am a stranger to half measures. With life I am on the attack, restlessly ferreting out each pleasure, foraging for answers, wringing from it even the pain. I ransack life, hunt it down. I am the hungry peasants storming the palace gates. I will have my share. No matter how it tastes.

★★★

My parents watched my transformation, stung by its ferocity and the fierceness of my allegiance to gods they had never known. My mother retreated into befuddled silence, watching me from the corner of her eyes, as though I were a stranger following her down a dark alley. My father said nothing for many months. Then, one afternoon, he waylaid me. He had stalked my moves, waited for my confidence to blossom before breaking it at the root. "I don't like what I see when I look at you now." His face was granite and my uneasy smile chipped away not one particle.

"What's wrong?"

"I want you to take off that makeup. I hate that lipstick, the mascara." His lips curled in disgust as he threw the words like sharpened darts.

"But, Daddy, there's nothing wrong—"

"And I want you to get rid of that natural."

"But why? You always taught me to be proud."

"Sure, I taught you to be proud. But you're still my little girl. My daughter." He said the words almost kindly, asserting his still pivotal role in a life I was wrestling out of his hands. "You're not a woman yet, Marita. You have to do what I say."

His voice was stretched taut with a threat I was afraid to name. I had never even received a spanking from my father. Yet now, as I sat facing him in the front seat of his taxi, my heart was cringing, my hand reaching for the door. I tried to imagine what he would do if I refused. But the bitterness in his eyes, which accused me of betrayal because of my lurching journey into womanhood, left no room for denial. He searched my face for assent, for a request for forgiveness. I clenched my teeth and turned away from him, the window witnessing the tears sliding down my cheeks in thin ribbons that he could not see.

I obeyed him and the next day walked into the Soul Corner of A.U.'s cafeteria to stares and questions that peeled the skin from my cheeks. A few months later I got a work-study job at school. No longer financially dependent on my father, I willfully disobeyed him and Afroed my hair once again. I was my own woman, I reasoned, forgetting, with a carelessness for which I would later pay, that I would always be his child.

Alice Walker, novelist, short story writer, and poet, was born in 1944 in Eatonton, Georgia. Walker has received numerous honors and awards for her writing. Her works include *Revolutionary Petunias and Other Poems* and the novels *The Third Life of Grange Copeland, Meridian,* the Pulitzer Prize–winning *The Color Purple,* and, most recently, *Temple of My Familiar.*

ALICE WALKER

Beauty: When the Other Dancer Is the Self

(1 9 8 3)

IT IS A BRIGHT summer day in 1947. My father, a fat, funny man with beautiful eyes and a subversive wit, is trying to decide which of his eight children he will take with him to the county fair. My mother, of course, will not go. She is knocked out from getting most of us ready: I hold my neck stiff against the pressure of her knuckles as she hastily completes the braiding and then beribboning of my hair.

My father is the driver for the rich old white lady up the road. Her name is Miss Mey. She owns all the land for miles around, as well as the house in which we live. All I remember about her is that she once offered to pay my mother thirty-five cents for cleaning her house, raking up piles of her magnolia leaves, and washing her family's clothes, and that my mother—she of no money, eight children, and a chronic earache—refused it. But I do not think of this in 1947. I am two and a half years old. I want to go everywhere my daddy goes. I am excited at the prospect of riding in a car. Someone has told me fairs are fun. That there is room in the car for only three of us doesn't faze me at all. Whirling happily in my starchy frock, showing off my biscuit-polished patent-leather shoes and lavender socks, tossing my head in a way that makes my ribbons bounce, I stand, hands on hips, before my father. "Take me, Daddy," I say with assurance; "I'm the prettiest!"

Later, it does not surprise me to find myself in Miss Mey's shiny black car, sharing the back seat with the other lucky ones. Does not surprise me that I thoroughly enjoy the fair. At home that night I tell the unlucky ones all I can remember about the merry-go-round, the man who eats live chickens, and the teddy bears, until they say: that's enough, baby Alice. Shut up now, and go to sleep.

It is Easter Sunday, 1950. I am dressed in a green, flocked, scalloped-hem dress (handmade by my adoring sister, Ruth) that has its own smooth satin petticoat and tiny hot-pink roses tucked into each scallop. My shoes, new T-strap patent leather, again highly biscuit-polished. I am six years old and have learned one of the longest Easter speeches to be heard that day, totally unlike the speech I said when I was two: "Easter lilies/pure and white/blossom in/the morning light." When I rise to give my speech I do so on a great wave of love and pride and expectation. People in the church stop rustling their new crinolines. They seem to hold their breath. I can tell they admire my dress, but it is my spirit, bordering on sassiness (womanishness), they secretly applaud.

"That girl's a little *mess*," they whisper to each other, pleased.

Naturally I say my speech without stammer or pause, unlike those who stutter, stammer, or, worst of all, forget. This is before the word "beautiful" exists in people's vocabulary, but "Oh, isn't she the *cutest* thing!" frequently floats my way. "And got so much sense!" they gratefully add . . . for which thoughtful addition I thank them to this day.

It was great fun being cute. But then, one day, it ended.

I am eight years old and a tomboy. I have a cowboy hat, cowboy boots, checkered shirt and pants, all red. My playmates are my brothers, two and four years older than I. Their colors are black and green, the only difference in the way we are dressed. On Saturday nights we all go to the picture show, even my mother; Westerns are her favorite kind of movie. Back home, "on the ranch," we pretend we are Tom Mix, Hopalong Cassidy, Lash LaRue (we've even named one of our dogs Lash LaRue); we chase each other for hours rustling cattle, being outlaws, delivering damsels from distress. Then my parents decide to buy my brothers guns. These are not "real" guns. They shoot "BBs," copper pellets my brothers say will kill birds. Because I am a girl, I do not get a gun. Instantly I am relegated to the position of Indian. Now there appears a great distance between us. They shoot and shoot at everything with their new guns. I try to keep up with my bow and arrows.

One day while I am standing on top of our makeshift "garage"— pieces of tin nailed across some poles—holding my bow and arrow and looking out toward the fields, I feel an incredible blow in my right eye. I look down just in time to see my brother lower his gun.

Both brothers rush to my side. My eye stings, and I cover it with my hand. "If you tell," they say, "we will get a whipping. You don't want that to happen, do you?" I do not. "Here is a piece of wire," says the older brother, picking it up from the roof; "say you stepped on one end of it and the other flew up and hit you." The pain is beginning to start. "Yes," I say. "Yes, I will say that is what happened." If I do not say this is what happened, I know my brothers will find ways to make me wish I had. But now I will say anything that gets me to my mother.

Confronted by our parents we stick to the lie agreed upon. They place me on a bench on the porch and I close my left eye while they examine the right. There is a tree growing from underneath the porch that climbs past the railing to the roof. It is the last thing my right eye sees. I watch as its trunk, its branches, and then its leaves are blotted out by the rising blood.

I am in shock. First there is intense fever, which my father tries to break using lily leaves bound around my head. Then there are chills: my mother tries to get me to eat soup. Eventually, I do not know how, my parents learn what has happened. A week after the "accident" they take me to see a doctor. "Why did you wait so long to come?" he asks, looking into my eye and shaking his head. "Eyes are sympathetic," he says. "If one is blind, the other will likely become blind too."

This comment of the doctor's terrifies me. But it is really how I look that bothers me most. Where the BB pellet struck there is a glob of whitish scar tissue, a hideous cataract, on my eye. Now when I stare at people—a favorite pastime, up to now—they will stare back. Not at the "cute" little girl, but at her scar. For six years I do not stare at anyone, because I do not raise my head.

Years later, in the throes of a mid-life crisis, I ask my mother and sister whether I changed after the "accident." "No," they say, puzzled. "What do you mean?"

What do I mean?

I am eight, and, for the first time, doing poorly in school, where I have been something of a whiz since I was four. We have just moved to the place where the "accident" occurred. We do not know any of the people around us because this is a different county. The only time I see the friends I knew is when we go back to our old church. The new school is the former state penitentiary. It is a large stone building, cold and drafty, crammed to overflowing with boisterous, ill-disciplined children. On the third floor there is a huge circular imprint of some partition that has been torn out.

"What used to be here?" I ask a sullen girl next to me on our way past it to lunch.

"The electric chair," says she.

At night I have nightmares about the electric chair, and about all the people reputedly "fried" in it. I am afraid of the school, where all the students seem to be budding criminals.

"What's the matter with your eye?" they ask, critically.

When I don't answer (I cannot decide whether it was an "accident" or not), they shove me, insist on a fight.

My brother, the one who created the story about the wire, comes to my rescue. But then brags so much about "protecting" me, I become sick.

After months of torture at the school, my parents decide to send me back to our old community, to my old school. I live with my grandparents and the teacher they board. But there is no room for Phoebe, my cat. By the time my grandparents decide there *is* room, and I ask for my cat, she cannot be found. Miss Yarborough, the boarding teacher, takes me under her wing, and begins to teach me to play the piano. But soon she marries an African—a "prince," she says—and is whisked away to his continent.

At my old school there is at least one teacher who loves me. She is the teacher who "knew me before I was born" and bought my first baby clothes. It is she who makes life bearable. It is her presence that finally helps me turn on the one child at the school who continually calls me "one-eyed bitch." One day I simply grab him by his coat and beat him until I am satisfied. It is my teacher who tells me my mother is ill.

My mother is lying in bed in the middle of the day, something I have never seen. She is in too much pain to speak. She has an abscess in her ear. I stand looking down on her, knowing that if she dies, I cannot live. She is being treated with warm oils and hot bricks held against her cheek. Finally a doctor comes. But I must go back to my grandparents' house. The weeks pass but I am hardly aware of it. All I know is that my mother might die, my father is not so jolly, my brothers still have their guns, and I am the one sent away from home.

"You did not change," they say.

Did I imagine the anguish of never looking up?

I am twelve. When relatives come to visit I hide in my room. My cousin Brenda, just my age, whose father works in the post office and whose mother is a nurse, comes to find me. "Hello," she says. And then she asks, looking at my recent school picture, which I did not want taken, and on which the "glob," as I think of it, is clearly visible, "You still can't see out of that eye?"

"No," I say, and flop back on the bed over my book.

That night, as I do almost every night, I abuse my eye. I rant and rave at it, in front of the mirror. I plead with it to clear up before morning. I tell it I hate and despise it. I do not pray for sight. I pray for beauty.

"You did not change," they say.

I am fourteen and baby-sitting for my brother Bill, who lives in Boston. He is my favorite brother and there is a strong bond between us. Understanding my feelings of shame and ugliness he and his wife take me to a local hospital, where the "glob" is removed by a doctor named O. Henry. There is still a small bluish crater where the scar tissue was, but the ugly white stuff is gone. Almost immediately I become a different person from the girl who does not raise her head. Or so I think. Now that I've raised my head I win the boyfriend of my dreams. Now that I've raised my head I have plenty of friends. Now that I've raised my head classwork comes from my lips as faultlessly as Easter speeches did, and I leave high school as valedictorian, most popular student, and *queen,* hardly believing my luck. Ironically, the girl who was voted most beautiful in our class (and was) was later shot twice through the chest by a male companion, using a "real" gun, while she was pregnant. But that's another story in itself. Or is it?

"You did not change," they say.

It is now thirty years since the "accident." A beautiful journalist comes to visit and to interview me. She is going to write a cover story for her magazine that focuses on my latest book. "Decide how you want to look on the cover," she says. "Glamorous, or whatever."

Never mind "glamorous," it is the "whatever" that I hear. Suddenly all I can think of is whether I will get enough sleep the night before the photography session: if I don't, my eye will be tired and wander, as blind eyes will.

At night in bed with my lover I think up reasons why I should not appear on the cover of a magazine. "My meanest critics will say I've sold out," I say. "My family will now realize I write scandalous books."

"But what's the real reason you don't want to do this?" he asks.

"Because in all probability," I say in a rush, "my eye won't be straight."

"It will be straight enough," he says. Then, "Besides, I thought you'd made your peace with that."

And I suddenly remember that I have.

I remember:

I am talking to my brother Jimmy, asking if he remembers anything unusual about the day I was shot. He does not know I consider that day the last time my father, with his sweet home remedy of cool lily leaves, chose me, and that I suffered and raged inside because of this. "Well," he says, "all I remember is standing by the side of the highway with Daddy, trying to flag down a car. A white man stopped, but when Daddy said he needed somebody to take his little girl to the doctor, he drove off."

I remember:

I am in the desert for the first time. I fall totally in love with it. I am so overwhelmed by its beauty, I confront for the first time, consciously, the meaning of the doctor's words years ago: "Eyes are sympathetic. If one is blind, the other will likely become blind too." I realize I have dashed about the world madly, looking at this, looking at that, storing up images against the fading of the light. *But I might have missed seeing the desert!* The shock of that possibility—and gratitude for over twenty-five years of sight—sends me literally to my knees. Poem after poem comes—which is perhaps how poets pray.

On Sight

I am so thankful I have seen
The Desert
And the creatures in the desert
And the desert Itself.

The desert has its own moon
Which I have seen
With my own eye.

There is no flag on it.
Trees of the desert have arms
All of which are always up
That is because the moon is up

The sun is up
Also the sky
The stars
Clouds
None with flags.

If there were *flags, I doubt*
the trees would point.
Would you?

But mostly, I remember this:

I am twenty-seven, and my baby daughter is almost three. Since her birth I have worried about her discovery that her mother's eyes are different from other people's. Will she be embarrassed? I think. What will she say? Every day she watches a television program called "Big Blue Marble." It begins with a picture of the earth as it appears from the moon. It is bluish, a little battered-looking, but full of light, with whitish clouds swirling around it. Every time I see I weep with love, as if it is a picture of Grandma's house. One day when I am putting Rebecca down for her nap, she suddenly focuses on my eye. Something inside me cringes, gets ready to try to protect myself. All children are cruel about physical differences, I know from experience, and that they don't always mean to be is another matter. I assume Rebecca will be the same.

But no-o-o-o. She studies my face intently as we stand, her inside and me outside her crib. She even holds my face maternally between her dimpled little hands. Then, looking every bit as serious and law-yerlike as her father, she says, as if it may just possibly have slipped my attention: "Mommy, there's a *world* in your eye." (As in, "Don't be alarmed, or do anything crazy.") And then, gently, but with great interest: "Mommy, where did you *get* that world in your eye?"

For the most part, the pain left then. (So what, if my brothers grew up to buy even more powerful pellet guns for their sons and to carry real guns themselves. So what, if a young "Morehouse man" once nearly fell off the steps of Trevor Arnette Library because he thought my eyes were blue.) Crying and laughing I ran to the bathroom, while Rebecca mumbled and sang herself off to sleep. Yes indeed, I realized, looking into the mirror. There *was* a world in my eye. And I saw that it was possible to love it: that in fact, for all it had taught me of shame and anger and inner vision, I *did* love it. Even to see it drifting out of orbit in boredom, or rolling up out of fatigue, not to mention floating back at attention in excitement (bearing witness, a friend has called it), deeply suitable to my personality, and even characteristic of me.

That night I dream I am dancing to Stevie Wonder's song "Always" (the name of the song is really "As," but I hear it as "Always"). As I dance, whirling and joyous, happier than I've ever been in my life, another bright-faced dancer joins me. We dance and kiss each other and hold each other through the night. The other dancer has obviously come through all right, as I have done. She is beautiful, whole and free. And she is also me.

John Edgar Wideman was born in Washington, D.C., in 1941. The author of *Brothers and Keepers, Damballah, Hurry, The Lynchers, Sent for Yesterday, Hiding Place,* and *Philadelphia Fire,* Wideman has received numerous honors, including a Rhodes scholarship. He has taught at Howard University, University of Pennsylvania, University of Wyoming, and, most recently, at the University of Massachusetts in Amherst as professor of English.

20

JOHN EDGAR WIDEMAN

From Brothers and Keepers

Summer 1982

(1984)

ONE MORE TIME. Summer 1982. The weather in Pittsburgh is unbearably hot. Two weeks of high temperatures and high humidity. Nights not much better than the days. Nights too hot for sleeping, days sapping what's left of the strength the sleepless nights don't replenish. You get sopping wet climbing in or out of a car. Especially if your car's little and not air-conditioned, like my mother's Chevette. Nobody remembers the last time they felt a cool breeze, nobody remembers pulling on clothes and not sweating through them in five minutes. "Unbearable" is my mother's word. She uses it often but never lightly. In her language it means the heat is something you can't escape. The sticky heat's a burden you wake up to every morning and carry till you're too exhausted to toss and turn anymore in your wet sheets. Unbearable doesn't mean a weight that gets things over with, that crushes you once and for all, but a burden that exerts relentless pressure. Whether you're lifting a bag of groceries from a shopping cart into the furnace your car becomes after sitting closed for twenty minutes in the Giant Eagle parking lot, or celebrating the birth of a new baby in the family, the heat is there. A burden touching, flawing everything. Unbearable is not that which can't be borne, but what must be endured forever.

Of course the July dog days can't last forever. Sooner or later they'll end. Abruptly. Swept away by one of those violent lightning-and-thunder storms peculiar to Pittsburgh summers. The kind signaled by a sudden disappearance of air, air sucked away so quickly you feel you're falling. Then nothing. A vast emptiness rubbing your skin. The air's gone. You're in a vacuum, a calm, still, vacated space waiting for the storm to rush in. You know the weather must turn, but part of the discomfort of being in the grip of a heat wave or any grave trouble is the fear that maybe it won't end. Maybe things will stay as miserable as they are.

Nothing changes. Nothing remains the same. One more visit to the prison, only this time, after I dropped my mother off at work, I tried a new route. The parkway had been undergoing repairs for two years. I'd used it anyway, in spite of detours and traffic jams. But this time I tried a shortcut my buddy Scott Payne had suggested. Scott was right; his way was quicker and freer of hassles. I'd arrived at Western Penitentiary in record time. Yet something was wrong. The new route transported me to the gates but I wasn't ready to pass through. Different streets, different buildings along the way hadn't done the trick, didn't have the power to take me where I needed to go because the journey to visit my brother in prison was not simply a matter of miles and minutes. Between Homewood and Woods Run, the flat, industrialized wasteland beside the river where the prison's hidden, there is a vast, uncharted space, a no-man's-land where the traveler must begin to forget home and begin to remember the alien world inside "The Walls." At some point an invisible line is crossed, the rules change. Visitors must take leave of the certainties underpinning their everyday lives.

Using the parkway to reach Woods Run had become part of the ritual I depended upon to get me ready to see my brother. Huge green exit signs suspended over the highway, tires screaming on gouged patches of road surface, the darkness and claustrophobia of Squirrel Hill Tunnel, miles of abandoned steel-mill sheds, a mosque's golden cupola, paddle-wheeled pleasure boats moored at the riverbank, the scenes and sensations I catalogue now as I write were stepping stones. They broke the journey into stages, into moments I could anticipate.

Paying attention to the steps allowed me to push into the back of my mind their inevitable destination, the place where the slide show of images was leading me.

I'd missed all that; so when I reached the last few miles of Ohio River Boulevard Scott's shortcut shared with my usual route, the shock of knowing the prison was just minutes away hit me harder than usual. I wasn't prepared to step through the looking glass.

Giving up one version of reality for another. That's what entering the prison was about. Not a dramatic flip-flop of values. That would be too easy. If black became white and good became bad and fast became slow, the players could learn the trick of reversing labels, and soon the upside-down world would seem natural. Prison is more perverse. Inside the walls nothing is certain, nothing can be taken for granted except the arbitrary exercise of absolute power. Rules engraved in stone one day will be superseded the next. What you don't know can always hurt you. And the prison rules are designed to keep you ignorant, keep you guessing, insure your vulnerability. Think of a fun-house mirror, a floor-to-ceiling sheet of undulating glass. Images ripple across its curved surface constantly changing. Anything caught in the mirror is bloated, distorted. Prison's like that mirror. Prison rules and regulations, the day-to-day operation of the institution, confront the inmate with an image of himself that is grotesque, absurd. A prisoner who refuses to internalize this image, who insists upon seeing other versions of himself, is in constant danger.

Somebody with a wry sense of humor had a field day naming the cluster of tiny streets bordering Western Penitentiary. Doerr, Refuge, Ketchum. When I reached the left turn at Doerr that would take me along the south wall of the prison to the parking-lot entrance, I still wasn't ready to go inside. I kept driving past the prison till the street I was on dead-ended. A U-turn in the lot of a chemical factory pointed me back toward the penitentiary and then for a few long minutes I sat in the car. . . .

In the half mile back to the prison as the walls loom higher and nearer I asked the question I always must when a visit is imminent: Is Rob still alive? The possibility of sudden, violent death hangs over

my brother's head every minute of every day so when I finally reach
the guard's cage and ask for P3468, my heart stands still and I'm filled
with the numbing irony of wishing, of praying that the guard will nod
his head and say, *Yes,* your brother's still inside.

Robby hugs me, we clasp hands. My arm goes round his body and
I hug him back. Our eyes meet. What won't be said, can't be said no
matter how long we talk, how much I write, hovers in his eyes and
mine. We know where we are, what's happening, how soon this tiny
opening allowing us to touch will be slammed shut. All that in our
eyes, and I can't take seeing it any longer than he can. The glance we
exchange is swift, is full of fire, of unsayable rage and pain. Neither
of us can hold it more than a split second. He sees in me what I see
in him. The knowledge that this place is bad, worse than bad. That
the terms under which we are meeting stink. That living under certain
conditions is less than no life at all, and what we have to do, *ought*
to do, is make our stand here, together. That dying with your hands
on an enemy's throat is better than living under his boot. Just a flash.
The simplest, purest solution asserting itself. I recognize what Rob is
thinking. I know he knows what's rushing through my mind. Fight.
Forget the games, the death by inches buying time. Fight till they kill
us or let us go. If we die fighting, it will be a good day to die. The
right day. The right way.

After that first contact, after that instant of threat and consolation
and promise flickers out as fast as it came, my eyes drop to the
vinyl-cushioned couches, rise again to the clutter of other prisoners
and visitors. I force myself to pretend the eye conversation never took
place, that Robby and I hadn't been talking about first things and last
things and hadn't reached a crystal-clear understanding of what we
must do. We'd lost the moment. The escape route closed down as he
looked away or I looked away. We're going to deal with the visit now.
We're going to talk, survive another day. I have to pretend the other
didn't happen because if I don't, disappointment and shame will spoil
the visit. And visits are all we have. All we're going to have for years
and years, unless we choose the other way, the solution burning in
Rob's eyes and mine before each visit begins.

270

The last iron gate, the last barred door. The visit proper doesn't begin until after we meet and touch and decide we'll do it their way one more time. Because the other way, the alternative is always there. I meet it every time. We know it's there and we consciously say, *No.* And the no lets everything else follow. Says yes to the visit. The words.

Whatever else the visit turns into, it begins as compromise, an acceptance of defeat. Maybe the rage, the urge to fight back doesn't rise from a truer, better self. Maybe what's denied is not the instinctual core of my being but an easily sidestepped, superficial layer of bravado, a ferocity I'd like to think is real but that winds up being no more than a Jonathan Jackson, George Jackson, Soledad-brother fantasy, a carryover from the old Wild West, shoot-em-up days as a kid. The Lone Ranger, Robin Hood, Zorro. Masked raiders attacking the bad guys' castle, rescuing trusty sidekicks in a swirl of swordplay, gunfire, thundering hooves. Maybe I needed to imagine myself in that role because I knew how far from the truth it was. Kidding myself so I could take the visits seriously, satisfy myself that I was doing all I could, doing better than nothing.

Point is, each visit's rooted in denial, compromise, a sinking feeling of failure. I'm letting Robby down, myself down, the team. . . . Always that to get through. The last gate. Sometimes it never swings all the way open on its hinges. A visit can be haunted by a sense of phoniness, hollowness. Who am I? Why am I here? Listening to my brother, answering him, but also fighting the voice that screams that none of this matters, none of this is worth shit. You missed your chance to put your money where your mouth is. A good day to die but you missed it. You let them win again. Humiliate you again. You're on your knees again, scrambling after scraps.

Sometimes we occupy one of the lawyer-client tables, but today a guard chases us away. Robby's had trouble with him before. I commit the guard's name to memory just in case. My personal shit list for close watching or revenge or whatever use it would serve if something suspicious happens to my brother. I consider making a fuss. After all, I'm a professional writer. Don't I have just as much right as a lawyer or social worker to the convenience of a table where I can set down the tools of my trade, where my brother and I can put a little distance between ourselves and the babble of twenty or thirty simultaneous conversations?

The guard's chest protrudes like there's compressed air instead of flesh inside the gray blouse of his uniform. A square head. Pale skin except on his cheeks, which are bluish and raw from razor burn. His mustache and short curly hair are meticulously groomed, too perfect to be real. The stylized hair of comic-book superheroes. A patch of blue darkness etched with symmetrical accent lines. His eyes avoid mine. He had spoken in a clipped, mechanical tone of voice. Not one man talking to another but a peremptory recital of rules droned at some abstraction in the middle distance where the guard's eyes focus while his lips move. I think, Nazi Gestapo Frankenstein robot motherfucker, but he's something worse. He's what he is and there's no way to get around that or for the moment get around him because he's entrenched in this no-man's-land and he is what he is and that's worse than any names I can call him. He's laying down the law and that's it. The law. No matter that all three tables are unoccupied. No matter that I tell him we've sat at them before. No matter that we'll vacate if and when lawyers need them. No matter that I might have a case, make a case that my profession, my status means something outside the walls. No matter, my pride and anger and barely concealed scorn. I move on. We obey because the guard's in power. Will remain in power when I have to leave and go about my business. Then he'll be free to take out on my brother whatever revenge he couldn't exact from me and my smart mouth. So I take low. Shake my head but stroll away (just enough nigger in my walk to tell the guard I know what he thinks of me but that I think infinitely less of him) toward the least crowded space in the row of benches against the wall.

Not much news to relate. Robby cares about family business and likes to keep up with who's doing what, when, how, etc., but he also treats the news objectively, cold-bloodedly. Family affairs have everything and nothing to do with him. He's in exile, powerless to influence what goes on outside the walls, so he maintains a studied detachment; he hears what I say and quickly mulls it over, buries the worrisome parts, grins at good news. When he comments on bad news it's usually a grunt, a nod, or a gesture with his hands that says all there is to say and says, A million words wouldn't make any difference, would they. Learning to isolate himself, to build walls within the walls enclosing him is a matter of survival. If he doesn't insulate himself against those things he can't change, if he can't discipline himself to ignore and forget, to narrow the range of his concerns to what he can immediately, practically effect, he'll go crazy. The one exception is freedom. Beneath whatever else Robby says or does or thinks, the dream of freedom pulses. The worst times, the lowest times are when the pulse seems extinguished. Like in the middle of the night, the hour of the wolf when even the joint is quiet and the earth stops spinning on its axis and he bursts from sleep, the deathly sleep that's the closest thing to mercy prison ever grants, starts from sleep and for a moment hears nothing. In the shadow of that absolute silence he can't imagine himself ever leaving prison alive. For hours, days, weeks, the mood of that moment can oppress him. He needs every ounce of willpower he possesses to pick up the pieces of his life, to animate them again with the hope that one day the arbitrary, bitter, little routines he manufactures to sustain himself will make sense because one day he'll be free.

I arrange my pens and yellow pad atop the table. But before we begin working on the book I tell Robby my sawing dream.

I am a man, myself but not myself. The man wakes up and can't see the stars. The smell of death surrounds him. Fifteen hundred other men sleep in the honeycomb of steel that is his home forever. The fitful stirrings, clattering bars, groaning, the sudden outcries of fear, rage, madness, and God knows what else are finally over at this hour of the night or morning as he lies in his cell listening to other men sleep. The monotonous sawing sound reminds him of the funny papers, the little cloud containing saw and log drawn above a character's head so you can see the sound of sleeping. Only the man doesn't see logs floating above the prisoner's heads. As he listens and shuts his eyes and gets as close to praying as he ever does anymore, praying for sleep, for blessed oblivion, the cartoon he imagines behind his closed eyes is himself sawing away the parts of his own body. Doggedly, without passion or haste, drawing a dull saw up and back, up and back through his limbs. Slices drop away on the concrete floor. The man is cutting himself to pieces, there is less of him every time he saws through a section. He is lopping off his own flesh and blood but works methodically, concentrating on the up-and-back motion of the saw. When there's nothing left, he'll be finished. He seems almost bored, almost asleep, ready to snore like the saw's snoring as it chews through his body.

Robby shakes his head and starts to say something but doesn't, and we both leave the dream alone. Pass on to the book, the tasks still to be accomplished.

Robby had said he liked what he'd seen of the first draft. Liked it fine, but something was missing. Trouble was, he hadn't been able to name the missing ingredient. I couldn't either but I knew I had to try and supply it. By the book's conclusion I wanted a whole, rounded portrait of my brother. I'd envisioned a climactic scene in the final section, an epiphany that would reveal Robby's character in a powerful burst of light and truth. As the first draft evolved, I seemed to settle for much less. One early reader had complained of a "sense of frustration . . . By the end of the book I want to know more about Robby than I actually know. I know a lot of facts about his life but most of his inner self escapes me." On target or not, the reaction of this early reader, coupled with Robby's feeling that something crucial was lacking, had destroyed any complacency I had about the book's progress. I reread Robby's letters, returned to the books and articles that had informed my research into prisons and prisoners. I realized no apotheosis of Robby's character could occur in the final section because none had transpired in my dealings with my brother. The first draft had failed because it attempted to impose a dramatic shape on a relationship, on events and people too close to me to see in terms of beginning, middle, and end. My brother was in prison. A thousand books would not reduce his sentence one day. And the only denouement that might make sense of his story would be his release from prison. I'd been hoping to be a catalyst for change in the world upon which the book could conceivably have no effect at all. I'd been waiting to record dramatic, external changes in Robby's circumstances when what I should have been attuned to were the inner changes, his slow, internal adjustment day by day to an unbearable situation. The book was no powerful engine being constructed to set my brother free; it was dream, wish, song.

No, I could not create a man whose qualities were self-evident cause for returning him to the world of free people. Prison had changed my brother, not broken him, and therein lay the story. The changes were subtle, incremental; bit by bit he had been piecing himself together. He had not become a model human being with a cure for cancer at his fingertips if only the parole board would just give him a chance, turn him loose again on the streets of Homewood. The character traits that landed Robby in prison are the same ones that have allowed him to survive with dignity and pain and a sense of himself as infinitely better than the soulless drone prison demands he become. Robby knows his core is intact; his optimism, his intelligence, his capacity for love, his pride, his dream of making it big, becoming somebody special. And though these same qualities helped get him in trouble and could derail him again, I'm happy they are still there. I rejoice with him.

The problem with the first draft was my fear. I didn't let Robby speak for himself enough. I didn't have enough confidence in his words, his vision, his insights. I wanted to clean him up. Manufacture compelling before-and-after images. Which meant I made the bad too bad and good too good. I knew what I wanted; so, for fear I might not get what I needed, I didn't listen carefully, probe deeply enough. As I tried his story again I began to recognize patterns, a certain consistency in his responses, a basic impetuous honesty that made him see himself and his world with unflinching clarity. He never stopped asking questions. He never allowed answers to stop him. The worst things he did followed from the same impulse as the best. He could be unbelievably dumb, corrupt, selfish, and destructive but those qualities could keep him down no more than his hope, optimism, his refusal to accept a dull, inferior portion could buoy him above the hell that engulfed black boys in the Homewood streets.

Robby watched it all. Ups and downs. Rises and falls. What was consistent was the watching, the consciousness, the vision in which he saw himself as counting, as being worth saving at any cost. If he had lost that vision, if he loses it now, then we will all matter a little less.

To repair the flawed first draft I had asked for more from Robby. He'd responded sporadically with poems, anecdotes, meditations on his time behind bars. What he was giving me helped me turn a corner. I was closer to him. I was beginning to understand what had been missing in the first version of his story. I was learning to respect my brother's touch, his vision. Learning what was at stake in this give-and-take between us, initiated by the idea of a book.

A letter from Robby had added this coda to Garth's story, the story he thought might be one place to begin telling his own:

> After Garth's funeral, me, Mike, and Cecil, our ladies, and Garth's lady sat in Mike's car and waited for all the other cars to leave. We weren't doing any talking, just crying and sniffling. It was raining outside and the silence was broken only by the pitter-patter of the rain on the car. Now I was always the oldest of our crew and Garth had always been my little brother though always taller. So when Mike finally started up the car the radio came on and a song by the group War was on the box. The name of the song was "Me and Baby Brother" and the chorus goes: "Me and baby brother used to run together. . . . Running over one another headed for the corner." It was like it was just for me. I sat there in the backseat with tears just running down my face.

His new girl friend Leslie claims Robby lives through the words of songs and movies. Robby admits maybe it's true. He's sent me the lyrics of a Sly and the Family Stone jam, "Family Affair." The song was popular at about the time Robby was breaking up with his first wife, Geraldine. For him the song says everything there is to say about that period in his life. Part of the magic's in the words, the line-by-line correspondence between what was happening to him and the situations and people the song described:

> Newlyweds a year ago but they're still
> Checking each other
> Nobody wants to blow
> Nobody wants to be left out
> You can't leave cause your heart is there. . . .

But another part was the music itself, what transfigures the personal, the unique with universals of rhythm, tone, and harmony, what must always remain unspoken because words can't keep up with the flood of feeling, of experience music releases.

The music Robby loves is simple; the lyrics often seem sentimental, banal. Though rhythm and blues and rock 'n' roll are rooted in traditional African music, the soul sounds Robby listened to in the sixties had been heavily commercialized, exploited by whites. Fortunes were made by whites who produced, performed, wrote, and distributed this so-called black music. About the only thing whites didn't do to black music was destroy it. Miraculously, the best black singers and musicians transcended the destructive incursions on their turf. Afro-American musical styles passed through one more crucible and emerged on the other side modified externally but intact at the core. Robby could see himself, recognize his world in the music called soul.

Over 125 years before Robby discovered visions of himself reflected in "Family Affair," young Frederick Douglass learned in the music of fellow slaves truths about his life, about the ordeal of slavery and the capacity of the spirit to rise above it, truths that were articulated in the form of strange chants, cries, percussive clapping and stomping, call-and-response cadences created by black field hands as they marched from one back-breaking job to another. "Their songs still follow me," Douglass later wrote; and certain songs continue to haunt my brother. Simple songs. Lyrics as uncomplicated, transparent as the poetry of the gospels and spirituals we sang in Homewood A.M.E. Zion church: *Let my people go. Farther along we'll understand why. Amazing Grace. How sweet the sound. One bright morning. His eye is on the sparrow so I know He watches me.*

The messages are simple. The mysteries they enfold are not. What Robby hears is the sound of what he has been, where he has been, the people he traveled with, the ones here, the ones there, the ones gone forever. The best, the authentic black music does not unravel the mysteries, but recalls them, gives them a particular form, a specific setting, attaches the mysteries to familiar words and ideas. Simple lyrics of certain songs follow us, haunt us because the words floating in the music are a way of eavesdropping on the mysteries, of remembering the importance of who we are but also experiencing the immensity of Great Time and Great Space, the Infinite always at play around the edges of our lives.

You are my sunshine, my only sunshine. You make me happy when skies are gray. Our grandfather John French loved that song. Hummed it, crooned it high on Dago Red, beat out its rhythm on his knee, a table's edge, the bottom of a pot. *Froggy went a-courtin'* was another favorite, and we'd ride like Froggy jiggedy-jig, jiggedy-jig on Daddy John's thigh while he sang. Those songs had survived. John French found them and stored them and toted them on his journey from Culpepper, Virginia, to Pittsburgh, Pennsylvania, the place where we began to know him as our mother's father. He saved those songs and they documented his survival. All of that hovered in the words and music when he passed them on to us.

Here are some more of the lines Robby remembered from "Family Affair":

> *One child grows up to be somebody*
> *who just loves to learn.*
> *And the other child grows up to be*
> *somebody who just loves to burn.*
> *Mom loves the both of them*
> *You see it in the blood*
> *Both kids are good to Mom*
> *Blood thicker than the mud . . .*
> *It's a family affair.*

What do these words tell me about my brother? Why did he share them with me? One reason may be his dissatisfaction with the picture of him I'd drawn in the first draft of this book. There will necessarily be distance, vast discrepancy between any image I create and the mystery of all my brother is, was, can be. We both know that. And he'll never be satisfied, but he's giving me the benefit of the doubt. Not complaining overtly, but reminding me that there's more, much, much more to know, to learn. He's giving me a song, holding open a door on a world I can never enter. Robby can't carry me over to the other side, but he can crack the door and I can listen.

Robby refuses to be beaten down. Sly said in another song that everybody wants to be a star. That wish contains the best of us and the worst. The thrust of ego and selfishness, the striving to be better than we are. If Robby fell because the only stardom he could reasonably seek was stardom in crime, then that's wrong. It's wrong not because Robby wanted more but because society closed off every chance of getting more, except through crime. So I'm glad to see Robby's best (worst) parts have survived. Can't have one without the other.

I let Robby know I've rewritten the book, virtually from start to finish. Plenty of blurred, gray space, lots of unfilled gaps and unanswered questions and people to interview, but the overall design is clearer now. I'm trying to explain to Robby how I feel released rather than constrained by the new pattern beginning to emerge. The breakthrough came when I started to hear what was constant, persistent beneath the changes in his life. The book will work if the reader participates, begins to grasp what I have. I hadn't been listening closely enough, so I missed the story announcing itself. When I caught on, there I was, my listening, waiting self part of the story, listening, waiting for me.

Yet I remained apprehensive about the prison section of the book. Robby wouldn't be able to help me as much in this last section as he had with the others. The method we'd evolved was this: Robby would tell his stories. I'd listen, take notes, reconstruct the episodes after I'd allowed them time to sink in, then check my version with Rob to determine if it sounded right to him. Letters and talk about what I'd written would continue until we were both satisfied. We'd had lots of practice performing that operation and I was beginning to feel a measure of confidence in the results it eventually produced. "Doing Time" was a different matter. The book would end with this section. Since I was writing the book, one way or another I'd be on center stage. Not only would the prison section have to pull together many loose ends, but new material had to surface and be resolved. Aside from logical and aesthetic considerations, finishing the book as object, completing the performance, there was the business of both rendering and closing down the special relationship between my brother and myself that writing the book had precipitated. All the questions I'd decided to finesse or sidestep or just shrug off in order to get on with writing would now return, some in the form of issues to be addressed in concluding the book, some as practical dilemmas in the world outside the book, the world that had continued to chug along while I wrote.

Robby was still a prisoner. He was inside and I was outside. Success, fame, ten million readers wouldn't change that. The book, whether it flopped or became a best-seller, would belong to the world beyond the prison walls. Ironically, it would validate the power of the walls, confirm the distance between what transpired inside and outside. Robby's story would be "out there," but he'd still be locked up. Despite my attempts to identify with my brother, to reach him and share his troubles, the fact was, I remained on the outside. With the book. Though I never intended to steal his story, to appropriate it or exploit it, in a sense that's what would happen once the book was published.

His story would be out there in a world that ignored his existence. It could be put to whatever uses people chose. Of course I was hoping Robby would benefit from a book written about him, but the possible benefits did not alter the fact that imprisonment profoundly alienated him from the finished product of our collaboration.

Simple things like sharing financial profits could be handled; but how could I insure a return on the emotional investment my brother had made? Once I'd gotten the book I'd come for, would I be able to sustain the bond that had grown between us? Would I continue to listen with the same attention to his stories? Would he still possess a story? Much of what he'd entrusted to me had nothing to do with putting a book together. Had I identified with him because I discovered that was the best way to write the book? Would the identification I'd achieved become a burden, too intense, too pressurized to survive once the book was completed? Was the whole thing between us about a book or had something finer, truer been created? And even if a finer, truer thing had come into being, would it be shattered by the noisy explosion (or dull thud) of the book's appearance in the world beyond the prison walls?

Some of these questions could be asked outright. Others were too intimidating, too close to the bone to raise with my brother. Yet we had to deal with all of them. In the world and in the prison section. The book, if there was to be a book, must end, must become in some senses an artifact. I wanted to finish it but I didn't want to let it go. I might be losing much more than a book.

The fears I could put into words I tried to share with Robby. He nodded, clenched and unclenched his big hands, smiled at the funny parts, the blackly comic pratfalls and cul de sacs neither of us nor anybody in the world can avoid. Yeah, shit's gon hit the fan. Yeah, sounds like it might get rough . . . but then again . . . what can you do but do? Many of my worries clearly were not his. I was the writer, that was *my* kitchen, *my* heat. He'd thought about some of the stuff worrying me but I could tell he hadn't spent lots of time fretting over it. And wouldn't. Many of the troubles I anticipated were too far down the line to tease out Robby's concern. In prison he had learned to walk a very fine line. On one side of the line was the minute-by-minute, day-by-day struggle for survival to which he must devote his undivided attention. On the other side his vision of something better, a life outside the walls, an existence he could conceive only if he allowed himself the luxury of imagination, of formulating plans in a future divorced from his present circumstances. The line was thin, was perilous because any energy he squandered on envisioning the future was time away, a lapse in the eternal vigilance he must maintain to stay alive in his cage. Yet the struggle to survive, the heightened awareness he must sustain to get through each moment, each day made no sense unless his efforts were buying something other than more chunks of prison routine. And plans for the future were pipe dreams unless he could convince himself he possessed the stamina and determination to make it step by step through the withering prison regimen. These options, realities, consequences defined the straight and narrow path Robby was forced to tread. Like Orpheus ascending from Hades or Ulysses chained to the mast or a runaway slave abandoning his family and fleeing toward the North Star, my brother knew the only way he might get what he desperately wanted was to turn his back on it, pretend it didn't exist.

Walking the line, leaning neither too far to the left nor too far to the right, balancing, always balancing the pulls of heart and head in one direction against the tugs wrenching him in the other—that was Robby's unbearable burden, made more unbearable because to escape it all he had to do was surrender, tilt one way or the other, and let the weight on his shoulders drag him down.

The source of my brother's strength was a mystery to me. When I put myself in his shoes, tried to imagine how I'd cope if I were sentenced to life imprisonment, I couldn't conceive of any place inside myself from which I could draw the courage and dignity he displayed. In prison Robby had achieved an inner calm, a degree of self-sufficiency and self-reliance never apparent when he was running the streets. I didn't know many people, inside or out, who carried themselves the way he did now. Like my mother, he'd grown accustomed to what was unbearable, had named it, tamed it. He'd fallen, but he'd found the strength to rise again. Inch by inch, hand over hand, he'd pulled himself up on a vine he'd never known was there, a vine still invisible to me. I knew the vine was real because I'd watched my brother grasp it, because I could feel its absence in the untested air when I thought of myself in his situation. To discover the source of my brother's strength I found myself comparing what I'd accomplished outside the walls with what he'd managed inside. The comparison made me uncomfortable.

I didn't envy my brother. I'd learned enough about the hell of prison life not to mistake what I was feeling for envy. No, I wouldn't trade my problems for his. I'd take my chances on the outside. Yet something like envy was stirring. Worse than envy. The ancient insatiability of ego kicking up. Why hadn't I ever been able to acknowledge a talent, success, or capacity in another person without feeling that person's accomplishment either diminished me or pointed to some crucial deficiency in my constitution? What compound of greed, insecurity, and anger forced me always to compare, compete? Why couldn't I just leave myself out of it and celebrate Robby's willpower, his grace under pressure? Why couldn't I simply applaud and be grateful for whatever transformation of self he'd performed? Were my visits to prison about freeing him or freeing myself from the doubt that perhaps, after all, in spite of it all, maybe my brother has done more with his life than I've done with mine. Maybe he's the better man and maybe the only way I can face that truth about him, about myself, is to demystify the secret of his survival. Maybe I'm inside West Pen to warm myself by his fire, to steal it. Perhaps in my heart of hearts or, better, my ego of egos, I don't really want to tear down the walls, but tear my brother down, bring him back to my level, to the soft, uncertain ground where my feet are planted.

If somebody has sung the praises of a book or movie, I go in looking for flaws, weaknesses. No matter how good these books or movies, my pleasure is never unalloyed because I'm searching for the bad parts, groping for them even when they're not there; so I usually come away satisfied by my dissatisfaction. I'm stuck with a belief that nothing can stand too close an examination. The times when I experience the world as joy, as song, some part of me insists even in the midst of the joy, the song, that these moments will pass and nothing, nothing promises they will ever come again. My world is fallen. It's best to be suspicious, not to trust anything, anyone too far. Including myself. Especially the treacherous, layered reality of being whatever I think I am at a given moment. It's a fallen world. My brother is rising from the ashes but because he is my brother, another fall is as certain as this rising and my particular burden is to see both always. I can't help it.

Does what he's achieved in the narrow confines of a cell mock the cage I call freedom? What would I do in his place? How would I act? Are the walls between us permanent? Do we need them, want them? Is there a better place without barred windows and steel doors and locked cells where there's room for both of us, all of us?

What it comes down to is saying yes. Yes to the blood making us brothers. Blood bonding us, constraining us to the unspoken faith that

I'm trying to do my best and he's trying to do his best but nothing we do can insure the worst won't happen so we keep at it, as best we can, doing the book and hoping it will turn out okay.

He's been thinking a lot about the time on the road, the three months as a fugitive when he and his partners crisscrossed the country, playing hide and seek with the law. He's tried to write some of it down but he's been too busy. Too much's been happening. School. He'll graduate in January. A little ceremony for the few guys who made it all the way through the program. An associate degree in engineering technology and three certificates. Rough. Real rough. The math he'd never had in high school. The slow grind of study. Hours relearning to be a student. Learning to take the whole business seriously while you hear the madness of the prison constantly boiling outside your cell. But I'm gon get it, Bruh. Few more weeks. These last exams kicking my ass but I'm gon get it. Most the fellows dropped out. Only three of us completed the program. It'll look good on my record, too. But I ain't had time to do nothing else. Them books you sent. I really enjoy reading them but lately I ain't been doing nothing but studying.

Amiri Baraka was born LeRoi Jones in Newark, New Jersey, in 1934. Teacher, writer, and political activist, he has taught at many universities, most recently at SUNY in Stony Brook as professor of Africana studies. His numerous publications include *Home, The Dead Lecturer,* and an autobiography. Baraka has received many fellowships, including a Guggenheim Fellowship and a Rockefeller Foundation Fellowship, as well as many awards for his plays.

21

AMIRI BARAKA

From The Autobiography of LeRoi Jones

(1984)

FOR ME, being here has always been a condition of struggle and, hopefully, growth. These are attempts to sum up my life, before having lived it all. Attempts to "make sense" where it has been difficult to see any sense.

> *Steps*
> *of a life*
> *turns*
> *under the sun*
> *& the sun*
> *turns &*
> *burns &*
> *finally one last day*
> *goes*
> *out*
> *Its history*
> *is a tail*
> *Tales for*
> *remembering*
> *words for*
> *understanding*

A long way (opens)
Back then &
there
we see now
again
To know
Seeing
& understand
Our
Being

Young

Growing up was a maze of light and darkness. I have never fully understood the purpose of childhood. Baby pictures nonplus me. It looks like me a little, I think. But what the hell, I don't know nuthin. It ain't that cute. Falling back like that, toothless grimace, mouth bare, legs bent, fat with diapers. And them probably wet.

Growing has obsessed me, maybe because I reached a certain point and stopped. My feeling is that I was always short. Maybe that's why people like those baby pictures, because you couldn't tell I was short then. Later, it became obvious and people started to rub it in.

I was not only short, little, a runt. But skinny too. Short & Skinny. But as a laughing contrast I got these big bulbous eyes. Big eyes. And that was no secret where they came from, my old man. Actually, you could say I got my whole "built" from him (Coyette Leroy Jones). But I don't want to slander him, because he is my father and I love him.

But people always would be sliding up to me saying, "You look just like your father," or to him, "Roy, he look just like you," or to my mother or some other hopeless "responsible" in whose charge I was placed, "Hey, he look just like Roy"—"He look just like his father." It made you wonder (even then) why they put so much insistence on this. Was this a miracle? Wasn't I spose to look like him? What was this wonder at creation?

That I was short and skinny with big eyes and looked just like my father. These were the most indelible. My earliest identity.

I knew, too, rather early, that I was brown. Brown with a round face and sometimes wavy hair. These were later *dis*sociations. Brown, round and wavy. OK.

I thought I looked OK when I wasn't too sparkly from my brown mom's Vaseline aspirations I didn't look bad.

Another thing is that we were always in motion. It seemed that way. But the expected chaos of such a situation never registered.

From Barclay Street, a "luxury" project we had to move out of, $24 a month was too much even though my ol' man had just got a good job at the Post Office. But he couldn't cut those prices, so we had to space. But I have some early memories of that place. Its park, its fire escapes (I nearly fell off and ended the saga right here), its red bricks and some light browns and yellows flittin round.

Earlier than this is a blank, though I have "memories" produced by later conversations. Like being hit by a car—banged in the head (or do I remember the steel grille smacking my face, trying to wake me up?).

A dude hit me in the head with a big rock. And I still carry the scar. I think I remember that sharp pain. A cold blue day. A brown corduroy jacket. And the whiz of wind as I broke round the corner to our crib.

I pulled a big brown radio down (also on my head). Another scar, still there. The radio had a knob missing and the metal rod sunk into my skull just left of my eye.

Tolchinski's Pickle Works across the street. A smell and taste so wonderful I been hooked ever since (every sense). Hey, man, in a wooden barrel, with them big green pimples on 'em. And good shit floatin around in the barrel with 'em.

A guy who flashed around and tried to teach us to play tennis. That's how "horizontal" our community was then. Almost all of us (them and us) right there, flattened out by the big NO. But I never learned. How to play tennis. That yellowness never got in. But it was different in my house than out in the street. Different conventions. Like gatherings—of folks & their histories. Different accumulations of life. So those references and their *enforcement*.

You see, I come from brown niggers from way back. Yeh. But some yellow niggers—let's say color notwithstanding—some yellow and even some factual, *a* factual, white motherfucker or fatherfucker in there.

I was secure in most ways. My father and mother I knew and related to every which way I can remember. They *were* the definers of my world. My guides. My standards.

I was a little brown boy on my mother's hand. A little brown big-eyed boy with my father. With a blue watch cap with Nordic design. At the World's Fair (1939) eyes stretched trying to soak up the days and their lessons.

But the motion was constant. And that is a standard as well. From Barclay to Boston (Street) and the half-dark of my grandmother's oil lamp across the street. They had me stretched out one night, and this red-freckle-face nigger was pickin glass outta my knee. There were shadows everywhere. And mystery.

My grandfather had had a grocery store on that same street earlier, but that was washed away in the 30's with a bunch of other stuff. My grandfather didn't shoot himself, or jump off a building. But after that, we was brown for sure!

And so for that branch of the family, there was a steep descent. My mother's folks. In Alabama the old man owned two funeral parlors and a grocery store. First funeral parlor burned down by "jealous crackers" (my grandmother's explanation). After the second arson, they had to hat.

First, to Pennsylvania (Beaver Falls) and then finally to Newark. My father was running from dee white folkz too. He had bopped some dude side the head in a movie he ushered in. The dude was an ofay. (*Natürlich!*) And so, again, the hat was called for.

To arrive, out of breath, in a place you thought was The Apple. But it turned out to be the *prune* (Newark). Jobless, detached from the yellow streak of the Jones (nee Johns) upward mobility, even there inside the brown. A part-time barber, for mostly white folks. With a high school diploma—though three of his sisters were bound for college. Projected from a teeny brown white-haired widow lady, daughter of another teeny brown white-haired widow lady, who shot the distaffs through on sewing for white folks.

So that's where we was coming from. The church of specific

reality. Inside the general (flight) our Johns-Jones/Russ lives merging. But see, they had sent my mother to Tuskegee (when it was a high school) and then to Fisk. I used to look at both yearbooks full of brown and yellow folks. She had one flick poised at the starting line, butt up, large eyes catching the whole world, about to take off. Her name then was "Woco-Pep," a Southern gasoline. She was that fast.

Where she was going to in her parents' head I ain't exactly hip. Except it's safe to say it was *up*. Storekeeper father, mother and brother assistants in the joint and what not. But somehow she ran into this big-eyed skinny dude. (M.F.) My father. A tipsy part-time barber or a barber who occasional got deep in his cups. The story goes he flipped his little Ford on top of his drunk self on 13th Avenue and come out from under swearing off.

You see an irony here? No? A split from off the upwardly mobile somehow molests (with permission) the scioness of the nigger rich. Except by 1929 all them social dynamics was put out by Uncle Sam's—Ugly Sissy's fatal flaw—capitalismus. And so the new day dawned with a pregnant coed who did not get to go to the Olympics and a new member of the family who didn't come from "bad stock" (aagh! hopeless!) but what the hell was his thoroughly brown ass going to do now?

Marrying your mama, jim. What else? And so flow the streams together. But wasn't one of the first Negroes to read in South Carolina, complete with plaque and multiple modest legend, your old man's Uncle Enoch? And them slender and fat sisters of his, wasn't they all got to be teachers and shit? Affirmative—J.A.M.F. So couldink you say they was all doing the same shit for a while?

You see, you doesink understand colored peoples or color peepas either. My mother's folks was in business. Them funeral parlor dudes was and is the actual colored rich guys. The bourgeoisie, dig? Them teachers and shit (His old man [M.F.'s] was a preacher part time and a chef, also bricklayed a taste. Got the flu and it took him off.), they just the petty bourgeoisie. And hell, they even had food smells and brick dust on 'em and some sew-for-white-ladies thread on 'em. Whew!

Later, it really cracked up. They was drug down! That's what the scuttlebutt was. Arguments in our weird orange house years later. My uncle called my father a "nincompoop." What is that? Because these Russes had been drug down, jim! Outta they funeral parlors, outta they stores, Granddaddy to be a night watchman, his wife on the bus to Essex Falls to curl up some white ladies' hairs, and wouldn't ya know it, M.F. "had" M.M. in a dusty-ass Jew factory doing piece-work. (But he did make a breakthrough, you got to admit. He wasn't jes a dumb nigger. He did get in the Post Office!) Thass rumblings all up in there as part of the collective psyche. On the X spot of the altar. The forebodings and nigger history. All stuffed into me gourd un-rapped on arrival. But ye gets used to hearing tumblings in the wind and words the leaves make spinning in the air like that.

But would ya tell from me mischievous ways the stuffings inside me round peapicker knot? A trained eye, ye say? Oh?

So, Boston Street. And "Bunny" and "Princess" across the street. His mother tortured him in the bathtub with green water. I couldn't help him—he was weeping and shit. I was froze and puzzled, standing there. What was in that water? Or was it just he didn't want no bath?

Boston Street.

Ellic the painter raved in them parts. Crawling over the fences in spotted coveralls, drunk as the social system. We lived in two houses on that street—at one address I tumbled off the stone porch and busted my collarbone. And a preacher blew his wife to smithereens around the corner. It was a spooky house with a narrow path. And Miss Rhapsody across the street gettin ready for evening so she could put on her purple flower and go out and sing the blues. (She had a fine-ass daughter. Blue, stiff and beautiful!)

But all that soon was in the wind. We moved, ya see? Looked up and we were way cross town near the Italian border. I was born in the center of the city (New Ark) in a hospital named for a yellow doctor, Kinney Memorial. But by age five or six we'd spaced. Wound up on a little street the other side of nowhere.

And we were all in there. Mama Daddy Nana Granddaddy Uncle Elaine and me. On Dey Street. The niggers were so cynical they called it *die*—the white folks so full of shit they called it *day*.

Orange house with a porch you sit on, or crawl under and plot shit. Living room, dining room, kitchen, left turn, bathroom. Back door and little yard, edged by cement and a two-car garage. Second floor: narrow bedroom (Uncle), middle bedroom with big oak bed with a back tall as a man and foot post taller than a six-year-old (Nana and Granddaddy). Front bedroom (Mama & Daddy and little kids, us).

A red-nosed Irishman (ol' man Doyle) and his wife on one side next to a vacant lot and right next door Angel Domenica Cordasca (female), a little non-romantic Italian playmate. Next to Doyle, the playground at the edge of which sat Central Avenue School. Next to Angel, a factory. Across the street from Central Avenue School, a row of brown houses. Clarence P. (funny), his older brother (weird), his mother (church stalker). Danny W., a confederate, short and curly-haired. Fast but plump. Another lot for an auto parts store. (They got the whole block now.) Then Pooky, a little Italian troublemaker, his twin sisters, snotty-nosed midgets. The Davises next, eight black curly-headed all-sized kids—actually light brown in color, black in socio-eco terms. Who knew Mr. D.? Mrs. D. was always called Miz as far as I know. And she ran that bunch, literally, up and down the street. Frank (big and away soon to the Army, never to return). Evelyn, big and fine with that wavy, straightish hair them kinda folks had, but way outta my generation. Sam, called "Lon-nell" (it was Lionel). Orland, called "Board," meaning Bud. Algernon, called "Angie." Jerome, real name "Fat." "Rookie," given name unknown, and Will, the peewee. The D.'s always seemed like more than they were. At least ten or twelve. They were a standard of measure around those parts. Their name called by my mother meant "many" or "dirty" or "wild" or something like that. Algy and Board were running buddies of ours. Board was a desperado. And my mother didn't dig us running together. Nutty as he was, I didn't dig it too much. Algy was wild too, but cooler. Lon-nell you liked to have on your team as one of the "big boys."

Next to the Davises, Domenick, an Italian iceman, and his brood. Some more Italians, a couple, next to him, with a red and white very clean house. Domenick's house was yellow and brown. The red and white house had cherries in the back of it and you know we hit on them whenever our ass stopped aching from the last hit reported to the mama authorities. But those cherries, and I think some hard green knot peaches, like that cause we never let 'em stay there long enough to ripen, were cause for much adventure and repeated instruction in cause and effect.

There was also contrast in that, and all along this one block center (Central Avenue to Sussex Avenue) there was a similar contrast from a similar dissimilarity—mixture. For now we'd (Jones/Russ) flashed into a *mixed* neighborhood. I was about six now. And already a veteran of three different abodes. This made the fourth (Barclay Street, two on Boston, and now Dey). But all those other places had been the Central Ward—or at that time the Third Ward—near round The Hill, center of black life. But this last move took us into the West (literally the Ward) and a place where the black community trailed off in a sputter of Italians. Or likewise where the Italian community thinned and more and more blacks had moved in. So that in our block and all around in that area, there was a kind of standoff. Central Avenue School, it seems to me, was heavier black. The life there more controlled in the playground, in the hallways, by the black students. And the year the Warren Street contingent came in it was The Hill for sure pouring in. So that even in that part of the West headed North, the ambassadors from Central and even South brought those places to us.

But that mixture carried contradictions in it far beyond we youth, hey, even beyond many of the grown folks. We were friends and enemies in the non-final caldron of growing up. We said things, did things, were things, and even became some other things which maybe could be understood on those streets, ca. 1940's.

So next to the red and white clean cherry and peach house, a lot with brown-gray gravel. A useless rusty lot that ended with a brick wall to nowhere. The back of some factory. And like a miniature boundary line, that 20 feet of lot separated the lower-middle-class Italian cleanie from Eddie Clay's brown and tan run-down clapboard shack.

And in that shack, like a ghost of the black South—a drunken building—were some living ghosts, poverty-struck and mad. Old toothless snuff-chumping ladies. Staring old men. People with hard rusty hands. A woman named Miss Ada (I always thought it was Ator, a weird radio-drama monster name) who wandered and staggered and stared and got outrageous drunk and cursed out history.

We made up stories about Eddie and teased Eddie. A veil hung over the house. A food like musk—an oldness, a strangeness. Yet Eddie was one of The Secret Seven (the kids who hung with us sometimes, my sister and I, Board, Algy, Norman, Danny, Eddie). We were The Secret Seven, which met under our porch at 19 Dey Street to plot the destruction of packs of Kits and jars of Kool-Aid.

And we'd all tease Eddie about his weird house. It was old and poor-looking, full of old country Negroes usually drunk. And sometimes Eddie'd chase one or a bunch of us when we talked about his creepy old house. Yet across the hard gravel were the anonymous cherry-growing Italians in their white spotless red-trimmed number. The best-looking house on the block.

Our orangish-brown clapboard number seemed merely like "headquarters." It seemed like it sagged a bit or leaned. Especially after a hurricane blew a big tree down on the bathroom and tore the bathroom roof off. It was on the street doing something, looking like something (to others), but what that was I really can't say. It was headquarters. Where I came out of and had to go back to—after school—after playground—after sneaking off—or after any stuff I'd got into, that leaning orangish-brown house was my center, and my fate.

Next to Eddie's was my fake cousin Lorraine's red job. Red shingles and short brick steps. Her name was Jones, so we could play cousins, though I liked her, from time to time, as a girlfriend, but that never went anywhere. But some older dudes thought she was my cousin on the real side and they would be trying to program me to drop their name on her. Some really vulgar types would tease me about what they was going to do to my cousin, like it mattered to me.

Lorraine's house was short and squat though it was three stories. Lorraine's mother looked just like her, chain smoking. A factory worker going back and forth during the war years like Rosie the

Riveter. When we all had house keys tied on strings around our necks.

Then Mattie's narrow tall porched brown joint. I guess like Mattie herself. Tall narrow brown . . . with glasses she'd be peering through. In streetwide gatherings when young and old kids big and little were together for some reason. Some summer happenings or chance gatherings, Mattie would be there, a big stringbean girl (no matter what age). She had a kind of horsiness to her face that set the boys to razzing her about it when they were in that frame of mind. Sometimes they'd be saying some other things and Mattie'd turn on her long narrow heel.

A fence next to Mattie's, then Joycee's yard (her family shared it with the New Hope Baptist Church). And that was the end of the block. On my side, across the street, after Angel's house, there was a factory that made boxes. They took up the rest of the block. The loading platform was the only interest, otherwise I remember wondering why they wanted to make our block dull with their gray building business.

And the block was, it seemed to me, fairly quiet. The scrambles of kids ran up and down and around the corner and around the other corner. I guess since Central Avenue School and playground sat on the block, it obviously couldn't have been quiet on school days, when those children ran screaming up and down the street. But Dey Street and, on either side, Newark Street to the west and Lock Street to the east, were like a swath of mixtures. Black-heavy, but still Italian and black. In fact, all the way to Orange Street, this mixture persisted. On the north side of Orange, you jumped into the Italian neighborhood. The old First Ward, now North Ward.

There was a mixture at the little-kid level which we carried most times successfully and at the tops of our voices. Adults fed us various poisons that pushed us apart as we grew, naturally. And by high school, almost miraculously, the relationships we'd had on the street level and in grammar school had disappeared. So quickly, I was startled. And I remember consciously taking note that this is what had happened. When I was a sophomore in high school I could see very clearly what had happened. That we had reached another stage, and those previous relationships were ended. And that while nobody spoke openly about this, we all, from our opposite sides of the nationality wall, knew what it meant, and acted accordingly. But that was a later stage; the open door onto it.

Kenneth A. McClane was born in 1951 in New York City. He has taught English and creative writing at several universities and has published his poetry in numerous periodicals. He is the recipient of many honors, including the Lamont Poetry Prize. He received the Clark Distinguished Teaching Award in 1983. He is a professor of English at Cornell University.

22

KENNETH A. MCCLANE

A Death in the Family

(1985)

> *He was a kid of about the same age as Rufus, from some insane place like Jersey City or Syracuse, but somewhere along the line he had discovered that he could say it with a saxophone. He had a lot to say. He stood there, wide-legged, humping the air, filling his barrel chest, shivering in the rags of his twenty-odd years, and screaming through the horn* Do you love me? Do you love me? Do you love me? *And, again,* Do you love me? Do you love me? Do you love me?
>
> James Baldwin, *Another Country*

I RECALL HOW difficult it was for me to realize that my brother loved me. He was always in the streets, doing this and that, proverbially in trouble, in a place, Harlem, where trouble indeed was great. At times we would even come to blows, when, for example, drunk as he could be, he wished to borrow my car and I had visions of his entrails splayed over the city. I remember one incident as if it were yesterday: Paul, my younger brother, physically larger than me, his hand holding a screw driver, poised to stab me, his anger so great that his brother, the college professor, wouldn't let him drive his "lady" home, even though he could barely walk. I can still see him chiding me about how

I had always done the right thing, how I was not his father, how I was just a poor excuse for a white man, the last statement jeweled with venom. And from his place, this was certainly true: I had done what I was expected to do; and the world, in its dubious logic, had paid me well. I was a college teacher; I had published a few collections of poems; I had a wonderful girlfriend; and what suffering I bore, at least to my brother's eyes, centered around my inability to leave him alone. Luckily, this confrontation ended when my father rushed in on us, our distress exceeded only by the distress in his eyes. Later, my brother would forget the events of that evening, but not the fact that I had not lent him the car. For my part I would never forget how we were both so angry, so hate-filled. I, too, that night, might have killed my brother.

As children we were often at each other's throats. The difference in our ages, just two years, was probably a greater bridge than either of us welcomed. And so we often went for each other's pressure points: the greater discomfort enacted, the more skillful our thrust. But this was child's play, in a child's world. On that November night when my brother and I confronted each other with hate and murder in our eyes, I realized I had mined a new intensity, full of terror and, though I didn't know it then, of love.

Though he was incredibly angry (bitter some might say), I always admired my brother's honesty and self-love. It seemed that everything he thrust into his body was a denial of self—alcohol, smoke, cocaine— yet his mind and his quick tongue demanded that he be heard. In a world full of weakness, he was outspoken, never letting anyone diminish him. When he was at the wheel in that torturous abandon euphemistically called "city driving," he invariably would maneuver abreast of a driver who had somehow slighted him, and tell him, in no uncertain language, where he could go and with utmost dispatch. Paul never cared how big, crazy, or dangerous this other driver might be. When I cautioned him, reliving again and again the thousand headlines of *Maniac Kills Two Over Words,* he would just shrug. "He's a bastard, needs to know it." I remember how scared I became when he would roll down the window—scared and yet proud.

My brother was unable to ride within the subway, moving immediately to the small catwalk between the cars, where the air might reach him. He complained that he was always too hot, that the people were too close; indeed, as soon as he entered the train, sweat began to cascade off him, as if he had just completed a marathon. Later this image would remain with me: my brother, feet apart, sweat pouring from his body, trying to keep his delicate balance between the two radically shifting platforms, while always maintaining that he was fine. "Bro, I'm just hot." I would later learn that these manifestations were the effects of acute alcoholism; I would later learn much about my brother.

Like the day's punctuation, Paul would make his numerous runs to the *bodega*, bringing in his small brown paper bags, then quickly returning to his room, where he would remain for hours. Some days you would barely see him; my father could never coax him out. Paul saw my father as the establishment, "fat man" he would call him, though this too was somewhat playful. With Paul play and truth were so intermeshed that they leased the same root. One had to be forever careful of traveling with a joke only to find that no joke was intended. Or, just as often, finding sympathy with something Paul said, one was startled to see him break out in the most wondrous smile, amusement everywhere. In this spectacle, one thing was enormously clear: Paul was a difficult dancer. And like all artists, his mastery was also, for the rest of us, cause for contempt. We enjoyed his flights; but we also sensed, and poignantly, that they were had at our expense. Clearly we had failed as listeners, for Paul had not sought to befuddle us; but we, as the majority, were in the position of power and could always depend on it as our last defense. And power, arguments to the contrary, is rarely generous.

My brother would stay in his room for hours, watching the box, playing his drums, talking to his endless friends who, until he was just about to die, came to sit and talk and smoke. Paul inevitably would be holding court: he knew where the parties were, could get anyone near anything, had entrée with the most beautiful girls, who sensed something in his eyes that would not betray them. Many of his friends would later become doctors, a few entertainers, all of them by the most incomprehensible and tortuous of routes. The black middle class—if it can really be termed that—is a class made up of those who are either just too doggedly persistent or too stupid to realize that, like Fitzgerald's America, their long sought-after future remains forever beckoning and endlessly retreating. And Paul's friends, who sensed his demise well before we did, as only the doomed or the near-doomed can, were as oddly grafted to class—or even the promise of respectability—as it is humanly possible to imagine. Like Paul, they sat waiting for the warden, knowing only that the walls exist, that the sentence is real. Indeed, if the crime were lack of understandable passion, they were guilty a hundredfold. But it is not understanding, alas, that the world is interested in. And the world—they rightfully sensed—was certainly not interested in them.

Paul was no saint. Like most of us, he exhibited the confusions and the possibilities that intermittently set us on our knees or loose with joy. He wasn't political in the established way; his body, in its remoteness, was political. It said that the state of the world was nothing he cared to be involved with. Fuck it, he'd say.

In the language of the street, Paul was a "lover." And like all lovers he believed that the pounding of the bed frame testified to something that "his woman" best understood. And in the logic of his bed and of those who shared it, women's lib to the contrary, there seemed to be no complaints. Often I wondered about his use of the term "my woman," the possessiveness of it, the language that brought to mind the auction block and a brutal history that had profited neither of us. But Paul's woman was like his life: if I had my job and my poems, he had his woman. Feminists might complain of this uneasy pairing—I certainly share their concern—but within the brutal reward structure of the ghetto, where one's life is often one's only triumph, such a notion is understandable. My brother's woman was his only bouquet, the one thing that testified that he was not only a man, but a man whom someone wanted. Arguments notwithstanding, no manner of philosophy or word play can alter the truth. My brother loved his "woman" in the most profound sense of the word, since his love centered on the greatest offering he could give, the sharing of himself. And I do not mean to be coy here. For when you are, in

Gwendolyn Brooks's terms, "all your value and all your art," the gift of yourself is an unprecedented one.

But this is a brother's testimony; it is a way of a brother living with a brother dead. It doesn't have the violence of unknowing—the great violence that kept me for so long feeling guilty, which still makes the early morning the most difficult time. I remember how Paul volunteered to watch our cats when Rochelle and I, living for a three-month exile in Hartsdale, New York, had to be away. Max, the large white one, hell-bent on intercourse with the hardly possible, hid within the wall and Paul went nearly crazy, looking here and there, wondering if he should call, afraid that disaster had no shores. Strange how I recall this; it certainly isn't important. But Paul was scared—scared more so because he loved animals, saw in their pain more than he saw in ours, in his.

In July, my father called to say that I had best come to New York. Paul was ill. Very Ill. He would probably die. The whole thing was incredible. My father has the nagging desire to protect those he loves from the worrisome. What this tends to create, however, is the strangest presentiment: when he does finally communicate something, it is always at the most dire stage, and the onlooker can barely understand how something has become so involved, so horrible, so quickly; or is thrown, similarly, into the uncomfortable position of confronting the possibility that one failed to acknowledge something so momentous occurring. In either case, one is completely unprepared for revelation, and no matter what my father's heroic designs (and they were that), one's horror at not being allowed to participate in the inexorable, outdistances any possible feeling of gratitude. Although pain cannot be prepared for, neither can it be denied. But on this day, my father's voice was that of cold disbelief—the doctor without any possible placebo. And I was in the air in a few hours.

At that time I was involved in teaching summer school, and the day before one of my students had suggested that we read Baldwin's *Sonny's Blues.* I had read the story some years before and had been favorably impressed, though I couldn't remember any of its particulars. Well, at 6:15 I got on the airplane, armed with a few clothes and

Baldwin. Little did I know that that story would save my life, or at least make it possible to live with it.

Sonny's Blues is about an older brother's relationship with his younger brother, Sonny, who happens to be a wonderful jazz pianist and a heroin addict. The story, obviously, is about much more: it involves love, denial, and the interesting paradox by which those of us who persist in the world may in fact survive not because we understand anything, but because we consciously exclude things. Sonny's older brother teaches algebra in a Harlem high school, where algebra is certainly not the only education the students are receiving. There are drugs, dangers, people as hell-bent on living as they are fervent on dying. But most importantly, *Sonny's Blues* is about the ways in which we all fail; the truth that love itself cannot save someone; the realization that there are unreconcilable crises in the world; and, most importantly, the verity that there are people amongst us, loved ones, who, no matter what one may do, will perish.

Now, I read this story on the plane, conscious, as one is only when truly present at one's distress, of the millions of things going on about me. The plane was headed to Rochester, a course only capitalism can explain, for Rochester is west of Ithaca; and New York, my destination, is east of Ithaca, my place of origin. Clearly this makes no sense, but neither does serving gin and tonic at 6:15 A.M. And I was thankful for that.

The hospital was located in central Manhattan, some five blocks from my father's newly acquired office. My father had just moved from his long-held office at 145th Street, because he had routinely been robbed; the most recent robbery had taken on a particularly brutal nature, when the intruders placed a huge, eight-hundred-pound EKG machine atop him to pin him to the floor. Robberies in this neighborhood were not unusual: my father had been robbed some eight times within the previous four years. But with the escalation of the dope traffic, and the sense that every doctor must have a wonderful stash, doctors, whether, like my father, they had no narcotics at all, became prime targets. My father loved his office; he had been there since he first came to New York in 1941. Although he could have made much more money in midtown, he remained by choice in Harlem. As a child I could not understand this. I wanted him to be amongst the skyscrapers, with the Ben Caseys. Little did I know then that his forsaking of these things was the highest act of selflessness. As he once quietly stated, probably after a bout of my pestering, "Black people need good doctors, too." I imagine my father would have remained in his office until a bullet found his head had not my mother finally put her foot down and declared, "Honey, I know thirty-five years is a long time, but you've got to move."

I walked past my father's new office and headed into the Intensive Care Unit of Roosevelt Hospital. There I met my father and the attending physician—two doctors, one with a son—and listened to the prognosis. Medicine, as you know, has wonderful nomenclature for things: the most horrible things and something as slight as hiccups have names that imply the morgue. But the litany of my brother—septicemia, pneumonia—had the weight, rehearsed in my father's face, of the irreconcilable. My brother was *going* to die. The doctor said my brother was *going to die.* They would try like hell, but the parameters (the word parameters had never before been so important to me) left little in the way of hope.

It is difficult enough to be a parent and have a thirty-one-year-old child dying of alcoholism, his gut enlarged, his eyes red, lying in a coma. It is even more difficult, however, when you are a parent and also a doctor. For you have a dual obligation, one to a profession, a way of seeing, and one to nature, a rite of loving. As a doctor, my father knew what was medically possible—as surely as did any well-trained specialist—in my brother's precarious situation: he certainly knew what the parameters dictated. But as a parent, hoping like any parent that his child might live, he knew nothing, hope being a flight from what is known to the fanciful. And so these two extremes placed my father in a country rarely encountered, a predicament where I could sense, even then, his distress, but a place from which no one could save him.

In the two weeks that would follow, my mother, in grief, would ask my father what were Paul's chances. And he—doctor, parent, and husband—would be placed in that country again and again. As a parent every slight twitching of Paul, a slight movement of the lips, a small spasm of the hand, would move him to joy, to speculation—was that an attempt at words, was Paul reaching out? But as a doctor, he knew the terrible weight of parameters—how a word, no matter how strange its sound or source, does involve meaning. So, often he was placed in the terrible paradox of stating what he least wanted to hear. That yes, it was possible that Paul was reaching for us; but the parameters, the this test and the that test, suggested that Paul was still critical, very critical. And we never pressed him further, probably sensing that he would have to announce that these small skirmishes with the inevitable, like water pools just before turning to ice, could not remove the fact, no matter how much we or he would wish it so, that Paul was going to die. Moreover, for us, this dalliance with hope was a temporary waystation so that we could harden our own tools for the coming onslaught. My father did not have this privilege; he was, like all the greatest heroes, the angel without the hope of heaven.

In many ways the third factor in my father's difficult situation now came most into play, that of husband. My mother, like all of us, clung to hope, but more, she clung to her son. There is no way to detail the sense of a mother's love. In substance, a mother protects her son from the world, which, she rightly senses, is unceasingly bent on his destruction. Yet in my house, since Paul was an artist, so remote, my mother, in a sense, defended a phantom, defending him in much the way one supports the constitutional right of due process. For my mother, Paul was to be protected in theory: he was an artist; he was sensitive; he was silent. This identification with him and with those of his facets the world was bound not to respect—and indeed never did—made her involvement with Paul all the more intense, for he was not only the issue of her womb but the wellspring of her imagination.

My father certainly understood some of this, yet his way of reacting to any ostensible conundrum was conditioned by his medical school training. If there is a problem, he maintained, it can be reasonably addressed. And so he hoped that Paul would descend from his room and tell him what the problem was, why he wasn't finishing college, why he continued to drink so heavily, what, in God's name, did he do up in that room? And as it became obvious that the Socratic method demanded an interchange between two consenting mentors, my father became increasingly concerned and distressed. (The problem with any axiom is that it is valuable only as long as it works: my father's belief in reason had served him happily heretofore; yet now he was encountering an unforeseen circumstance. And he, like all of us when confronting Paul, had little in the bank.)

In any event, my father, in the hospital, was forced continually to grapple with three very difficult responsibilities all somehow connected. My mother, as Paul, miraculously, showed slight signs of rallying (the doctors had originally stated that he had a 10 percent chance of surviving), continued to find reasons, as all of us did, for hope. I recall how my wife and I visited one day and Paul actually extended his wobbling hand—and I, relating this later to my father, actually did press him, asking him if he thought Paul could possibly make it. My father, caught between a brother's hope and the sense that miracles do happen, and possibly even to him, said: "Yes, I think he could; but the parameters *(again that word)* are inconclusive." (Now I know that he didn't believe that Paul could live—the doctor in him didn't believe it, that is.)

But the most difficult moments for my father came, I think, when he had to explain to my mother, his wife, what he saw, trying always to remember that she was a grieving mother and a hopeful one; and no matter what was happening, might happen, he had to remain a source of strength for her, as she had so often been for him. In this difficult barter, my father also had to worry about my mother's natural inclination to believe the impossible, for hope would make us all immortal, while at the same time protecting that part of her which would permit her to bear this thing, no matter what the outcome. My father continued to caution my mother about the dire state of my brother. The word *parameter* became as palpable to my family as my brother's breath. And the boundaries, no matter what my brother's outward appearance, remained the same. It was enough to drive one crazy. With the weather, when the sun rises and the skin feels warm, the thermometer registers one's sense of new heat. Yet with my brother it seemed that our senses were at war with the medical reality. What, then, in this place, were cause and effect?

During the last week of my brother's life, my mother became increasingly angry with my father, blurting out, "You sound as if you want your son to die." Clearly this was an outburst culled out of anguish, frustration, and grief. And yet it adequately gave language to my father's paradox. Never have I seen the mind and the heart so irrefutably at odds.

My brother died after five coronaries at two A.M. thirteen nights after he was admitted to intensive care. His funeral took place some 250 miles from New York, on lovely Martha's Vineyard, where Paul and the family had spent our happiest years. The funeral was a thrown-together affair: 90 percent grief and the rest dogged persistence that something had to be done. The service was a plain one, with an Episcopal minister reading from the dreary *Book of Common Prayer*. My mother had hoped that someone could better eulogize my brother, someone who might get beyond the ashes-to-ashes bit and talk about the stuff of him, possibly so that we, his family, might finally get to know the person who had slowly drained away from us. The one reverend who knew my brother begged off, with the excuse that Paul had traveled a great distance from when he knew him. And that, to say the least, was the profoundest ministry that man had ever preached.

Although the funeral was a hasty affair, with little notice—and though we hardly knew many of Paul's friends—somehow a large contingent gathered, coming from Vermont, New York, and elsewhere, many of them for the first time at a funeral of one of their peers. I can't adequately describe the motley assemblage. Suffice it to say that these were the Lord's children, the ones who had tasted the bread of this world and waited, still, for manna. One young woman said a few words, choked them out, and then the sobbing began.

I think this meditation aptly ends with his friends, for they knew him and loved him as we did. In Baldwin's *Another Country,* one of the characters, Vivaldo, is described as feeling that "love is a country he knew nothing about." With the death of my brother, I learned about love: my love for him; my love for my parents; their love for one another; my love for those thin-shelled children who gathered on that small hillside to pay witness to one of theirs who didn't make it, who evidenced in his falling that death indeed is a possibility, no matter how young one is or how vigorous. I can't say that I know who my brother was, but I know that I miss him, more now than ever. And love, yes, is a country I know something about.

Brent Staples, born in 1951, is currently a member of the *New York Times* editorial board, where he writes on politics and culture. Prior to joining the *Times*, he worked as a reporter for the *Chicago Sun-Times*. Mr. Staples has published numerous magazine articles, book reviews, and drama criticism. He is the author of *Parallel Time: A Memoir*.

23

BRENT STAPLES

A Brother's Murder

(1986)

IT HAS BEEN more than two years since my telephone rang with the news that my younger brother Blake—just 22 years old—had been murdered. The young man who killed him was only 24. Wearing a ski mask, he emerged from a car, fired six times at close range with a massive .44 Magnum, then fled. The two had once been inseparable friends. A senseless rivalry—beginning, I think, with an argument over a girlfriend—escalated from posturing, to threats, to violence, to murder. The way the two were living, death could have come to either of them from anywhere. In fact, the assailant had already survived multiple gunshot wounds from an incident much like the one in which my brother lost his life.

As I wept for Blake I felt wrenched backward into events and circumstances that had seemed light-years gone. Though a decade apart, we both were raised in Chester, Pa., an angry, heavily black, heavily poor, industrial city southwest of Philadelphia. There, in the 1960's, I was introduced to mortality, not by the old and failing, but by beautiful young men who lay wrecked after sudden explosions of violence. The first, I remember from my 14th year—Johnny, brash lover of fast cars, stabbed to death two doors from my house in a fight over a pool game. The next year, my teen-age cousin, Wesley, whom

I loved very much, was shot dead. The summers blur. Milton, an angry young neighbor, shot a crosstown rival, wounding him badly. William, another teen-age neighbor, took a shotgun blast to the shoulder in some urban drama and displayed his bandages proudly. His brother, Leonard, severely beaten, lost an eye and donned a black patch. It went on.

I recall not long before I left for college, two local Vietnam veterans—one from the Marines, one from the Army—arguing fiercely, nearly at blows about which outfit had done the most in the war. The most killing, they meant. Not much later, I read a magazine article that set that dispute in a context. In the story, a noncommissioned officer—a sergeant, I believe—said he would pass up any number of affluent, suburban-born recruits to get hard-core soldiers from the inner city. They jumped into the rice paddies with "their manhood on their sleeves," I believe he said. These two items—the veterans arguing and the sergeant's words—still characterize for me the circumstances under which black men in their teens and 20's kill one another with such frequency. With a touchy paranoia born of living battered lives, they are desperate to be *real* men. Killing is only *machismo* taken to the extreme. Incursions to be punished by death were many and minor, and they remain so: they include stepping on the wrong toe, literally; cheating in a drug deal; simply saying "I dare you" to someone holding a gun; crossing territorial lines in a gang dispute. My brother grew up to wear his manhood on his sleeve. And when he died, he was in that group—black, male and in its teens and early 20's—that is far and away the most likely to murder or be murdered.

I left the East Coast after college, spent the mid- and late-1970's in Chicago as a graduate student, taught for a time, then became a journalist. Within 10 years of leaving my hometown, I was overeducated and "upwardly mobile," ensconced on a quiet, tree-lined street where voices raised in anger were scarcely ever heard. The telephone, like some grim umbilical, kept me connected to the old world with news of deaths, imprisonings and misfortune. I felt emotionally beaten up. Perhaps to protect myself, I added a psychological dimension to the physical distance I had already achieved. I rarely visited my hometown. I shut it out.

As I fled the past, so Blake embraced it. On Christmas of 1983, I traveled from Chicago to a black section of Roanoke, Va., where he then lived. The desolate public housing projects, the hopeless, idle young men crashing against one another—these reminded me of the embittered town we'd grown up in. It was a place where once I would have been comfortable, or at least sure of myself. Now, hearing of my brother's forays into crime, his scrapes with police and street thugs, I was scared, unsteady on foreign terrain.

I saw that Blake's romance with the street life and the hustler image had flowered dangerously. One evening that late December, standing in some Roanoke dive among drug dealers and grim, hair-trigger losers, I told him I feared for his life. He had affected the image of the tough he wanted to be. But behind the dark glasses and the swagger, I glimpsed the baby-faced toddler I'd once watched over. I nearly wept. I wanted desperately for him to live. The young think themselves immortal, and a dangerous light shone in his eyes as he spoke laughingly of making fools of the policemen who had raided his apartment looking for drugs. He cried out as I took his right hand. A line of stitches lay between the thumb and index finger. Kickback from a shotgun, he explained, nothing serious. Gunplay had become part of his life.

I lacked the language simply to say: Thousands have lived this for you and died. I fought the urge to lift him bodily and shake him. This place and the way you are living smells of death to me, I said. Take some time away, I said. Let's go downtown tomorrow and buy a plane ticket anywhere, take a bus trip, anything to get away and cool things off. He took my alarm casually. We arranged to meet the following night—an appointment he would not keep. We embraced as though through glass. I drove away.

As I stood in my apartment in Chicago holding the receiver that evening in February 1984, I felt as though part of my soul had been cut away. I questioned myself then, and I still do. Did I not reach back soon or earnestly enough for him? For weeks I awoke crying from a recurrent dream in which I chased him, urgently trying to get him to read a document I had, as though reading it would protect him from what had happened in waking life. His eyes shining like black diamonds, he smiled and danced just beyond my grasp. When I reached for him, I caught only the space where he had been.

Houston A. Baker, Jr. a renowned educator and African-American scholar, was born in Kentucky in 1943. He has taught at a variety of institutions including Howard University, Yale University, University of Virginia, and the University of Pennsylvania, where he is the Albert M. Greenfield Professor of Human Relations and director of the Center for Study of Black Literature and Culture. His publications include several volumes of poetry and numerous books of criticism, among them *The Journey Back: Issues in Black Literature and Criticism; Blues, Ideology and Afro-American Literature; Modernism and the Harlem Renaissance;* and *Workings of the Spirit.*

24

HOUSTON A. BAKER, JR.

From An Apple for My Teacher: Twelve Writers Tell About Teachers Who Made All the Difference

What Charles Knew

(*1987*)

HE WAS A tobacco brown, soft-eyed, angular man. He had transformed himself from a poor, Bluefield, West Virginia, mountain boy into an American intellectual. He had crafted an Oxonian mask behind which one could only surmise black beginnings. I caught glimpses of that ethnic past in the twinkle—the almost break-loose and "signifying" laughter—of his eyes when he told us of his dissertation. The title of that work in progress, according to him, was: "Some Ontological and Eschatological Aspects of the Petrarchan Conceit." He never dreamed of writing such a work, but he enjoyed using philosophical words that he knew would send the curious among us scurrying to the dictionary. I believe he actually wrote on the *Canterbury Tales.* He intrigued us. Slowly puffing on the obligatory pipe, he would chide us for the routineness of our analyses of revered works in the British and American literary canons. He wore—always—a tie and tweed of Ivy provenance, and at the end of the first session of his "World Litera-ture" course at Howard University in the fall of 1963, I had but one response—I wanted to be exactly like him.

The task was to prove myself worthy. I labored furiously at the beginning assignment—an effort devoted to Marvellian Coy mis-tresses and pounding parodies thereof. The result was a D and the comment: "This is a perfunctory effort. You have refused to be creative. There are worlds on worlds rolling ever. Try to make contact with them." I was more than annoyed; I was livid. Who did he think he was? I'd show him. My next essay would reveal (cleverly, of course) that I didn't give a tinker's dam for his grade or his comments. "Creative"—Indeed!

At the conclusion of his initial class, he said: "I want you to take these texts home and have intercourse with them and derive a satisfying orgasm." The sharp and shocked intake of breath from all of us surely kept us from seeing the merriment playing over his face. I had scant wisdom vis-à-vis orgasm, and I didn't have a clue what he considered creative. So I followed the general American procedure for such cases: I winged it.

My second essay might properly have been entitled: Love's labor loosed on William Blake. I strained to see every nuance of the *Songs of Innocence*. I combed the poems for every mad hint that would help forward my own mad argument. I never turned my eyes from the text as I sought to construct the most infuriating (yet plausible) analysis imaginable. I felt my feet dancing to Muhammed Ali rhythms as I slaved away, darting logical jabs at Professor C. Watkins who would (I was certain) be utterly undone when I threw my irreverent straight right. The paper came back with the comment: "This is a maverick argument, but stubbornly logical—'A–'." Bingo! The grade in itself gave me almost enough courage to seek him out during office hours— but not quite. I corralled a friend to make the pilgrimage with me.

He was extraordinarily gracious on the mid-autumn afternoon when we had our first long talk. "Come in, Mr. Baker—Miss Pierce. How are you?" His tie was loose; he was reared back in his desk chair. There was a clutter of papers and blue books, and they provided a friendly setting for a two-hour conversation. (Apparently no one else had sufficiently overcome the effects of his intimidating intellectualism to brave office hours.) He talked easily, describing his odyssey from Ohio State to a first teaching position at San Francisco State University and then to Howard. He was currently a doctoral candidate for an Ohio State Ph.D. in English. He was serving time, so to speak, at Howard until his dissertation was completed and his degree conferred. His real love was philosophy, and the New World metaphysics of Emerson set his blood warming and brought out his best polemical instincts. He held his Howard colleagues in low esteem because they were wedded to an old, old literary history while he was an enlightened devotee of the New Criticism. They were rattling Model Ts of a socio-historical approach, while he occupied a smoothly non-referential world of the Cleanth Brooks and Robert Penn Warren Mercedes. We were thrilled that he considered us (potentially) enough like him to invite us to visit him and his wife two weeks hence—for dessert.

There was far more than dessert. His wife was hospitable, witty, attractive—and white. She was the first such person I had met. For partners in interracial marriages were not common in my hometown of Louisville, Kentucky. The evening surprisingly took on (in my youthful imagination) the cast of Greenwich Village "Beats" and *verboten* revelations. The greatest stimulation, however, came when he played the Library of Congress recording of T. S. Eliot reading "The Waste Land." In that moment, I became, willy-nilly, a party to "modernism" in its prototypical form. I was surprised and delighted. I had heard nothing like it before. The Eliotian reading initiated my habit of "listening" for poems rather than "looking" for them. (I spent hours thereafter in the library listening to the sounds of English, French, and American poets. And later in the term when we were assigned "The Waste Land" for analysis, the echoes of that evening were constant.) I stepped into a late fall evening with an entirely new sense of myself and of "worlds on worlds" rolling ever.

I began self-consciously to craft a critical vocabulary. (An instructor commented at the end of one of my assignments: "Are 'ontological' and 'eschatological' the only words you know?") I talked in an American literature class about the dynamics of speech and silence—with the raven as representative of the "ontological foundations" of silence—in Poe's famous poem. I felt I had acquitted myself with verve. The Model T in charge said: "Mr. Baker, that's a lot of gobbledy-gook." When I told Professor Watkins of the incident, he simply said: "Mr. Baker, there are people here who have not read a book or had an original idea for years." (Then, I didn't know he meant not simply Howard but the entire academic world.)

I was reassured. I began to wear ties to class and abandoned my old satchel for a green bookbag. I was happy that I could appear in such attire when he called one day for my assistance. He had suffered the indignity of *two* flat tires, and his call brought me like a shot. Ironically, though, as we kneeled in the late-November snow, I noticed how threadbare *he* was. A frayed collar belied his intellectual elegance. His down-at-the-heels shoes were closer to West Virginia than Oxford. His face was prematurely kneaded and lined. I began to glean then (but only comprehended much, much later) the enormous price he had paid (and continued to pay) for his intellectual being in the world. I felt sorry for him at that instant, but also prodigiously attracted to such ascetic brilliance.

The semester rolled to a wintry climax, and I received an A for "World Literature." By the end of the term, I had made up my mind that I not only wanted to remain an English major, but also wanted to become a Ph.D.—a university professor. The project seems abundantly feasible in today's world where graduate fellowships for Afro-Americans go begging. But in 1963, it was a rare occurrence for a black person to set his sights on a traditional Ph.D.—not a doctorate in education, or social work, or physical education—but a traditional Ph.D. in arts and sciences. The person most influential in the decisions I made over the next several years was Charles Watkins. He encouraged my ambitions, guided me to fellowships, quieted my doubts, wrote letters of recommendation, and sketched vistas of intellectual work that glowed in my imagination.

I was overjoyed to see him at the Columbus, Ohio, airport in the spring of 1966. He had returned to Ohio State, where he completed his dissertation and took a position as assistant professor in English. We had a wonderful time during my visit. We conversed on every topic of which I was capable, including Emersonian essays. He read my fledgling poetry, and the twinkle in his eye told me I had many rivers to cross. He was generously complimentary of my scholarly progress, and I knew, on leaving, that I loved this West Virginia man who, by dint of main force, had shaped himself into an American Scholar.

News of his death came quite unexpectedly. I received it, quite indirectly, while attending a black writers conference. He died of heart trouble. He and I lost touch during the years he was in Seattle. He had taken a post at the University of Washington. I felt that he had little sympathy for my recently acquired interests in black literature and black studies. (A lack of sympathy that was, perhaps, justified since he had received threats and ugly harassment from black power advocates at San Francisco State who were displeased with his interracial marriage and insisted that he either join them or suffer.) He was a man of the New Criticism, and I was moving under gloriously socio-historical and polemical banners of The Black Aesthetic, where referentiality was of the utmost importance. I had joyfully allied myself with black critics who were repudiating traditional, Oxonian masks—making, so we thought, the world all "new"—redefining it in BLACK terms. I felt that I had outgrown Charles. But the wisdom of hindsight allows me to see that "growth" is merely a sign for "moving things around"—outrageous posturing designed to convince those we love that we are still worthy of consideration, to solicit from them an acknowledgment of our changing sameness. I felt profoundly lonely. I also felt guilty and helpless because Charles and I had lost touch. The only thing I could offer as a gesture of appeasement and love was the dedication of my book *Singers of Daybreak*. I sent a copy to his wife with a feeling that someone I cared for had virtually vanished, leaving no tangible trace.

In the fall of 1985, however, I received a telephone call that began: "Hello, Houston, this is Rita Watkins." Charles and Rita's son Jonathan is currently employed as a Senate aide in the District of Columbia, and his mother wondered if I would mind calling him on one of my trips to Washington. She hoped I would tell him about his father because he was only nine when Charles died. I assured her that I would be happy to call. As soon as I hung up, I began to think of what I would say to Charles' firstborn. I will tell him, I believe, that

Charles was a courageous black man who carved from the granite of racism and impoverishment a role for himself as master of the best that has been thought and said in the world.

He was a teacher par excellence. He knew, better than anyone I have encountered since, how to convey the worth and excitement of a demanding intellectual enterprise to a country boy from Louisville, Kentucky. I am certain I will tell Jonathan that his father knew consummately well how to bless, inspire, and encourage the threadbare thinkers among us. He suggested to us a scholarly ideal that he would have been both amused and delighted to see described in the following words:

> Ful threadbare was his overeste courtepy,
> For he had feten him yit no benefice.
> Nor was so worldly for to have office.
> For him was levere have at his beddes heed
> Twenty bookes, clad in blak or reed
> Of Aristotle and his philosophye,
> Than robes riche, or filthele, or gay sautre.

I can see the twinkle in his eye as he might have said: "If you substitute 'Emerson' for 'Aristotle,' Mr. Baker, you will have a fair characterization." Like Chaucer's Clerk of Oxenforde, Charles would gladly "lerne, and gladly teche" because he knew the resonant and signal pleasure of creative intellectual thought in a land of "dust and dollars." "Emerson" is, surely, an appropriate substitution. It describes, in a word, what Charles knew so very, very well.

Samuel R. Delany was born in Harlem, New York, in 1942. He is a prolific author of science fiction novels, including *The Einstein Intersection; Triton; Dhalgren; The Bridge of Lost Desire;* and *The Straits of Messina.* He has also published several books of essays and an autobiography, *The Motion of Light in Water.*

S A M U E L   R.   D E L A N Y

From The Motion of
Light in Water

Sentences: An Introduction

(1988)

MY FATHER HAD been sick almost a year. Already he'd had one lung
removed. But after a time home—which he spent mostly in bed,
listening to programs of eclectic classical music (Penderecki, Kodaly's
Sonata for Unaccompanied Cello) on WBAI-FM, all of which were
new to him and pleased him greatly, or sitting up in his robe and
pajamas working on a few ordered and geometric paintings of city-
scapes in which there were no people (he'd always wanted to paint)—
he began to grow weaker. Soon he was in pain. Toward the end of
September, an ambulance was sent for, to take him to the hospital.
But the attendants who arrived to strap him into their stretcher, there
in the apartment hall in his dark robe and pale pajamas, were too
rough, yanking down the straps and buckles over his thin legs that,
by now, could not fully straighten. After asking them twice to loosen
them, he began to shout: "Stop it! You're hurting me! Stop—!" Lips
tight, my mother stood, flustered, embarrassed, and worried at once,
perfectly still.

My father bellowed at the two white-jacketed young men, one
black, one white, "Get out—!"

An hour later, my grown cousin (called Brother) and I helped him
down the hall, into the elevator, out to the car, and drove him over

325

to the hospital. Each bump in the rutted Harlem streets made him gasp or moan. The day was shot through with his fear and exhaustion. The pain made him cry when, in his awkward white smock, he had to stretch out on the black, cold X-ray table. I held his hand. ("I'm going to fall. I'm falling . . . ! Hold me. I'm falling." "No you're not, Dad. I've got you. You're okay." "I'm falling . . . !" Tears rolled down his bony cheeks. "It's too cold.") He had difficulty urinating into the enameled bedpan as I sat with him in his hospital room, and he made little whisperings to imitate the fall of water to induce his own to fall.

For most of my life, if it came up, I would tell you: "My father died of lung cancer in 1958 when I was seventeen."

Behind that sentence is my memory of a conversation with my older cousin Barbara, who was staying with us. She was a doctor. I said: "I guess it's going to take an awful long time for him to get well."

Carefully, Barbara put her teacup down on the glass-topped table, with the woven wicker beneath. "He's not going to get well," she said. Then, very carefully, she said: "He's going to die."

It was, of course, the truth; and, of course, I knew it.

It was also the kindest thing she could have said.

"How long will it be?" I asked.

"You can't say for sure," she said. "Two or three weeks. Two or three months."

Later, I went downstairs to see Mr. Jackson.

"Is Jesse in?" I asked his wife.

"Sure." Ann was a little woman with glasses and meticulous hair. "He's in the back." She stepped from the door. "Just go on in."

Sitting in the room that served him for an office, with its floor-to-ceiling bookshelves and the framed illustrations from the young peoples' novels he'd written about black children growing up in the Midwest looking down at us from the walls, I told him what Barbara had said. Jesse was a teak-colored man, with short gray hair. Somehow he'd managed to be equally close to both my father and me, an extraordinary accomplishment as we'd been so often at loggerheads.

"Yes." He put his pipe carefully on the desk, recalling Barbara with her cup. "That's probably true."

He let me sit there without saying anything else, while he puttered around in his office, a full twenty minutes before I went back to our apartment upstairs.

An early October afternoon a heavy handful of days later, we were called in the morning to go over, and, in the darkened hospital room, I smiled and said, "How're you feeling . . . ?" while my younger sister reached through the oxygen tent's plastic, scored with light from the floor lamp, to squeeze my father's long hand with its slightly clubbed fingers. His face was lax and unshaven. "Yes," he said hoarsely, "I'm feeling a little better . . ." After I followed her into the hall, her own face broke slowly apart before she covered it with her hands to cry, while some of my aunts stood in the corridor, speaking quietly of the kindnesses of one particular white nurse from Texas.

My sister and I rode home on the bus, together, alone.

Sometime near five, I had just stepped from the living room as my sister came out of her room in the back, when the lock on the hall door between us ratcheted. The door swung in. Then my mother and aunts erupted through, between us, all at once:

"It's all over! It's all over—the poor boy—he's gone! Oh, the poor boy!"

(That was one of my father's older sisters. As the announcement broke through the women's sobs, why, I wondered, feeling distant, do we turn in stress to such banalities?)

"No more suffering! It's all over!" My Aunt Virginia's voice might have been that of a traffic policeman clearing the road, as she led in my mother, an arm around her shoulders. "He's out of his pain."

The four of my father's sisters, as well as my mother, were in tears. (Only Virginia, my mother's sister, was not crying.) All six women—I realized—already wore black.

That evening, over Mom's protests, I went walking by Riverside Park. Dead leaves mortared the pavement around Grant's Tomb. For some reason, sitting on one of the benches beside the public mausoleum, I took my shoes and socks off to amble barefoot on the chill concrete, beneath the mercury-vapor lights, notebook under my arm. I'd been trying to write an elegy. It began, "They told me you were not in any pain . . ." because, for some reason, that's what people had been saying to me about him a week now, even though every movement had made him gasp, grunt, or grate his teeth.

Days later, in suit and tie, I sat beside my mother in the front row of folding chairs in the funeral chapel, watching Brother (the same cousin who had driven us to the hospital, and who had been running my father's funeral business a year now, since Dad had been too ill to work) go up at the end of the service to the casket banked left and right by flowers, take the corpse's hand in his, and, with a sharp tug, remove my father's ring. Then he reached up to lower dark, gleaming wood. Moments afterward, outside the funeral home on Seventh Avenue among milling relatives and friends, he handed the ring to me and I slipped it into the inside pocket of my suit jacket, before I got into the gray, nestlike softness of the funeral car for the ride to the cemetery.

Ten years ago, in 1978, while I was at the typewriter table in my office one afternoon, with Amsterdam Avenue's commercial traffic growling by five stories down, I opened an envelope giving its return address as the English department of a Pennsylvania state college. Two scholars were undertaking a book-length bibliography of my then-sixteen years of published writing, to be introduced with a biographical essay of some fifty or sixty pages.

Honesty? Accuracy? Tact? These are the problems of all biographers, auto- or otherwise. But the very broadness of the questions obscures the specific ways each can manifest itself. Few of us are ever biographized—especially during our lifetime. No one is born a biographical subject, save the odd and antiquated royal heir; I have never seen a book on how to be a good one. But, like anything else, having your life researched and written about is an experience, with particular moments that characterize it, mark it, and make it what it is.

"My father died of lung cancer in 1958 when I was seventeen." This is just not a sentence that, when an adult says it in a conversation seven or a dozen or twenty years after the fact, people are likely to challenge.

And when, to facilitate my Pennsylvania scholars, I put together a chronology of my life, starting with my birth (April Fools' Day, 1942), that sentence, among many, is what I wrote.

I don't remember the specific letter in which one of them pointed out gently that, if I was born in 1942, in 1958 I could not possibly have been seventeen. In 1958 I was fifteen up until April 1 and sixteen for the year's remaining nine months. (Certainly my father didn't die when I was fifteen or sixteen . . . ?) WBAI-FM did not begin to broadcast till 1960. There *were* no Penderecki recordings available in 1958. Various researches followed, along with more questions; a sheaf of condolence letters to my mother turned up—one from a man I'd never heard of, now living somewhere in Europe, who recalled teaching my father to drive in North Carolina, when my father was seventeen or eighteen—the first time it ever occurred to me that, at some time, he must have learned. Finally, in an old Harlem newspaper, a small article was unearthed that confirmed it: my father died in the early days of October 1960.

I was eighteen.

Here's a pretty accurate chronology that we prepared for the year and a half that straddled my nineteenth birthday, starting from the summer before, covering my father's death, and ending a year later.

In June 1960 when I was eighteen, because of disagreements over school policy, I cut my graduation so as not to be present to receive my high school creative writing award. My father was ill. My parents did not understand; I probably made little or no effort to explain it to them. But a few days later at the beginning of July, with the son of our downstairs neighbor, Peter, a talented banjo player a year older than I and with whom I had gone to summer camp some years before, I drove up to the Newport Folk Festival, where we attended concerts in the evening and slept on the beaches at night, with thousands of other young people. The notebook I filled over our four days there was typed over the next week to become an 80-page memoir of the trip, whose title "The Journals of Orpheus," I rolled around on my tongue for weeks, for months.

A few days later, I left New York City by Greyhound for the Breadloaf Writers' Conference, in Middlebury, Vermont, where I'd received a work scholarship at the recommendation of an editor from Harcourt, Brace, on the strength of one of my several adolescent novels. Along with half a dozen or more young people who'd received similar scholarships, I supplemented the partial tuition by working at the conference as a waiter. My roommate was a young black poet, Herbert Woodward Martin. The evening I got back to New York City, my father came out to the living room, in his blue pajamas and robe, to listen, with my mother, to my accounts of my summer with Robert Frost, John Frederick Nims, Allen Drury, and X. J. Kennedy, smiling at my anecdotes, now and then hawking into the galvanized zinc pail Mom had set by his slippered feet, with a little water and detergent in it—till, in the midst of something I was saying, he rose and walked back into the bedroom, and I realized just how sick he'd grown.

In September, I began classes at the College of the City of New York: Greek, Latin, and English, along with Chemistry, Speech (a required freshman course), and Art History. I joined the staff of the college literary journal, *The Promethean.* At the end of that month, my father went into the hospital—as I've told. I also resumed weekly therapy sessions with a psychologist, Dr. Harold Esterson, which were to continue, somewhat intermittently, through the early months of 1961.

In the last days of October, after Dad's death, I moved in with Bob Aarenberg, a nineteen-year-old friend who lived, as my family and I had since I was fifteen, in Morningside Gardens. He had taken a small student apartment on the third floor of a grimy building on West 113th Street. Bob was an amateur shortwave radio operator, and the place was jammed with ham equipment. Upstairs in the same building lived SF writer Randall Garrett, whom I met, with whom I became friends, and to whom I showed some of my early (non-SF) novels. That Halloween, dressed as Medusa and Perseus, Marilyn Hacker and I, with a friend named Gail (Medea), hiked through a chill Washington Square evening to a costume party at NYU's Maison Française, where a number of our friends, among them Judy (dressed as Comedy/Tragedy) were celebrating. Our regalia was inspired by a verse play of Marilyn's, called *Perseus,* whose sections she had read to me over the phone, some weeks before, day by day as she'd written them.

Over this same period (September, October, November), during which I started school and my father died, I produced translations of Brecht's "Vom ertrunkenen Mädchen," Rimbaud's "Le Bateau ivre" (also a pastiche of his sonnet "Voyelles"), and Catullus's "Vivamus, mea Lesbia," as well as an original English version of "The Song of Songs Which Is Solomon's," and some of Chatterton's "Middle English" Rowley forgeries—using various English texts as cribs, such as Stanley Burnshaw's international anthology *The Poem Itself* (purchased while at Breadloaf) or a recent paperback translation of "The Song of Songs"; no, my French, German, or Latin (not to mention Hebrew) was not up to the job unassisted.

On the day before Christmas Eve, a City College companion, who shared both my Speech and my Art classes and whom I'd nicknamed "Little Brother" when we became friends in the first days of school, came over to spend the night with me at my mother's apartment. At about three o'clock in the morning, an hour after we'd stopped talking and were, presumably, asleep, he suddenly sat up in his underwear at the edge of his bed and said, "I have to go home . . ."

"Hm?" I said, sleepily, from mine. "Why . . . ?"

"Because if I don't," he said, "I'm going to try and get in bed with you."

"That's okay," I said. "Come on."

"I don't think you understand," he said, softly. "I want to go to bed with you."

"Sure I do." I held back the covers for him. "I want to go to bed with you, too. Come on. Get in."

And, a moment later, he slid down beside me.

The next afternoon, when he left, I wrote some dozen rather jejune sonnets about it all—though I did not see him again for some three or four years. When the Christmas break was over, he did not return to school.

Christmas passed, and on that snowy New Year's Eve, I went to a party at a young musician and composer's, Josh Rifkin's, where the two of us went upstairs and, secreted in Josh's room, listened to carefully and analyzed for hours the Robert Craft recording, just released, of the complete works of Anton Webern, while people celebrated downstairs.

Midnight passed.

In January 1961, I began my second term at City, continuing with Latin and Greek, dropping English, Speech, and Art, and adding History, Calculus Two (I'd received advanced placement in math, allowing me to skip Calculus One), and an obligatory Physical Education course. I became *The Promethean*'s poetry editor.

In February I directed some friends, Eric and Esther, and myself in Marilyn's *Perseus: An Exercise for Three Voices.* Marilyn was then a student at NYU: she had been my close friend since our first year together at the Bronx High School of Science. Shortly David Litwin replaced Eric. *Perseus* was performed in the "grand ballroom" of the Student Center of City College on a Wednesday, once in the afternoon and again in the evening. It ran just under fifteen minutes.

In March I was spending little time at my schoolwork; rather I would devote desultory bursts of energy to my own writing. I all but ceased attending classes. Here and there at various places in the Village, I played with the folksinging group I'd pulled together around me, the Harbor Singers (who rehearsed through the whole period at Dave's mother's apartment in Hell's Kitchen regularly on Tuesday evenings), and, sometimes, banjo-playing Pete. I was an indifferent singer, but a passable guitarist. Possibly in that month, possibly in April, Randall Garrett took me to a party probably at John and Ann Hamilton's, in Greenwich Village, at which I met SF writer and critic Judith Merril, whose work I was familiar with through her anthologies and stories; late that night, I rode with her on the subway up to Port Authority, where she caught the bus back to Milford, Pennsylvania (famous to SF readers as the home of numerous SF writers, back then), then returned to 113th Street.

Toward the end of April, I restaged *Perseus* for the Coffee Gallery, a small, second-floor art gallery and coffee shop, then on Tenth Street, between Second and Third Avenues, this time with Daniel Landau in the role of Voice Three. The program was expanded with a recitation by Marilyn and a reading by me. The program now ran slightly over half an hour. The Coffee Gallery was just upstairs from the print shop where Diane Di Prima and LeRoi Jones were producing *The Floating Bear*. At least once Diane and some of her friends stopped in to see the performance. The program ran on weekends, Friday and Saturday nights, for ten weeks, with audiences ranging from three to fifteen.

In May, I cut all my final exams. Unofficially, I had dropped out of school. (I managed, however, to fulfill my duties on the college magazine.) Over the previous six months I had written a number of short novels, with titles like *The Flames of the Warthog*, *The Lovers*, and *The Assassination*. Along with some earlier novels, I regularly submitted these to a number of New York publishers—by whom they were regularly rejected.

In June Marilyn became pregnant with our second sexual experiment.

In the first week of July, after *Perseus* closed, I took a bus up to the Newport Jazz Festival, which it had been suggested to me that I write about by an editor at *Seventeen* Magazine.

Back in New York, after the festival, I went with Marilyn to rent a four-room apartment on the Lower East Side.

In August, with a loan from another old high school friend, Sharon, Marilyn and I took a three-day trip to Detroit, Michigan, where we were married.

At the beginning of September, I got a job at Barnes & Noble on Fifth Ave. and Eighteenth Street as a stockclerk, in time for the September textbook rush.

In October, almost exactly a year after my father's death, Marilyn miscarried.

She recuperated at my mother's apartment. Two or three weeks later, she got a job as a "salesgirl" at B. Altman's Department Store. Let go even before New Year's, almost immediately she got a job as an editorial assistant at Ace Books. Probably within a week (certainly no more than ten days), after a set of obsessively vivid dreams, I began what, not quite a year later, would be my first published novel, *The Jewels of Aptor*.

★★★

Looking over this bare and untextured chronology, it's easy to read a fairly clear emotional story. My father's death, my subsequent dropping out of school, and my hasty marriage speak of a young man, interested in writing and music, but still under fair emotional strain. With the facts that I was black and Marilyn was white, that I was gay and both of us knew it, the implication of strain—for both of us—only strengthens.

The story is so clear, I wouldn't even think, at this date, to deny it.

Still, it is not the story *I* remember from that time. While all the incidents listed are, in my own mind, associated with vivid moments, rich details, complexes of sensation, deep feelings, and the texture of the real (so indistinguishable from that of dream), their places on the list are wholly a product of research. And my inaccurate statement, "My father died when I was seventeen in 1958 . . ." is an emblem of the displacements and elisions committed upon that more objective narrative, if not a result of that strain.

I have clear memories of my father's death.

I have clear memories of my first weeks of classes at City College, of my new teachers, of the new friends I made there, of surprises and disappointments and great excitement, of lunches with new and old acquaintances in the cafeteria, of trips between classes through crowded halls, of extracurricular activities, including a small choral group I sang with during the afternoons, under the direction of Allan Sklar (a former music counselor of mine at Camp Rising Sun), where we prepared for a recording of an *a cappella* version of the Orlande de Lassus's *Two-Part Motets*.

But there's no connection between those memories and those of my father's death in my mind. I retain no sense that one came along to interrupt the other. My entrance into college and my father's death, instead of incidents separated by weeks, seem rather years apart. To the extent I retain any context around my father's dying at all, it is some vague and uncertain time during my last two years of high school—possibly because I saw a friend or two I connected with that period right before or right after he died. Or because that was when he first became ill. Or because . . .

But I don't know why memory separates it so completely from the time in which, objectively, it occurred.

From the October a year later, I have clear—and painful—memories of Marilyn's miscarriage.

I also have clear memories of the afternoon back at East Fifth Street, when, waking from a nap, I became aware of the recurrent dreams that, a day or so later, impelled me into the writing of my first science fantasy novel. In the same months when I was writing and autumn gave way to winter, Marilyn, thinking back on her miscarriage a few weeks before, wrote:

> . . . *The waxing body swells with seeds of death.*
> *The mind demands a measure to its breath . . .*
> *Change is neither merciful nor just.*
> *They say Leonard of Vinci put his trust*
> *in faulty paints: Christ's Supper turned to dust . . .*

Some of these lines I quoted *in* the novel. Still, I have no sense that the book began within a week or so of the miscarriage: only the chronology tells me that. In memory, the two seem months, many months, from one another; several times, when I've recounted the happenings to other people, I've spoken of them as if they actually were.

In both cases, the disjunction in memory was strong enough to make me, now and again, even argue the facts, till their proximities were fixed by document and deduction:

A careful and accurate biographer can, here and there, know more about the biographical subject than the subject him- or herself.

My favorite autobiographical memoirs are Osip Mandelshtam's *The Noise of Time,* Louise Bogan's *Journey Around My Room,* Maxine Hong Kingston's *The Woman Warrior: Memoirs of a Girlhood Among Ghosts,* Goethe's *Italian Journey,* Paul Goodman's *Five Years: Thoughts During a Useless Time,* Frederick Douglass's *Narrative of the Life of an African Slave,* Michael McClure's and Frank Reynold's

Freewheelin' Frank, sections of Walter Benjamin's *One Way Street,* and parts of *Barthes* by Barthes.

With those brief and intense models shamelessly in mind (with the exception of the Goethe, the longest is just over 250 pages), I am not about to try here for the last word on event and evidential certainty. I hope it's clear: despite the separate factual failing each is likely to fall into, the autobiographer (much less the memoirist) cannot replace the formal biographer. Nor am I even going to try. I hope instead to sketch, as honestly and as effectively as I can, something I can recognize as my own, aware as I do so that even as I work after honesty and accuracy, memory will make this only one possible fiction among the myriad—many in open conflict—anyone might write of any of us, as convinced as any other that what he or she wrote was truth.

But bear in mind two sentences:

"My father died of lung cancer in 1958 when I was seventeen."

"My father died of lung cancer in 1960 when I was eighteen."

The first is incorrect, the second correct.

I am as concerned with truth as anyone—otherwise I would not be going so far to split such hairs. In no way do I feel the incorrect sentence is privileged over the correct one. Yet, even with what I know now, a decade after the letter from Pennsylvania, the wrong sentence still *feels* to me righter than the right one.

Now a biography or a memoir that contained only the first sentence would *be* incorrect. But one that omitted it, or did not at least suggest its relation to the second on several informal levels, would be incomplete.

Bell Hooks, leading black feminist theorist and activist, is currently a professor at Oberlin College. She was educated at the University of California at Santa Cruz. Her works include *Ain't I Woman?*, *Feminist Theory: From Margin to Center*, *Talking Back*, and *Yearnings*.

26

BELL HOOKS

Black Is a Woman's Color

(1989)

GOOD HAIR—that's the expression. We all know it, begin to hear it when we are small children. When we are sitting between the legs of mothers and sisters getting our hair combed. Good hair is hair that is not kinky, hair that does not feel like balls of steel wool, hair that does not take hours to comb, hair that does not need tons of grease to untangle, hair that is long. Real good hair is straight hair, hair like white folks' hair. Yet no one says so. No one says your hair is so nice, so beautiful because it is like white folks' hair. We pretend that the standards we measure our beauty by are our own invention—that it is questions of time and money that lead us to make distinctions between good hair and bad hair. I know from birth that I am lucky, lucky to have hair at all for I was bald for two years, then lucky finally to have thin almost straight hair, hair that does not need to be hot combed.

We are six girls who live in a house together. We have different textures of hair, short, long, thin, thick. We do not appreciate these differences. We do not celebrate the variety that is ourselves. We do not run our fingers through each other's dry hair after it is washed. We sit in the kitchen and wait our turn for the hot comb, wait to sit in the chair by the stove smelling grease, feeling the heat warm our scalp like a sticky hot summer sun.

For each of us, getting our hair pressed is an important ritual. It is not a sign of our longing to be white. It is not a sign of our quest to be beautiful. We are girls. It is a sign of our desire to be women. It is a gesture that says we are approaching womanhood. It is a rite of passage. Before we reach the appropriate age we wear braids and plaits that are symbols of our innocence, our youth, our childhood. Then we are comforted by the parting hands that comb and braid, comforted by the intimacy and bliss. There is a deeper intimacy in the kitchen on Saturday when hair is pressed, when fish is fried, when sodas are passed around, when soul music drifts over the talk. We are women together. This is our ritual and our time. It is a time without men. It is a time when we work to meet each other's needs, to make each other beautiful in whatever way we can. It is a time of laughter and mellow talk. Sometimes it is an occasion for tears and sorrow. Mama is angry, sick of it all, pulling the hair too tight, using too much grease, burning one ear and then the next.

At first I cannot participate in the ritual. I have good hair that does not need pressing. Without the hot comb I remain a child, one of the uninitiated. I plead, I beg, I cry for my turn. They tell me once you start you will be sorry. You will wish you had never straightened your hair. They do not understand that it is not the straightening I seek but the chance to belong, to be one in this world of women. It is finally my turn. I am happy. Happy even though my thin hair straightened looks like black thread, has no body, stands in the air like ends of barbed wire; happy even though the sweet smell of unpressed hair is gone forever. Secretly I had hoped that the hot comb would transform me, turn the thin good hair into thick nappy hair, the kind of hair I like and long for, the kind you can do anything with, wear in all kinds of styles. I am bitterly disappointed in the new look.

A senior in high school, I want to wear a natural, an afro. I want never to get my hair pressed again. It is no longer a rite of passage, a chance to be intimate in the world of women. The intimacy masks betrayal. Together we change ourselves. The closeness, an embrace before parting, a gesture of farewell to love and one another.

***

Jazz, she learns from her father, is the black man's music, the working man, the poor man, the man on the street. Different from the blues because it does not simply lament, moan, express sorrow; it expresses everything. She listens to a record he is playing, to a record that is being played on the radio. It is the music of John Coltrane. Her father says this is a musician who understands all the black man is longing for, that he takes this longing and blows it out of his saxophone. Like the alchemist, he turns lead into gold. To listen, her father tells her, is to feel understood. She listens, wanting this jazz not to be beyond her, wanting it to address the melancholy parts of her soul. To her, black people make the most passionate music. She knows that there is no such thing as natural rhythm. She knows it is the intensity of feeling, the constant knowing that death is real and a possibility that makes the music what it is. She knows that it is the transformation of suffering and sorrow into sound that bears witness to the black past. In her dreams she has seen the alchemist turning lead into gold.

On communion Sundays they sing without musical accompaniment. They keep alive the old ways, the call and response. They sing slow and hold each note as if it is caught in the trap of time and struggling to be free. Like the bread and the wine, they do it this way so as not to forget what the past has been. She listens to the strength in the voices of elderly women as they call out. She sings in the choir. She loves the singing. She looks forward to choir practice on Wednesday night. It is the only weekday night that they are away from home. They sit in the basement of the church singing. They sing "hush children, hush children, somebody's calling my name, oh my lord, oh my lordy, what shall I do."

At home her mama listens to music. On Friday nights she sits in her corner on the couch, smoking one cigarette, drinking one can of beer, playing records, staring sadly into the smoke as Brooke Benton sings "you don't miss you water till your well runs dry." Saturday morning they clean house and listen to music. They listen to the soul music on the radio. It is the only time they can hear a whole program with black music. Every other day is country and western or rock 'n roll. In between vacuuming, dusting, and sweeping they listen to the latest songs and show each other the latest dances. She likes to dance, but they make fun of her. She cannot slow dance. She does not know how to follow the lead. She gives up dancing, spends her time listening to the music.

She likes to hear the music of Louis Armstrong. She likes to see the pleasure he brings to her father's face. They watch him on the Ed Sullivan show, making funny faces, singing in his deep voice. It is the trumpet sound that they are waiting for. When he pulls the handker- chief from his pocket to wipe away the dripping sweat she is reminded of the right-hand men of God weeping into thin squares of cotton. She imagines tears mingled with Satchmo's sweat, that they are tears of gratitude, that he too is giving thanks for finding in his horn yet another sweet stretching sound he did not know was there.

She wants to express herself—to speak her mind. To them it is just talking back. Each time she opens her mouth she risks punish- ment. They punish her so often she begins to feel they are persecuting her. When she learns the word *scapegoat* in vocabulary lesson, she is sure it accurately describes her lot in life. Her wilderness, unlike the one the goat is led into, is a wilderness of spirit. They abandon her there to get on with the fun things of life. She lies in her bed upstairs after being punished yet again. She can hear the sound of their laughter, their talk. No one hears her crying. Even though she is young, she comes to understand the meaning of exile and loss. They say that she is really not a young girl but an old woman born again into a young girl's body. They do not know how to speak the old woman's language so they are afraid of her. She might be a witch. They have given her a large thick paperback of original fairy tales. On page after page, an old woman is eating children, thinking some wicked deed, performing evil magic. She is not surprised that they fear the old woman inside her. She understands that the old women in the fairy tales do evil because they are misunderstood. She is a lover of old women. She does not mind at all when they look at her and say she must be ninety, look at the way she walks. No! They say she must be at least a hundred. Only a hundred-year-old woman could walk so slow.

Their world is the only world there is. To be exiled from it is to be without life. She cries because she is in mourning. They will not let her wear the color black. It is not a color for girls. To them she already looks too old. She would just look like a damn fool in a black dress. Black is a woman's color.

She finds another world in books. Escaping into the world of novels is one way she learns to enjoy life. However, novels only ease the pain momentarily as she holds the book in hand, as she reads. It is poetry that changes everything. When she discovers the Romantics it is like losing a part of herself and recovering it. She reads them night and day, all the time. She memorizes poems. She recites them while ironing or washing dishes. Reading Emily Dickinson she senses that the spirit can grow in the solitary life. She reads Edna St. Vincent Millay's "Renascence," and she feels with the lines the suppression of spirit, the spiritual death, and the longing to live again. She reads Whitman, Wordsworth, Coleridge. Whitman shows her that language, like the human spirit, need not be trapped in conventional form or traditions. For school she recites "O Captain, My Captain." She would rather recite from *Song of Myself*, but they do not read it in school. They do not read it because it would be hard to understand. She cannot understand why everyone hates to read poetry. She cannot understand their moans and groans. She wishes they did not have to recite poems in school. She cannot bear to hear the frightened voices stumbling through lines as if they are a wilderness and a trap. At home she has an audience. They will turn off the television set and listen to her latest favorite.

She writes her own poetry in secret. She does not want to explain. Her poems are about love and never about death. She is always thinking about death and never about love. She knows that they will think it better to discover secret poems about love. She knows they never speak of death. The punishments continue. She eases her pain in poetry, using it to make the poems live, using the poems to keep on living.

★★★

They have never heard their mama and daddy fussing or fighting. They have heard him be harsh, complain that the house should be cleaner, that he should not have to come home from work to a house that is not cleaned just right. They know he gets mad. When he gets mad about the house he begins to clean it himself to show that he can do better. Although he never cooks, he knows how. He would not be able to judge her cooking if he did not cook himself. They are afraid of him when he is mad. They go upstairs to get out of his way. He does not come upstairs. Taking care of children is not a man's work. It does not concern him. He is not even interested—that is, unless something goes wrong. Then he can show her that she is not very good at parenting. They know she is a good mama, "the best." Even though they fear him they are not moved by his opinions. She tries to remember a time when she felt loved by him. She remembers it as being the time when she was a baby girl, a small girl. She remembers him taking her places, taking her to the world inhabited by black men, the barber shop, the pool hall. He took his affections away from her abruptly. She never understood why, only that they went and did not come back. She remembered trying to do whatever she could to bring them back, only they never came. Growing up she stopped trying. He mainly ignored her. She mainly tried to stay out of his way. In her own way she grew to hate wanting his love and not being able to get it. She hated that part of herself that kept wanting his love or even just his approval long after she could see that he was never, never going to give it.

Out of nowhere he comes home from work angry. He reaches the porch yelling and screaming at the woman inside. Yelling that she is his wife and that he can do with her what he wants. They do not understand what is happening. He is pushing, hitting, telling her to shut up. She is pleading, crying. He does not want to hear, to listen. They catch his angry words in their hands like lightning bugs. They store them in a jar to sort them out later. Words about other men, about phone calls, about how he had told her. They do not know what he has told her. They have never heard them in an angry discussion, an argument.

344

She thinks of all the nights she lies awake in her bed hearing the woman's voice, her mother's voice, hearing his voice. She wonders if it is then that he is telling her the messages he refers to now. Yelling, screaming, hitting, they stare at the red blood that trickles through the crying mouth. They cannot believe that this pleading, crying woman, this woman who does not fight back, is the same person they know. The person they know is strong, gets things done, is a woman of ways and means, a woman of action. They do not know her still, paralyzed, waiting for the next blow, pleading. They do not know her afraid. Even if she does not hit back they want her to run, to run and to not stop running. She wants her to hit him with the table light, the ash tray near her hand. She does not want to see her like this, not fighting back. He notices them long enough to tell them to get out, go upstairs. She refuses to move. She cannot move. She cannot leave her alone. When he says "What are you staring at, do you want some too," she is afraid enough to move, but she does not take her orders from him. She asks the woman if it is right to leave her alone. The woman nods her head yes. She still stands still. It is his movement in her direction that sends her up the stairs. She cannot believe they are not taking a stand, that they go to sleep. She cannot bear their betrayal. When he is not looking she creeps down the steps. She wants the woman to know that she is not alone. She wants to bear witness.

All that she does not understand about marriage, about men and women, is explained to her one night. In her dark place on the stairs she is seeing over and over again the still body of the woman pleading, crying, the moving body of the man angry, yelling. She sees that the man has a gun. She hears him tell the woman that he will kill her. She sits in her place on the stair and demands to know of herself if she is able to come to the rescue, if she is willing to fight, if she is ready to die. Her body shakes with the answers. She is fighting back the tears. When he leaves the room she comes to ask the woman if she is all right, if there is anything she can do. The woman's voice is full of tenderness and hurt. She is now in her role as mother. She tells her daughter to go upstairs and go to sleep, that everything will be all right. The daughter does not believe her. Her eyes are pleading. She does not want to be told to go. She hovers in the shadows. When he returns he tells her that he has told her to get her ass upstairs. She does not look at him. He turns to the woman, tells her to leave, tells her to take the daughter with her.

The woman does not protest. She moves like a robot, hurriedly throwing things into suitcases, boxes. She says nothing to the man. He is still screaming, muttering. When she tried to say to him he was wrong, so wrong, he is more angry, threatening. All the neat drawers are emptied out on the bed, all the precious belongings that can be carried, stuffed, are to be taken. There is sorrow in every gesture, sorrow and pain. It is so thick she feels that she could gather it up in her hands. It is like a dust collecting on everything. She is seeing that the man owns everything, that the woman has only her clothes, her shoes, and other personal belongings. She is seeing that the woman can be told to go, can be sent away in the silent, long hours of the night. She is hearing in her head the man's threats to kill. She can feel the cool metal against her cheek. She can hear the click, the blast. She can see her body falling. No, it is not her body, it is the body of love. It is the death of love she is witnessing. If love were alive she believes it would stop everything. It would steady the man's voice, it would calm his rage. It would take the woman's hand, caress her cheek and with a clean handkerchief wipe her eyes. The gun is pointed at love. He lays it on the table. He wants her to finish her packing and go.

She is again in her role as mother. She tells the daughter that she does not have to flee in the middle of the night, that it is not her fight. The daughter is silent. She is staring into the woman's eyes. She is looking for the bright lights, the care and adoration she has shown the man. The eyes are dark with grief, swollen. She feels that a fire inside the woman is dying out, that she is cold. She is sure the woman will freeze to death if she goes out into the night alone. She takes her hand. She wants to go with her. Yet she hopes there will be no going. She hopes that when the mother's brother comes he will be strong enough to take love's body, and give it mouth to mouth the life it has lost. She hopes he will talk to the man, guide him. She cannot believe the calm way he lifts suitcase, box, sack, carries it to the car without question.

She cannot bear the silent agreement that the man is right, that he has done what men are able to do. She cannot take the bits and pieces of her mother's heart and put them together again.

I am always fighting with mama. Everything has come between us. She no longer stands between me and all that would hurt me. She is hurting me. This is my dream of her—that she will stand between me and all that hurts me, that she will protect me at all cost. It is only a dream. In some way I understand that it has to do with marriage, that to be the wife to the husband she must be willing to sacrifice even her daughters for his good. For the mother it is not simple. She is always torn. She works hard to fulfill his needs, our needs. When they are not the same she must maneuver, manipulate, choose. She has chosen. She has decided in his favor. She is a religious woman. She has been told that a man should obey God, that a woman should obey man, that children should obey their fathers and mothers, particularly their mothers. I will not obey.

She says that she punishes me for my own good. I do not know what it is I have done this time. I know that she is ready with her switches, that I am to stand still while she lashes out again and again. In my mind there is the memory of a woman sitting still while she is being hit, punished. In my mind I am remembering how much I want that woman to fight back. Before I can think clearly, my hands reach out, grab the switches, are raised as if to hit her back. For a moment she is stunned, unbelieving. She is shocked. She tells me that I must never ever as long as I live raise my hand against my mother. I tell her I do not have a mother. She is even more shocked; she is enraged. She lashes out again. This time I am still. This time I cry. I see the hurt in her eyes when I say "I do not have a mother." I am ready to be punished because I did not want to hurt. I am ashamed. I am torn. I do not want to stand still and be punished but I do not want to hurt her. It is better to hurt than to cause her pain. She warns me that she will tell him when he comes home, that I may be punished again. I cannot understand her acts of betrayal. I cannot understand that she must be against me to be for him. He and I are strangers. Deep in the night we parted from one another, knowing that nothing would ever be the same. He did not say goodbye. I did not look him in the face. Now we avoid one another. He speaks to me through her.

Although they act as if everything between them is the same, that life is as it was, it is only a game. They are only pretending. There is no pain in the pretense. All pain is hidden. Secrets find a way out in sleep. They say to the mother she cries in her sleep, calls out. In her sleep is the place of remembering. It is the place where there is no pretense. She is dreaming always the same dream. A movie is showing. It is a tragic story of jealousy and lost love. It is called "A Crime of Passion." In the movie a man has killed his wife and daughter. He has killed his wife because he believes she has lovers. He has killed the daughter because she witnesses the death of the wife. At his job he is calm and quiet, a hardworking man, a family man. Neighbors come to testify that the dead woman was young and restless, that the daughter was wild and rebellious. Everyone sympathizes with the man. His story is so sad that they begin to weep. All their handkerchiefs are clean and white. They are like flags waving. They are a signal of peace, of surrender. They are a gesture to the man that he can go on with life.

John Hope Franklin has had a long and distinguished career as
educator. Born in 1915 in Oklahoma, Franklin taught at Fisk
University, University of Chicago, and, most recently, Duke
University, where he is the James B. Duke Professor of History
Emeritus and professor of legal history. His publications include
*From Slavery to Freedom: A History of Negro Americans; Racial
Equality in America;* and *A Southern Odyssey: Travelers in the
Antebellum North.* He has served as president of many scholarly
organizations, including the American Historical Association
and the Society of Phi Beta Kappa. He has also been the recipi-
ent of numerous awards and honors, including a Guggenheim
Fellowship and more than eighty honorary degrees.

27

JOHN HOPE FRANKLIN

From Race and History:
Selected Essays 1938–1988

A Life of Learning

(1990)

AS I BEGAN the task of putting the pieces together that would describe
how I moved from one stage of intellectual development to another,
I was reminded of a remark that Eubie Blake made as he approached
his ninety-ninth birthday. He said, "If I had known that I would live
this long I would have taken better care of myself." To paraphrase
him, if I had known that I would become a historian I would have kept
better records of my own pilgrimage through life. I may be forgiven,
therefore, if I report that the beginnings are a bit hazy, not only to
me but to my parents as well. For example, they had no clear idea of
when I learned to read and write. It was when I was about three or
four, I am told.

My mother, an elementary school teacher, introduced me to the
world of learning when I was three years old. Since there were no
daycare centers in the village where we lived, she had no alternative
to taking me to school and seating me in the rear of her classroom
where she could keep an eye on me. I remained quiet but presumably
I also remained attentive, for when I was about five my mother

This essay was the Charles Homer Haskins Lecture, delivered before the American
Council of Learned Societies, New York City, April 14, 1988, and printed in the
Council's *Occasional Papers, Number 4* (New York, 1988).

noticed that on the sheet of paper she gave me each morning, I was no longer making lines and sketching out some notable examples of abstract art. I was writing words, to be sure almost as abstract as my art, and making sentences. My mother later said that she was not surprised much less astonished at what some, not she, would have called my precocity. Her only reproach—to herself, not me—was that my penmanship was hopelessly flawed since she had not monitored my progress as she had done for her enrolled students. From that point on, I would endeavor to write and, through the written word, to communicate my thoughts to others.

My interest in having some thoughts of my own to express was stimulated by my father who, among other tasks, practiced law by day and read and wrote by night. In the absence of any possible distractions in the tiny village, he would read or write something each evening. This was my earliest memory of him and, indeed, it was my last memory of him. Even after we moved to Tulsa, a real city, and after we entered the world of motion pictures, radio, and television, his study and writing habits remained unaffected. I grew up believing that in the evenings one either read or wrote. It was always easy to read something worthwhile, and if one worked at it hard enough he might even write something worthwhile. I continue to believe that.

Two factors plagued my world of learning for all of my developing years. One was race, the other was financial distress; and each had a profound influence on every stage of my development. I was born in the all-Negro town of Rentiesville to which my parents went after my father had been expelled from court by a white judge who told him that no black person could ever represent anyone in his court. My father resolved that he would resign from the world dominated by white people and try to make it among his own people. But Rentiesville's population of less than two hundred people could not provide a poverty-free living even for one who was a lawyer, justice of the peace, postmaster, farmer, and president of the Rentiesville Trading Company which, incidentally, was not even a member of the New York Stock Exchange.

The quality of life in Rentiesville was as low as one can imagine. There was no electricity, running water, or inside plumbing. There was no entertainment or diversion of any kind—no parks, playgrounds, libraries, or newspapers. We subscribed to the Muskogee *Daily Phoenix,* which was delivered by the Missouri, Kansas, and Texas Railroad as it made its way southward through the state each morning. The days and nights were lonely and monotonous, and for a young lad with boundless energy there was nothing to do but read. My older sister and brother were away in private school in Tennessee, and one did not even have the pleasure of the company of older siblings. Now and then one went to Checotah, six miles away, to shop. That was not always pleasant, such as the time when my mother, sister, and I were ejected from the train because my mother refused to move from the coach designated for whites. It was the only coach we could reach before the train moved again, so my mother argued that she would not move because she was not to blame if the train's white coach was the only one available when the train came to a halt. Her argument was unsuccessful, and we had to trudge back to Rentiesville through the woods.

There were the rare occasions when we journeyed to Eufala, the county seat, where I won the spelling bee for three consecutive years. There was Muskogee to the north, where I went at the age of five for my first pair of eye glasses—the malady brought on, I was told, by reading by the dim light of a kerosene lamp. It was a combination of these personal and family experiences that forced my parents to the conclusion that Rentiesville was not a viable community. They resolved to move to Tulsa. First, my father would go, find a place, set himself up in the practice of law, and we would follow six months later, in June, 1921, when my mother's school closed for the summer recess.

That June, however, we received word that in Tulsa there was a race riot, whatever that was, and that the Negro section of that highly segregated community was in flames. At the age of six I sensed from my mother's reaction that my father was in danger. We were all relieved several days later, therefore, when a message arrived that he had suffered no bodily harm, but that the property he had contracted to purchase was destroyed by fire. He practiced law in a tent for several months, and our move to Tulsa was delayed by four years.

In the month before I reached my eleventh birthday, we arrived in Tulsa. It was quite a new world, and although a city of less than moderate size at the time, it was to my inexperienced eyes perhaps the largest city in the country. I did not see much of it, however, for racial segregation was virtually complete. I thought that Booker T. Washington, the school where I enrolled in grade seven, was the biggest and best school until one day I saw Central High for whites. It was a massive, imposing structure covering a city block. I was later to learn that it had every conceivable facility such as a pipe organ and a theater-size stage, which we did not have. I also learned that it offered modern foreign languages, and calculus, while our school offered automobile mechanics, home economics, typing, and shorthand. Our principal and our teachers constantly assured us that we need not apologize for our training and they worked diligently to give us much of what was not even in the curriculum.

Now that the family was together again I had the example and the encouragement of both of my parents. My mother no longer taught but she saw to it that my sister and I completed all of our home assignments promptly. Quite often, moreover, she introduced us to some of the great writers, especially Negro authors, such as Paul Laurence Dunbar and James Weldon Johnson, who were not a part of our studies at school. She also told us about some of the world's great music such as Handel's Oratorio "Esther," in which she had sung in college. While the music at school was interesting and lively, especially after I achieved the position of first trumpet in the band and orchestra, there was no Handel or Mozart, or Beethoven. We had a full fare of Victor Herbert and John Philip Sousa, and operettas, in more than one of which I sang the leading role.

Often after school I would go to my father's office. By the time I was in high school, the Depression had yielded few clients but ample time, which he spent with me. It was he who introduced me to ancient Greece and Rome, and he delighted in quoting Plato, Socrates, and Pericles. We would then walk home together, and after dinner he went to his books and I went to mine. Under the circumstances, there could hardly have been a better way of life, since I had every intention after completing law school of some day becoming his partner.

It was in secondary school that I had a new and wonderful experience which my parents did not share. It was the series of concerts and recitals at Convention Hall, perhaps even larger than the theater at Central High School which I never saw. As in the other few instances where whites and blacks were under the same roof, segregation was strict, but I very much wanted to go with some of my teachers who always held season tickets. My parents would *never* voluntarily accept segregation; consequently, the concerts were something they chose to forgo. Even at court my father refused to accept segregation. Whenever I accompanied him, which was as often as I could, he would send me to the jury box when it was empty or, when there was a jury trial, have me sit at the bench with him. They took the position, however, that if I could bear the humiliation of segregation, I could go to the concerts.

Thus, I could purchase my own tickets with the money I earned as a paper boy. To be more accurate, I was not the paper boy, but the assistant to a white man who had the paper route in the black neighborhood. It was at one of these concerts that I heard Paul Whiteman present Gershwin's "Rhapsody in Blue" while on a nationwide tour in 1927. I also attended the annual performances of the Chicago Civic Opera Company, which brought to Tulsa such stellar singers as Rosa Raisa, Tito Schipa, and Richard Bonelli. I am not altogether proud of going to Convention Hall; there are times, even now, while enjoying a symphony or an opera, when I reproach myself for having yielded to the indignity of racial segregation. I can only say that in the long run it was my parents who knew best, though later I made a conscious effort to regain my self-respect.

There were many sobering experiences at Fisk, which I entered on a tuition scholarship in 1931. The first was my encounter with at least two dozen valedictorians and salutatorians from some of the best high schools in the United States. The fact that I had finished first in my high school class did not seem nearly as important in Nashville as it had in Tulsa. Imagine my chagrin when a whiz kid from Dayton made all A's in the first quarter while I made two B's and a C+. My rather poor grades were somewhat mitigated by my having to hold three jobs in order to pay my living expenses. I was also absolutely certain that the C+ resulted from whimsical grading by the teaching assistants in a course called "Contemporary Civilization." As I think of it now I still become infuriated, and if there was anyone to listen to my case today I would insist that my examinations be reevaluated and my grade raised accordingly! I *was* consoled by my salutatorian girl friend, now my wife of forty-seven years, who over the years has lent a sympathetic ear to my rantings about the injustices in that course. She can afford to be charitable; she received a grade of B+.

Another sobering experience was my first racial encounter in Nashville. At a downtown streetcar ticket window, I gave the man the only money I possessed, which was a $20 bill. I apologized and explained that it was all I had and he could give me my change using any kind of bills he wished. In an outburst of abusive language and using vile racial epithets, he told me that no nigger could tell him how to make change. After a few more similar statements he proceeded to give me $19.75 in dimes and quarters. From that day until I graduated, I very seldom went to Nashville, and when I did I never went alone. It was about as much as a sixteen-year-old could stand. I thought of that encounter some three years later, and felt almost as helpless, when a gang of white hoodlums took a young black man from a Fisk-owned house on the edge of the campus and lynched him. As president of student government I made loud noises and protests to the mayor, the governor, and even President Franklin D. Roosevelt, but nothing could relieve our pain and anguish or bring Cordie Cheek back. Incidentally, the heinous crime he had committed was that, while riding his bicycle, he struck a white child who was only slightly injured.

Still another sobering, even shattering, experience was my discovery at the end of my freshman year that my parents had lost our home and had moved into a four-family apartment building which they had built. I knew that the country was experiencing an economic depression of gigantic proportions, that unemployment had reached staggering figures, and that my father's law practice had declined significantly. I was not prepared for the personal embarrassment that the Depression created for me and my family, and frankly I never fully recovered from it. The liquidation of all debts became an obsession with me, and because of that experience my determination to live on a pay-as-you-go basis is as great today as it was when it was not at all possible to live that way.

Despite these experiences my years in college were pleasant if hectic, rewarding if tedious, happy if austere. Most classes were rigorous, and everyone was proud of the fact that the institution enjoyed an A rating by the Southern Association of Colleges and Secondary Schools. The faculty was, on the whole, first-rate, and they took pride in their scholarly output as well as in their teaching. Although the student body was all black, with the exception of an occasional white exchange student or special student, the faculty was fairly evenly divided between white and black. It was an indication of the lack of interest in the subject that we never thought in terms of what proportion of the faculty was white and what proportion was black.

Since I was merely passing through college en route to law school, I had little interest in an undergraduate concentration. I thought of English, but the chairman of that department, from whom I took freshman English, discouraged me on the ground that I would never be able to command the English language. (Incidentally, he was a distinguished authority in American literature and specialized in the traditions of the Gullah-speaking people of the Sea Islands. I was vindicated some years later when he chaired the committee that awarded me the Bancroft Prize for the best article in the *Journal of Negro History*.) My decision to major in history was almost accidental. The chairman of that department, Theodore S. Currier, who was white, had come into that ill-fated course in contemporary civilization and had delivered the most exciting lectures I had ever heard. I decided to see and hear more of him.

During my sophomore year I took two courses with Professor Currier, and my deep interest in historical problems and the historical process and what he had to say was apparently noted by him. Soon we developed a close personal relationship that developed into a deep friendship. Soon, moreover, I made the fateful decision to give up my plan to study and practice law and to replace it with a plan to study, write, and teach history. My desire to learn more about the field resulted in his offering new courses, including seminars, largely for my benefit. He already entertained the hope that I would go to Harvard, where he had done his own graduate work. I had similar hopes, but in the mid-1930s with the Depression wreaking its havoc, it was unrealistic to entertain such hopes. With a respectable grade point average (that C+ prevented my graduating *summa cum laude*), and strong supporting letters from my professors, I applied for admission to the Harvard Graduate School of Arts and Sciences.

Harvard required that I take an aptitude test that must have been the forerunner to the Graduate Records Examination. It was administered at Vanderbilt University, just across town but on whose grounds I had never been. When I arrived at the appointed place and took my seat, the person in charge, presumably a professor, threw the examination at me, a gesture hardly calculated to give me a feeling of welcome or confidence. I took the examination but cannot imagine that my score was high. As I left the room a Negro custodian walked up to me and told me that in his many years of working there I was the only black person he had ever seen sitting in a room with white people. The record that Fisk made that year was more important. The Association of American Universities placed Fisk University on its approved list. On the basis of this new recognition of my alma mater, Harvard admitted me unconditionally. Apparently this was the first time it had given a student from a historically black institution an opportunity to pursue graduate studies without doing some undergraduate work at Harvard. The university declined, however, to risk a scholarship on me.

Admission to Harvard was one thing; getting there was quite another. My parents were unable to give me more than a very small amount of money and their good wishes. I was able to make it back to Nashville, where Ted Currier told me that money alone would not keep me out of Harvard. He went to a Nashville bank, borrowed $500, and sent me on my way.

Shortly after my arrival in Cambridge in September, 1935, I felt secure academically, financially, and socially. At Fisk I had even taken two modern foreign languages in order to meet Harvard's requirement, and in Currier's seminars I had learned how to write a research paper. Since I was secretary to the librarian at Fisk for four years, I had learned how to make the best use of reference materials, bibliographical aids, and manuscripts. Even when I met my advisor, Professor A. M. Schlesinger, Sr., I did not feel intimidated, and I was very much at ease with him while discussing my schedule and my plans. After I got a job washing dishes for my evening meal and another typing dissertations and lectures, a feeling of long-range solvency settled over me. Although I had a room with a Negro family that had taken in black students since the time of Charles Houston and Robert Weaver, I had extensive contact with white students who never showed the slightest condescension toward me. I set my own priorities, however, realizing that I had the burden of academic deficiencies dating back to secondary school. I had to prove to myself and to my professors that the Association of American Universities was justified in placing Fisk University on its approved list. I received the M.A. degree in nine months and won fellowships with which I completed the Ph.D. requirements.

There were few blacks at Harvard in those days. One was completing his work in French history as I entered. As in Noah's Ark, there were two in the law school, two in zoology, and two in the college. There was one in English and one in comparative literature; there were none in the Medical School and none in the Business School.

The most traumatic social experience I had there was not racist but antisemitic. I was quite active in the Henry Adams Club, made up of graduate students in United States history. I was appointed to serve on the committee to nominate officers for the coming year which, if one wanted to be hypersensitive, was a way of making certain that I would not be an officer. When I suggested the most active, brightest graduate student for president, the objection to him was that although he did not have some of the more reprehensible Jewish traits, he was still a Jew. I had never heard any person speak of another in such terms, and I lost respect not only for the person who made the statement but for the entire group that even tolerated such views. Most of the members of the club never received their degrees. The Jewish member became one of the most distinguished persons to get a degree in United States history from Harvard in the last half-century.

The course of study was satisfactory but far from extraordinary. Mark Hopkins was seldom on the other end of the log, and one had to fend for himself as best he could. I had no difficulty with such a regimen, although I felt that some of my fellow students needed more guidance than the university provided. In my presence, at the beginning of my second year, one of the department's outstanding professors verbally abused a student visiting from another institution and dismissed him from his office because the student's question was awkwardly phrased the first time around. Another professor confessed to me that a doctoral committee had failed a candidate because he did not *look* like a Harvard Ph.D. When the committee told him that he would have to study four more years before applying for reconsideration, the student was in the library the following morning to begin his four-year sentence. At that point, the chairman of the committee was compelled to inform the student that under no circumstances would he be permitted to continue his graduate studies there.

When I left Harvard in the spring of 1939 I knew that I did not wish to be in Cambridge another day. I had no desire to offend my advisor or the other members of my doctoral committee. I therefore respectfully declined suggestions that I seek further financial aid. It was time, I thought, to seek a teaching position and complete my dissertation *in absentia.* I had taught one year at Fisk following my first year at Harvard. With five preparations in widely disparate fields and with more than two hundred students, I learned more history than I had learned at Fisk *and* Harvard. I early discovered that teaching had its own very satisfying rewards. For some fifty-two years, there have been many reasons to confirm the conclusions I reached at Fisk, St. Augustine's, North Carolina College at Durham, Howard, Brooklyn, Chicago, Duke, and short stints in many institutions here and abroad.

After I committed myself to the study, teaching, and writing of history, I was so preoccupied with my craft that I gave no attention to possible career alternatives. Less than two years into my career, however, when I was working on my second book, the president of a small but quite respectable historically black liberal arts college invited me to become dean of his institution. It was at that point that I made a response that was doubtless already in my mind but which I had not yet articulated. I thanked him and respectfully declined the invitation on the grounds that my work in the field of history precluded my moving into college administration. When the president received my letter, he sent me a telegram informing me that he was arriving the following day to explain his offer. During the three hours of conversation with him I had ample opportunity to state and restate my determination to remain a teacher and writer of history. Each time I did so I became more unequivocal in my resistance to any change in my career objectives. I believe that he finally became convinced that he was indeed wrong in offering me the deanship in the first place. From that day onward, I had no difficulty in saying to anyone who raised the matter that I was not interested in deanships, university presidencies, or ambassadorships. And I never regretted the decision to remain a student and teacher of history.

There is nothing more stimulating or satisfying than teaching bright, inquisitive undergraduates. It was puzzling, if dismaying, when a student complained, as one did at Howard, that my lengthy assignments did not take into account the fact that his people were only eighty-five years removed from slavery. It was sobering, but challenging, when an undergraduate asked, as one did at Brooklyn, if I would suggest additional readings since he had already read everything in the syllabus that I distributed on the first day of class. It was reassuring to find that some students, such as those at Chicago, came to class on a legal holiday because I neglected to take note of the holiday in my class assignments. It was refreshing, even amusing, when students requested, as some did at Duke, that the date for the working dinner at my home be changed because it conflicted with a Duke–Virginia basketball game. As Harry Golden would say, only in America could one find undergraduates with so much *chutzpah*.

There came a time in my own teaching career when I realized that with all my frantic efforts at research and writing I would never be able to write on all the subjects in which I was deeply interested. If I only had graduate students who would take up some of the problems regarding slavery, free blacks, the Reconstruction era and its overthrow, it would extend my own sense of accomplishment immeasurably. That was a major consideration in my move in 1964 from Brooklyn College to the University of Chicago where for the next eighteen years I supervised some thirty dissertations of students who subsequently have published more than a dozen books. In view of Chicago's free-wheeling attitude toward the time for fulfilling degree requirements, there is a possibility that eight years after retirement, I might have more doctoral students to complete their work and write more books. Meanwhile, I continue to revel in the excitement of teaching in still another type of institution, the law school at Duke University.

I could not have avoided being a social activist even if I had wanted to. I had been barred from entering the University of Oklahoma to pursue graduate studies, and when the National Association for the Advancement of Colored People asked me to be the expert witness for Lyman Johnson, who sought admission to the graduate program in history at the University of Kentucky, I was honored to do so. After all, it was easy to establish the fact that Johnson could not get the same training at the inferior Kentucky State College for Negroes that he could get at the University of Kentucky. Johnson was admitted forthwith. To me it was one more blow against segregation in Oklahoma as well as Kentucky. The defense argument collapsed when the University of Kentucky placed one of its history professors on the stand and asked him about teaching Negroes. He replied soberly that he did not teach Negroes, he taught history, which he was pleased to do!

Then, Thurgood Marshall asked me to serve on his nonlegal research staff when the NAACP Legal Defense Fund sought to eliminate segregation in the public schools. Each week in the late summer and fall of 1953 I journeyed from Washington to New York, where I worked from Thursday afternoon to Sunday afternoon. I wrote historical essays, coordinated the work of some other researchers, and participated in the seminars that the lawyers held regularly, and provided the historical setting for the questions with which they were wrestling. I had little time for relaxing at my home away from home, the Algonquin Hotel, but each time I entered this establishment, I made eye contact with an imaginary Tallulah Bankhead, Agnes De-Mille, or Noël Coward, who were among the more famous habitués of its lobby.

The historian, of all people, must not make more of his own role in events, however significant, even if it is tempting to do so. It would be easy to claim that I was one of the 250,000 people at the March on Washington in 1963. I was not there and perhaps the truth is even more appealing. Since I was serving as Pitt Professor at the University of Cambridge that year, I was something of a resource person for the BBC-TV. On Richard Dimbleby's popular television program, *Panorama,* I tried to explain to the British viewers what had transpired when James Meredith sought to enter the University of Mississippi. I suspect there was a bit of advocacy even in the tone of my voice. In the summer of 1963 I took British viewers through what the BBC called "A Guide to the March on Washington." Here again, with film clips on Malcolm X, James Baldwin, A. Philip Randolph, and others, I explained why the march was a very positive development in the history of American race relations. Finally, in 1965, I was actually on the Selma march. No, I did not march *with* Martin, as some imaginative writers have claimed. I doubt that Martin ever knew that I was there, far back in the ranks as I was. I was *not* at Pettus Bridge in Dallas County, but joined the march at the city of St. Jude on the outskirts of Montgomery. I took pride in marching with more than thirty historians who came from all parts of the country to register their objection to racial bigotry in the United States. And I want to make it clear that I was afraid, yes, frightened out of my wits by the hate-filled eyes that stared at us from the sidewalks, windows, businesses, and the like. It was much more than I had bargained for.

One must be prepared for any eventuality when he makes any effort to promote legislation or to shape the direction of public policy or to affect the choice of those in the public service. This came to me quite forcefully in 1987 when I joined with others from many areas of activity in opposing the Senate confirmation of Robert H. Bork as associate justice of the Supreme Court of the United States. In what I thought was a sober and reasoned statement, I told the Judiciary Committee of the United States Senate that there was "no indication—in his writings, his teachings, or his rulings—that this nominee has any deeply held commitment to the eradication of the problem of race or even of its mitigation." It came as a shock, therefore, to hear the president of the United States declare that the opponents of the confirmation of Judge Bork constituted a "lynch mob." This was a wholly unanticipated tirade against those activists who had merely expressed views on a subject in which all citizens had an interest.

It was necessary, as a black historian, to have a personal agenda, as well as one dealing with more general matters, that involved a type of activism. I discovered this in the spring of 1939 when I arrived in Raleigh, North Carolina, to do research in the state archives, only to be informed by the director that in planning the building the architects did not anticipate that any Afro-Americans would be doing research there. Perhaps it was the astonishment that the director, a Yale Ph.D. in history, saw in my face that prompted him to make a proposition. If I would wait a week he would make some arrangements. When I remained silent, registering a profound disbelief, he cut the time in half. I waited from Monday to Thursday, and upon my return to the archives I was escorted to a small room outfitted with a table and chair which was to be my private office for the next four years. (I hasten to explain that it did not take four years to complete my dissertation. I completed it the following year, but continued to do research there as long as I was teaching at St. Augustine's College.) The director also presented me with keys to the manuscript collection in order to avoid requiring the white assistants to deliver manuscripts to me. That arrangement lasted only two weeks, when the white researchers, protesting discrimination, demanded keys to the manuscript collection for themselves. Rather than comply with their demands, the director relieved me of my keys and ordered the assistants to serve me.

Nothing illustrated the vagaries of policies and practices of racial segregation better than libraries and archives. In Raleigh alone, there were three different policies: the state library had two tables in the stacks set aside for the regular use of Negro readers. The state supreme court library had no segregation while, as we have seen, the archives faced the matter as it arose. In Alabama and Tennessee, the state archives did not segregate readers, while Louisiana had a strict policy of excluding Negro would-be readers altogether. In the summer of 1945 I was permitted by the Louisiana director of archives to use the manuscript collection since the library was closed in observance of the victory of the United States over governmental tyranny and racial bigotry in Germany and Japan. As I have said elsewhere, pursuing southern history has been for me a strange career.

While World War II interrupted the careers of many young scholars, I experienced no such delay. At the same time, it raised in my mind the most profound questions about the sincerity of my country in fighting bigotry and tyranny abroad. And the answers to my questions shook my faith in the integrity of our country and its leaders. Being loath to fight with guns and grenades, in any case, I sought opportunities to serve in places where my training and skills could be utilized. When the United States entered the war in 1941 I had already received my doctorate. Since I knew that several men who had not been able to obtain their advanced degrees had signed on as historians in the War Department, I made application there. I was literally rebuffed without the department giving me any serious consideration. In Raleigh, where I was living at the time, the Navy sent out a desperate appeal for men to do office work, and the successful ones would be given the rank of petty officer. When I answered the appeal, the recruiter told me that I had all of the qualifications except color. I concluded that there was *no* emergency and told the recruiter how I felt. When my draft board ordered me to go to its staff physician for a blood test, I was not permitted to enter his office and was told to wait on a bench in the hall. When I refused and insisted to the draft board clerk that I receive decent treatment, she in turn insisted that the doctor see me forthwith, which he did. By this time, I had concluded that the United States did not need me and did not deserve me. I spent the remainder of the war successfully outwitting my draft board, including taking a position at North Carolina College for Negroes whose president was on the draft appeal board. Each time I think of these incidents, even now, I feel nothing but shame for my country—not merely for what it did to me, but for what it did to the million black men and women who served in the armed forces under conditions of segregation and discrimination.

One had always to be mindful, moreover, that being a black scholar did not exempt one from the humiliations and indignities that a society with more than its share of bigots can heap upon a black person, regardless of education or even station in life. This became painfully clear when I went to Brooklyn College in 1956 as chairman of a department of fifty-two white historians. There was much fanfare accompanying my appointment, including a front-page story with picture in the New York *Times*. When I sought to purchase a home, however, not one of the thirty-odd realtors offering homes in the vicinity of Brooklyn College would show their properties. Consequently, I had to seek showings by owners who themselves offered their homes for sale. I got a few showings including one that we very much liked, but I did not have sufficient funds to make the purchase. My insurance company had proudly advertised that it had $50 million to lend to its policy holders who aspired to home ownership. My broker told me that the company would not make a loan to me because the house I wanted was several blocks beyond where blacks should live. I cancelled my insurance and, with the help of my white lawyer, tried to obtain a bank loan. I was turned down by every New York bank except the one in Brooklyn where my attorney's father had connections. As we finally moved in after the hassles of more than a year, I estimated that I could have written a long article, perhaps even a small book, in the time expended on the search for housing. The high cost of racial discrimination is not merely a claim of the so-called radical left. It is as real as the rebuffs, the indignities, or the discriminations that many black people suffer.

★★★

Many years ago, when I was a fledgling historian, I decided that one way to make certain that the learning process would continue was to write different kinds of history, even as one remained in the same field. It was my opinion that one should write a monograph, a general work, a biography, a period piece, and edit some primary source and some work or works, perhaps by other authors, to promote an understanding of the field. I made no systematic effort to touch all the bases, as it were, but with the recent publication of my biography of George Washington Williams, I believe that I have touched them all. More recently, I have started the process all over again by doing research for a monograph on runaway slaves.

Another decision I made quite early was to explore new areas or fields, whenever possible, in order to maintain a lively, fresh approach to the teaching and writing of history. That is how I happened to get into Afro-American history, in which I never had a formal course, but which attracted a growing number of students of my generation and many more in later generations. It is remarkable how moving or even drifting into a field can affect one's entire life. More recently, I have become interested in women's history, and during the past winter I prepared and delivered three lectures under the general title of "Women, Blacks, and Equality, 1820–1988." I need not dwell on the fact that for me it was a very significant learning experience. Nor should it be necessary for me to assure you that despite the fact that I have learned much, I do not seek immortality by writing landmark essays and books in the field of women's history.

I have learned much from my colleagues both at home and abroad. The historical associations and other learned societies have instructed me at great length at their annual meetings, and five of them have given me an opportunity to teach and to lead by electing me as their president. Their journals have provided me with the most recent findings of scholars and they have graciously published some pieces of my own. Very early I learned that scholarship knows no national boundaries, and I have sought the friendship and collaboration of historians and scholars in many parts of the world. From the time that I taught at the Salzburg Seminar in American Studies in

1951, I have been a student and an advocate of the view that the exchange of ideas is more healthy and constructive than the exchange of bullets. This was especially true during my tenure on the Fulbright Board, as a member for seven years and as the chairman for three years. In such experiences one learns much about the common ground that the peoples of the world share. When we also learn that this country and the western world have no monopoly of goodness and truth or of skills and scholarship, we begin to appreciate the ingredients that are indispensable to making a better world. In a life of learning that is, perhaps, the greatest lesson of all.

Itabari Njeri is currently a staff reporter for the *Los Angeles Times*. She has written previously for the *Miami Herald* and the *Greenville News* and has received many reporting awards and major fellowships. Njeri, who is also a professional singer and actress, is the author of *Every Good-bye Ain't Gone* and *Personal Escapades*.

From Every Good-bye Ain't Gone

Who's Bad?

(1990)

MY COUSIN JEFFREY looked like Ricky Nelson and always wanted to be the baddest nigger on the block.

"Little girl, come here. What you doin' with that white man?" the black supermarket clerk asked, eyeing me with concern.

"He's not white, that's my cousin," I told him, then ran to catch up with Jeff several aisles away in the Safeway.

"That man wanted to know if I was white, didn't he?" Jeff asked.

"No he didn't," I said, my face as fixed as granite. Jeff looked me straight in the eyes but I didn't blink. I knew nothing made him feel worse than people calling him a white man.

We paid for our groceries—the candy we lifted was in our pockets—then walked up the hill from Amsterdam Avenue to my parents' apartment on Convent and 129th Street.

"You make a really good sandwich," he said, seated at the dining table. I glowed. Jeff didn't often hang out with me. He and my cousin Karen were the oldest grandchildren. I was only number five, and there were a lot of cousins after me, most of them Jeffrey's brothers and sisters. His mother, my aunt Glo, had six kids. It was hard to get any attention in that house when I visited.

An old white man, Mr. Javitz, lived there, too. His family couldn't figure why he chose to spend his last years rooming with my aunt in the heart of Harlem, 116th Street and Seventh Avenue. But I guess Mr. Javitz had the same attitude as my grandmother, who lived there most of the time, as well: "I'm a Harlemite," she boasted, though she'd yet to give up her Jamaican citizenship after more than forty years in America. She loved the neighborhood's insomnia—sirens in the night suggesting a death, a fight, a fire. The constant bustle of humanity hustling to earn a cent below her bedroom window from daylight to dark.

Brooklyn, where I lived most of my life, was just too quiet, my grandmother said. Jeff felt the same way. The lure of the neighborhood streets and the incessant household traffic at my aunt's kept me an afterthought in Jeffrey's world—not to mention my age. But he was in my living room now, eating my hero. I stared at him mutely, watching his jaws move. I was eleven and a half, counting the days till twelve, and he was almost seventeen.

"Where you goin'?" I asked. He stood up and smoothed his puckered shirt.

"I got to go back downtown."

"I can go with you," I told him, rushing to clear his plate from the table.

"I'm not going straight downtown," he said, following me into the kitchen. He washed his hands in the sink, dried them on a paper towel, then quickly inspected his nails. "I got to make a couple of stops first."

"Oh," I said simply. Some girl, I thought. I followed him down the long hallway in our apartment to the front door. He bent down and kissed me softly on the cheek.

"Thanks for the sandwich. See ya later," he said, and ran down the six flights instead of taking the elevator.

It was the usual chaos the next time I saw him at Aunt Glo's.

"Hey man *stoooop,*" Jeff screamed as he fell back in the kitchen chair, laughing and yelling at Karen, our oldest cousin. She was pouring a pitcher of grape Kool-Aid over his head. He had put ice down her back.

Aunt Glo, a useless disciplinarian dressed in a muumuu, marched into the kitchen waving a big yellow spoon dangerously close to

Jeffrey's head. "What are you guys doing," she yelled, then burst out laughing.

Ducking, Jeff yelled, "Don't hit me. Karen's the one."

Karen—all the younger cousins called her Kay-Kay—was pretty, twenty, and had her arms folded across her infinitesimal bosom. Her smile was villainous. Her nostrils flared and I started giggling uncontrollably.

"What are you laughing at, Linkatara head?" she demanded. Kay-Kay had all sorts of pet names for me.

"Your face," I said weakly, doubled over from laughing.

"You better stop," she warned, "or you know what's gonna happen, you'll be peeing on the floor."

"Oh no she won't, you uncouth children." Aunt Glo giggled. "My niece only urinates. She was the only four-year-old I ever met who said 'urinate' instead of 'pee.' "

Not only that, in my house one didn't have a belly button, or even a navel: "Make sure your umbilicus is clean," my mother instructed at bathtime. She was the oldest of four children. Aunt Glo was the youngest, and a fast-and-high-liver by profession.

She looked down at me knotted on the kitchen linoleum, holding my stomach. "Girl, go to the bathroom."

"Not before me," Karen yelled—also the inheritor of a weak bladder—and dashed past me.

The ruckus didn't seem to faze Mr. Javitz, who was in bed, in the room-with-bath, right off the kitchen. He never complained about the noise. He either slept right through it or was too removed from reality to care. On these visits to Aunt Glo, I'd occasionally see him shuffle out of his room to dish up dinner from the always present pots on the stove. He'd eat in silence then return to his room. He was never unfriendly, just a bent, yellowing man with liver spots and nothing left to say.

How he and Aunt Glo found each other, I don't know. From my mother's perspective, everything about Aunt Glo is best kept hermetically sealed. When it came to her sister, my mother would just shake her head and say, "Going to hell in a chariot."

Like her son, Aunt Glo never wanted people to think she was

white. When she shopped in fancy department stores in the 1950s with my brown-skinned mother, white people would approach her *tsk, tsk, tsking,* at their intimate chatter. "You shouldn't be with that colored woman," they'd take my aunt aside and say.

"That's my sister," she'd spit at them.

Aunt Glo had many personas before her expanding figure was relegated to the capacious muumuu she wore in the kitchen that afternoon, waving the big yellow spoon.

St. Patrick's Day, circa 1950, she stepped off a jet wrapped in a white ermine coat, her dyed-green hair framing her naturally alabaster face. My mother looked for a place to hide as this portent of punk approached her in the airport terminal.

I was born too late to hang with Aunt Glo in her salad days. Back then, she'd take Kay-Kay to the Harlem hot spots and let her sip Shirley Temples at the bar. After a night out, she'd get to sleep in Aunt Glo's bed with a mink coat as a quilt.

Aunt Glo had theatrical aspirations. Burl Ives—Burl Ives? right, that's what Kay-Kay told me—was supposed to have thought her very talented. He planned to help her break into show business, Kay-Kay said. Promises, promises. She missed out on stage fame, but her connections with Harlem's underworld in the 1940s and 1950s did generate some notice—a few inches in one of the New York tabloids, family legend has it.

The ignominious publicity compelled my mother to leave Harlem after college and escape to the more genteel borough of Brooklyn.

But we were living in Harlem now, as well, and would for another few years. Living in Harlem kept me straight, kept me balanced, kept me from being culturally denuded. And Aunt Glo was a counterweight—if an extreme one—to my mother's sometimes sterile primness.

My mother's healthier bourgeois values, however, could not be undermined merely by contact with school friends who were thugs-in-the-making, whose mothers hooked, whose fathers ran numbers and worse, or by the general hustling into which certain members of my own family delved. Instead, their influence kept me in touch with the complex realities of a race constantly under siege and endlessly adapting to survive. Between my mother and my extended family of relatives and friends, I had the opportunity to experience, synthesize or discard—very early—the variegated elements of black urban culture.

But Jeffrey never had the consistent guidance I had. He was raised, initially, not by his mother, but by a childless couple old enough to be his grandparents. When his foster mother died, Aunt Glo married his foster father—dead a few years by the time Kay-Kay poured Kool-Aid over Jeffrey's jet black hair.

Jeff jiggled when he laughed, I remember now. He was tall but tended to be pudgy in his teens. The extra flesh added to the altar boy innocence of his face. He was a good Catholic kid who attended parochial school for years. He could take apart and put together anything electrical. He could have been an engineer. But he was a black male surrounded by the hustling life without a counterweight, without a sense of options—and since it was the early sixties, without the reality of many options. He bought into the street life, but because of his looks, the price of admission was made exceedingly high. He looked too much like the enemy, and always had to prove how bad he was.

Jeff was about nineteen, I think, and just out of jail, the last time we had friendly dealings. He was living with Karen's mother in that shattered urban zone called the South Bronx. I lived there, too, off and on for a year because it was closer to the junior high school I was attending—one of the best in the city but far from my Harlem neighborhood.

I was walking from Willis Avenue up 147th Street, past vast, junk-heaped lots, past five-story walk-ups with broken-down front stoops, their iron railings supporting the tight asses of fine, lean Borinquen young men posturing—legs spread open, hands on their balls—and pimple-faced, fatter ones spreading their cheeks on the iron to less effect.

"Pssst pssst, pssst pssst." One called me. I was thirteen now and my flat-chested cousin, Kay-Kay, didn't call me Linkatara anymore. She called me Milk Maid Bessie. The block was full of Borinquen gang members at war with neighboring black gangs. Black people lived on the block, most of them middle-aged and older, but few my age. I ignored them and kept walking. My aunt's building was still a half block away. I passed another occupied stoop.

"Somebody back there wants you," a Borinquen said. "How come you not talking to my friends?" he asked, moving down the steps toward me. Jeffrey suddenly appeared behind him on the stoop.

"Hey Jill," he called to me. He told the men on the steps, "That's my cousin."

"For real?" one of them asked, looking him up and down.

"Yeah," he said.

No one on the street bothered me after that. If someone even tried, another Borinquen would warn him off. "No man, that's Jeff's cousin."

It had gotten to the point where Jeffrey was tired of denying he was white to black people, especially in the joint. Borinquens, as Jeff explained it, assumed he was a spic born in the States who never learned Spanish. They never thought he was a nigger. Out of jail, on the street, bloods told him he was so white why deal with the hassle of being black? Just go on and pass.

I realize Jeffrey didn't look like a redbone, a high yellow or anything else in the nomenclature of color African-Americans use to distinguish our varied complexions. He looked like one of Ozzie and Harriet's kids. But African-Americans are the product of a New World culture: it's been estimated that 80 percent of us are of mixed-race backgrounds. And while U.S. social custom and law have denied that miscegenated reality to perpetuate their own system of apartheid, it wouldn't be the first trick bag black people got hip to and out of.

But more than twenty years after I walked down that South Bronx block, a whole new generation of African-Americans are either hyping or putting down each other based on skin complexion, still perpetuating what Alice Walker calls colorism and what Spike Lee scratched the surface of in his film about color and class conflict among African-Americans, *School Daze*.

And as I write this, Jeffrey's sister—fair-skinned, golden-haired and living in a tenement above crack-infested Harlem—hopes her second baby looks *black, black, black,* 'cause that will validate her in the eyes of other black people, she says. In the meantime, she'd like to give her older son to somebody else to raise, like her mother, Aunt Glo, 'cause he's so *light, light, light* . . .

The judge, preparing to sentence him, put down Jeffrey's arrest record and looked at him from the bench. My cousin was into drugs now and into theft to support his habit. The judge opened his mouth to speak; Jeffrey beat him to it.

"I'd like something corrected, Your Honor. I am not white, I am black," he said, and demanded the racial classification in his records be changed.

"I'm looking right at you and you look white to me," the judge replied.

"That's my grandmother right there," Jeffrey persisted, pointing to the brown woman in the black felt hat. Physical appearance is always a matter of genetic roulette among so mixed a race of people as the descendants of Africans in the New World. Her light brown skin had grayed with age and actually looked the color of taupe now. "If she's black, I'm black," he said with increased belligerence.

The judge changed his racial designation and added a year to his sentence, too.

Jeff seemed straight for a long time after he left the penitentiary. But it didn't last. He started using heroin again. He stole from my mother. He stole from our grandmother. After that, I wouldn't have anything to do with him.

I was cold and formal the last time we spoke. He was staring out the living room window of my aunt's latest apartment when I walked in. The apartment was just a few blocks from the one on Seventh Avenue where Mr. Javitz had roomed. Mr. Javitz was long dead. The building was sprawling, half inhabited, run-down and poised for urban renewal. "Hello, Jeffrey," I said stiffly.

He looked at me sideways, said "Hi," then quickly averted his eyes, fixing his gaze on the cityscape of Harlem rooftops, crumbling crowns on stone, gray prisons.

He did not look like Ricky Nelson anymore. His face was pasty and pocked. His hair was sandy and thin. But he really had stopped using drugs. He had a daughter. Her Borinquen mother was an addict. Jeff didn't want that for his child. He put her in a Catholic school and took a job as superintendent of the tenement where he and Aunt Glo lived.

I talked with my aunt but said nothing to Jeff. When I was ready to leave, I moved toward him to say good-bye, but couldn't. I felt him shrink away from me; I felt him shrinking inside. I simply said, "Bye."

A few months later, his bloated body was found on one of those crumbling Harlem rooftops. Parties to a drug deal gone sour more than a year before had tracked him down and shot him.

I came to New York for the funeral from Miami, where I was working as a journalist. My aunt wanted a big funeral. My mother said there was no money for a big funeral, but she'd do the best she could. She caught a priest on the fly in the funeral home and said, "Father, my nephew is dead and I'd like you to say a few words over him before he's buried." The priest was glad to oblige.

I waited in a vestibule with my other cousins while dozens of friends from Aunt Glo's and Jeff's neighborhood filed into the room where he lay in the alloyed equivalent of a plain pine box. There were no flowers. Thelma, my mother's first cousin, got up from her seat and placed a small bunch of violets on top of the coffin.

"This ain't the type of funeral Jeffrey should have," complained one of his brothers.

"Then you should have paid for it, motherfucker," I told him and walked away. He was peddling drugs and had gotten a younger brother, not even in his teens, busted in a deal.

They carried Aunt Glo in wailing, a person on each side supporting her obese, tented frame. For years she had rarely been seen in public. She almost never left her house.

The priest entered. It was obvious from his slightly quizzical expression and darting eyes that he was trying to figure out what the white man in the coffin had to do with all these very dark and very light and everything-between people.

My mother had told him Jeffrey's full name, and after a few stock religious phrases he began the Hail Mary. ". . . the Lord is with thee, blessed art thou amongst women, and blessed is the fruit of thy womb Jesus—"

"Amen," a voice rose.

"Yes Lord," another black Protestant cried, injecting an unaccustomed emotionalism into the prayer. I spotted my mother and Thelma exchanging quick glances. I tried not to laugh when my mother turned and rolled her eyes at me.

"Holy Mary, mother of God, pray for us sinners—"

"Please Jesus, yes."

"—now, and at the hour of our death, Ah-men," the priest concluded.

"Amen," a voice echoed.

Aunt Glo stood in the kitchen of yet another apartment after the funeral. "It was nice of you to come all the way from Miami," she told me. "How come Kay-Kay wouldn't come?"

"She's angry," I said.

"Angry at what?" she snapped. "What has she got to be mad at me about?" I peered into my aunt's eyes and wondered what was behind them. "I don't know what I did wrong," she said. "Your mother is lucky, two fine kids. But my kids, I lose them to the streets."

Jeffrey's daughter, a beautiful girl of about eight, sat quietly in the living room. Her father was dead and her mother had last been seen shooting up in a hallway. Aunt Glo was going to raise her. I looked around the room. The furniture was old, worn and different from the solid pieces she'd had in previous apartments, but she still had her complete set of encyclopedias. I crossed my fingers and hoped by the time Jeff's daughter reached puberty she wouldn't be pregnant and lost to the streets, too.

When I returned to that apartment three years later, Jeffrey's youngest sister was in college and planning to become an attorney. His daughter was a very independent young lady of about eleven. We went shopping one afternoon and she spent the night with me at my mother's house. The next morning, she had already carefully made her bed and was fixing a bowl of cereal when I found her in the kitchen.

Aunt Glo asked me later how she'd behaved and I said great. "I told her how you could take care of yourself and run the house when you were just a little girl. She's got to do the same thing," said my aunt, her once-green hair now in a short, pretty, salt-and-pepper Afro, all her teeth gone, emphysema cutting her breath short. "She's got to know how to do for herself," my aunt said. "I won't always be here."

After her thirteenth birthday, almost to the day, I learned my hopes for Jeffrey's daughter were in vain. The street now owns her and she can be found on it at the midnight hour, with my aunt's consent. And my aunt, who still rarely has the energy to leave home, can work up enough steam to flail her arms and shriek profanity to anyone who tells her someone else should be raising Jeffrey's child.

Acknowledgments

Grateful acknowledgment is made to the following for permission to reprint previously published material:

Beacon Press: "On Being Young—a Woman—and Colored" by Marita Bonner from *Frye Street and Environs: The Collected Works of Marita Bonner,* edited by Joyce Flynn and Joyce Occomy Stricklin. Copyright © 1987 by Joyce Flynn and Joyce Occomy Stricklin. Reprinted by permission of Beacon Press.

HarperCollins Publishers Inc.: "The Ethics of Living Jim Crow: An Autobiographical Sketch" from *Uncle Tom's Children* by Richard Wright. Copyright 1936 by Richard Wright, renewed 1964 by Ellen Wright. Reprinted by permission of HarperCollins Publishers.

Farrar, Straus & Giroux, Inc.: Excerpt from *The Big Sea* by Langston Hughes. Copyright © 1940 by Langston Hughes. Renewal copyright © 1968 by Anra Bontemps and George Houston Bass. Reprinted by permission of Hill and Wang, a division of Farrar, Straus and Giroux, Inc. Rights in the British Commonwealth administered by Serpent's Tail, London.

Esther E. Redding: Excerpt from *No Day of Triumph* by J. Saunders Redding. Reprinted by permission.

The Feminist Press: "Growing Out of Shadow" by Margaret Walker Alexander from *How I Wrote Jubilee and Other Essays on Life and Literature.* Copyright © 1990 by Margaret Walker Alexander. Published by The Feminist Press at CUNY. Reprinted by permission.

permission of Henry Holt and Company, Inc. Rights in the British Commonwealth administered by Wylie, Aitken & Stone.

Sterling Lord Literistic, Inc.: Excerpt from *The Autobiography of LeRoi Jones* by Amiri Baraka. Copyright © 1984 by Amiri Baraka. Reprinted by permission of Sterling Lord Literistic, Inc.

The Antioch Review: "A Death in the Family" by Kenneth A. McClane, originally published in *The Antioch Review,* Vol. 43, No. 2, Spring 1985. Copyright © 1985 by The Antioch Review, Inc. Reprinted by permission of the Editors.

The New York Times: "A Brother's Murder" by Brent Staples, originally published in *The New York Times Magazine,* March 30, 1986. Copyright © 1986 by The New York Times Company. Reprinted by permission.

Algonquin Books of Chapel Hill: "What Charles Knew." by Houston A. Baker, Jr., from *An Apple for My Teacher: Twelve Writers Tell About Teachers Who Made All the Difference,* edited by Louis D. Rubin, Jr. Copyright © 1990, 1987 by Algonquin Books of Chapel Hill. Reprinted by permission.

William Morrow & Company, Inc.: Excerpt from *The Motion of Light in Water* by Samuel R. Delany. Copyright © 1988 by Samuel R. Delany. Reprinted by permission of William Morrow & Company, Inc. Rights in the British Commonwealth administered by Henry Morrison Inc.

Callaloo/The Johns Hopkins University Press: "Black Is a Woman's Color" by Bell Hooks, originally published in *Callaloo,* Vol. 12, Issue 2, Spring 1989. Reprinted by permission.

Louisiana State University Press: "A Life of Learning" from *Race and History: Selected Essays 1938–1988* by John Hope Franklin. Copyright © 1990 by Louisiana State University Press. Reprinted by permission.

Random House, Inc.: Excerpt from *Every Good-Bye Ain't Gone* by Itabari Njeri. Copyright © 1982, 1983, 1984, 1986, 1990 by Itabari Njeri. Reprinted by permission of Random House, Inc.

Photo Credits

HENRY LOUIS GATES, JR., is the DuBois Professor of the Humanities at Harvard University. He is the author of *Figures in Black: Words, Signs, and the "Racial" Self* and *The Signifying Monkey: A Theory of Afro-American Literary Criticism.* He is the editor of many books, among them: *Reading Black, Reading Feminist,* the *Norton Anthology of Afro-American Literature,* and the 30-volume series *The Schomburg Library of Nineteenth-Century Black Women Writers.* He is recipient of a MacArthur Foundation Grant.